Emotional and Behavioural Difficulties in Middle Childhood

Emotional and Behavioural Difficulties in Middle Childhood:
Identification, Assessment and Intervention in School

Maurice Chazan, Alice F. Laing
and Diane Davies

 The Falmer Press

(A member of the Taylor & Francis Group)
London • Washington, D.C.

UK   The Falmer Press, 4 John Street, London WC1N 2ET
USA The Falmer Press, Taylor & Francis Inc., 1900 Frost Road, Suite 101, Bristol, PA 19007

First published in 1994

A catalogue record for this book is available from the British Library

Library of Congress Cataloging-in-Publication Data are available on request

ISBN 0 7507 0346 6 (cased)
ISBN 0 7507 0347 4 (paper)

Jacket design by Caroline Archer

Typeset in 10/12pt Bembo by
Graphicraft Typesetters Ltd., Hong Kong.

Printed in Great Britain by Burgess Science Press, Basingstoke on paper which has a specified pH value on final paper manufacture of not less than 7.5 and is therefore 'acid free'.

Contents

Authors' Note

The names of individuals and institutions in the case studies are all fictitious. The authors would like to thank Mrs. Letty Johns, Ms. Karen Glover and Mrs. Jill Edwards for secretarial assistance.

Abbreviations

BATPACK	Behavioural Approach to Teaching Package
BSAG	Bristol Social Adjustment Guides
CBCTRF	Child Behaviour Checklist Teachers' Report Form (Achenbach and Edelbrock)
CBRSC	Comprehensive Behaviour Rating Scale for Children (Neeper and Lahey)
CTRS	Conners Teacher's Rating Scale
DES	Department of Education and Science
DFE	Department for Education
DHSS	Department of Health and Social Security
EBDs	Emotional and Behavioural Difficulties
EWO	Educational Welfare Officer
GP	General Practitioner (Family Doctor)
HMSO	Her Majesty's Stationery Office
INSET	In-Service Education of Teachers
LEA	Local Education Authority
LDA	Learning Development Aids
LMS	Local Management of Schools
NERS	National Exclusions Reporting System
NFER	National Foundation for Educational Research
PE	Physical Education
SATs	Standard Assessment Tests
SCAA	School Curriculum and Assessment Authority
SENs/SNs	Special Educational Needs/Special Needs
SPS	School Psychological Service
STB	Support Teacher, Behaviour
UK	United Kingdom
USA	United States of America
WO	Welsh Office
Y1, 2 etc	Year 1 (age range 5 to 6+), Year 2 (age range 6 to 7+) and so on

Chapter 1

Introduction

Scope of Book

In recent years, increased attention has been given by both schools and researchers to emotional and behavioural difficulties (EBDs) in children. This has been particularly the case with EBDs occurring during middle childhood (here taken as the period roughly between 7+ and 11+ years), previously relatively neglected as a focus for action and research as compared with the under-5s and adolescents. Consequently, a considerable literature now exists on many aspects of EBDs in middle childhood which is of practical relevance to teachers and parents but is scattered widely in a variety of publications.

The nature of EBDs in middle childhood will be discussed in chapter 2. The term 'emotional and behavioural difficulties' has largely replaced 'maladjustment' in Britain, and is roughly equivalent to 'behaviour disorder' as used in the USA. Here, the focus is put on those EBDs presented in school which are serious enough to cause concern to parents and teachers, and which may take the form of 'externalized' behaviour (for example, aggressiveness, disruptiveness, bullying) or 'internalized' behaviour (for example, timidity, inhibition, withdrawal), or indeed a mixture of both outgoing and introverted behaviour. The usage of the term 'EBDs' in this book is very much in line with the definition of the 'behavioural problem' child put forward by Woody (1969) in relation to behaviour shown within the school, i.e. 'the child who cannot or will not adjust to the socially acceptable norms for behaviour and consequently disrupts his own academic progress, the learning efforts of his classmates, and interpersonal relations' (p. 19).

This book aims to highlight the main findings of studies relating to the identification, assessment and treatment of EBDs in middle childhood, in the context of the school. It is hoped that the content of the book will be of interest to parents as well as school staffs, as parents need to be closely involved in EBDs arising in school at all stages. EBDs in school cannot be fully understood without insight into the child's family background, even if the home is not a factor in the causation of problems of behaviour. However, limitations of space prevent children's emotional and behavioural difficulties at home from being fully considered in this book. In the main, EBDs will be discussed in the context of the educational system in England and Wales, but reference will be made to other countries, especially the USA.

This introductory chapter will briefly discuss the organization of educational provision for 7–11+ year-olds; the main features of normal emotional and social growth in this age group; developments in the education and treatment of children with EBDs over the years; and the effects of the 1988 Education Reform Act and subsequent legislation on the way in which pupils with EBDs are dealt with. The rest of the book will be divided into four parts.

In *Part I*, the book will explore the extent to which children aged 7–11+ years present EBDs in school, the nature of these difficulties, and the factors affecting estimates of prevalence. It will consider how EBDs can be identified and appropriately assessed.

In *Part II*, after an examination of the role of schools in the prevention of, and intervention in, EBDs and the ways in which teachers cope with behaviour problems in the classroom, a variety of possible approaches to intervention will be looked at, in particular behaviour modification strategies, social skills training, group work and problem-solving techniques. Working with parents and others will also be discussed.

Part III will consider the integration of pupils presenting EBDs in the mainstream school system as well as the contribution of special classes, units and schools to the education of these pupils. *Part IV* will deal with some specific problems that may arise in middle childhood, such as school refusal, disruptive behaviour, bullying, and anxiety/inhibition. The concluding chapter will summarize the issues raised in the book, and look forward to future developments in preventing and treating EBDs. Throughout the book, the evaluation of different approaches to prevention and intervention will be underlined, and general principles will be illustrated by a range of case studies.

Educational Provision for 7 to 11+-Year-Olds

In Europe and the USA many pupils aged 7–11+ form a somewhat separate sub-division within a school that caters for children from the ages of 5, 6 or 7 years up to 11, 12, 13 or even later. In Europe the primary school tends to span the years 6–12, with a linked pre-school system, though in Scandinavia the entry age is 7 and the schools cover most or all of compulsory education (Galton and Blyth, 1989). In the USA most children attend elementary school between 6 and 12, after a non-compulsory year in a kindergarten, but in some school districts the elementary school extends its coverage up to 13 or 14. Grades 4 to 6 (ages 9–11+) form an 'intermediate' sub-division within the elementary school (Gutek, 1988).

In England and Wales, some pupils within the 7–11+ age-range are to be found in junior schools, or middle schools, but most are in junior departments, after two or three years in infant schools or departments and possibly about two years before that in nursery schools/classes or playgroups. A junior school is separate from the infant school, which caters for pupils aged 5–7 years (some enter at 4+), while a junior department is a part of a primary school which includes children from 5–11+ years.

Following the Education Act of 1964, which made it possible for local education authorities (LEAs) in England and Wales to transfer pupils to secondary education at ages other than 11+, patterns of school reorganization emerged such as first schools catering for 5–8 or 9-year-olds and middle schools covering the years 8 or 9 to 12 or 13. The development of middle schools was primarily a consequence of political and economic pressures and helped to alleviate the problems associated with the shortage of buildings brought about by the move to comprehensive secondary education and the raising of the school leaving age to 16. However, middle schools were also intended to keep pupils free for a longer period from the pressures of class instruction and external examinations that affected secondary schools (Taylor and Garson, 1982; Sharp and Dunford, 1990). Middle schools flourished in some areas of the country during the 1970s, but now occupy only a minority position in the educational system of England and Wales.

During the late 1960s and 1970s, British primary schools tended to encourage a child-centred approach, emphasizing individual and group work rather than rote learning and whole-class instruction. American educationists became enthusiastic about this approach during this period. However, more recently in both Britain and the USA the pendulum has swung back, with a call for a return to an emphasis on the basic subjects and 'traditional' rather than 'progressive' teaching methods (Gutek, 1988; Alexander, 1992). The debate continues.

Emotional and Social Development in Middle Childhood

The period from about 5 years of age until puberty has tended to be seen as relatively free from emotional upheaval. This view has been largely the result of the influence of Sigmund Freud, who considered middle childhood to be a 'latency' or rest period, when the sexual and aggressive impulses are in a subdued state, and of less significance for the formation of personality than earlier or later periods. As Sula Wolff (1973) puts it, during latency the erotic longings of early childhood, its jealousies and its fears, become hidden until the psychological and social changes of puberty bring them to life again.

Erik Erikson (1950), too, perceived children as less prone to aggression during the latency period. However, Erikson considered middle childhood to be a most decisive stage socially, when children could develop a sense of inadequacy and inferiority if they failed to acquire appropriate skills or to achieve status among their contemporaries. Erikson also recognized that school life played a crucial role in children's emotional and social growth: it had its own goals and limits, achievements and disappointments, and involved doing things beside, and with, others.

Later work has confirmed that middle childhood is a time of significant growth in many spheres — physical, cognitive, emotional and social. New capacities emerge, and there is a gradual consolidation and extension of abilities. During this period, children achieve a greater self-regulation and a deeper understanding of others. Indeed, development in middle childhood appears to have considerable significance for behaviour patterns and adjustment later on; for example, behaviour problems become more resistant to change as the child gets older (Collins, 1984; Levine and Satz, 1984).

In attempting to understand EBDs in the context of normal development, it is useful to think in terms of the specific developmental tasks or challenges faced by children at particular stages of their growth (Havighurst, 1972). A developmental task is seen by Havighurst as midway between an individual need and a societal demand, and the concept assumes an active learner interacting with an active social environment. Successful achievement of age-appropriate tasks leads to happiness and success with later tasks; failure is likely to lead to adjustment problems, disapproval by society and difficulty in the future.

The main developmental tasks faced by children in middle childhood may be listed as follows:

(i) *the achieving of increased personal independence and self-reliance*
The child needs an increasing detachment from the parents (or other caretakers), especially perhaps from the mother, without losing the feeling of security derived from the knowledge that the responsible adults are always available to give affection, support and comfort when necessary. EBDs are likely to arise if this feeling of security is absent, or if child-parent relationships are over-intense.

(ii) *the acquisition and consolidation of physical skills*
During middle childhood, children make progress in physical strength and motor skills. Smoothness, accuracy and coordination all develop in skills such as running, catching, throwing, jumping, swimming and riding as well as in fine motor skills such as writing and drawing (Mussen *et al.*, 1992). The child who is clumsy, or who fails to stand up to the increasingly robust physical activities characteristic of the age group, may well be subject to social derision. The child's stage of physical maturation will greatly influence potential skills, and it needs to be recognized that some children (especially girls) will have entered puberty by the age of 11+. Whether or not a boy or girl has entered puberty influences not only self-image but the way the child is perceived and treated by his/her family, teachers and peers; late-developing boys may be particularly at risk in regard to emotional and behavioural difficulties (Gross, 1984).

(iii) *the achievement of success in the basic school subjects*
The child needs satisfaction from reasonable progress in school work, especially from the ability to read adequately. A link has been found between failure in school, particularly in reading, and behaviour difficulties. School life becomes more demanding as the child grows older, and some 7 and 8-year-olds may not easily adjust to the new pressures on them. Parents and teachers become increasingly concerned at failure to make adequate progress in the

basic subjects, and this concern is likely to communicate itself to the child and lead to frustration, loss of self-esteem and problem behaviour. If a pupil enters classes for 7-year-olds already showing some emotional disturbance, this may well interfere with his/her scholastic learning. Whether EBDs are primary or secondary factors in learning failure, the interaction between emotional disturbance and learning blockage tends to increase both behavioural and learning difficulties (Chazan, 1985; Croll and Moses, 1985).

(iv) *the development of psychological understanding*

As cognitive ability matures during this period, children become increasingly aware of their own strengths and weaknesses, as well as those of others significant in their lives, especially parents and teachers. They become better able to understand the complexity of emotions and to have insight into what others are feeling (Smith and Cowie, 1991). They come to know, too, that the emotional state of one person is influenced by the emotional state of another (Harris, 1989).

Failure in psychological understanding may lead to behavioural difficulties. Dodge (1986), for example, has suggested that some children may be highly aggressive because they tend to misinterpret the behaviour of others and mistakenly attribute hostile intentions to their peers (see also Shaffer, 1989). But psychological understanding may bring about problems of adjustment, in that the awareness of the reality of their situation may be painful for some children. When relationships at home are fragile, facing up to the real world may lead a child into emotional and behavioural disturbance.

Prior to middle childhood, children's self-esteem rests largely on identification with their parents. Now they are forced to begin evaluating themselves much more on the basis of their own skills and personal attributes. Their expectancies and judgments become more realistic, though the distinction between ability and effort is not clearly distinguished until about 10 to 13 years (Mussen *et al.*, 1992). Their self-judgments are also determined by their experience of success and failure. Competence is self-rewarding; a lack of competence leads to feelings of helplessness. In the terms of attribution theory (Weiner, 1974), those who experience success in the early years come to believe that this success is determined mainly by their own efforts and ability: they are encouraged to further achievements. Individuals whose early experiences are repeatedly unfulfilling and frustrating are likely to think that success is the result of chance or factors outside their control, and to give up trying (see also Brooks, 1984).

(v) *learning how to interact with peers*

In middle childhood, a child's peer group grows in size and influence. From about 6 to 9 years, groups or gangs are informal, with few fixed rules; thereafter groups become more highly structured. The child becomes anxious to be liked by his/her peers, and the values and attitudes of the peer group help to shape the developing personality of the individual. Children increasingly compare themselves with others in making judgments about their own performance (Mussen *et al.*, 1992).

Friendships are important in ensuring positive interaction with agemates, as well as in the acquisition of social skills. Children with friends tend to be more socially competent than those who are without them, and better adjusted emotionally (Hartup, 1992). Acceptance by peers depends greatly on what children can offer in the way of talents and skills. Children who are popular and have high social status in middle childhood are usually helpful, friendly and skilful at following the accepted rules in their interaction with peers (Coie *et al.*, 1990; Dunn and McGuire, 1992). Prowess in physical action and the ability to stand up for oneself may also be important factors, and aggressive behaviour can form a basis for social cohesion and friendship in both boys and girls, as in the case of many small gangs. Generally, however, aggressive encounters between individuals decrease from about 8 years on, being replaced by the use of verbal methods to assert dominance. During middle childhood, children come to evaluate dominance relationships and learn not to challenge them too often (Fishbein, 1984).

Children who fail to adapt to the values, standards and demands of the peer group are likely to become isolated or rejected by others. Dunn and McGuire (1992) suggest that there are several developmental routes to being disliked by peers, and that children can be rejected for a variety of reasons. However, whatever the reason for rejection, children tend to withdraw from attempts to be a part of a group once it is clear that they are not liked by the group; such withdrawal may lead to further rejection. Unpopular children tend to be less effective at entering groups than popular children (see also Putallaz and Wasserman, 1990). In middle childhood, it would seem that it is the combination of either aggressiveness or submissiveness with low levels of prosocial behaviour that is associated with rejection by peers. Middle childhood is likely to be a bad time for children who are solitary, social failures, or have disabilities; also for those who dislike sport, lack courage or are hypersensitive.

Acceptance by peers is also influenced by the child's conformity or otherwise to recognized sex-typed behaviours. Sex role development begins long before the age of 7, but awareness of the differences between boys and girls sharpens considerably during middle childhood. By 8 or 9, the sexes tend to segregate themselves in play, and there are pressures from parents and teachers to conform to sex-appropriate norms of appearance, clothing and behaviour. Boys and girls who appear different in any way are likely to encounter hostility or ridicule and to be excluded from the group, and behaving in ways considered to be inappropriate for one's sex may well arouse these reactions (Strommen *et al.*, 1977; Delamont, 1980; Burns, 1982).

(vi) *conforming to social rules*
In addition to having to adjust to the norms of the peer group, 7–11+ year-olds have to meet the demands made on them by parents, teachers and other

adults to conform to certain rules and standards of behaviour — demands that become heavier as the child grows older. An inability or unwillingness to respond to such demands usually results in conflict between child and adults which may lead to aggressive acts on the part of the child or else withdrawal behaviour. It is important that adults should make sure that the demands which they make on individual children are appropriate in the particular case, and that the reasons for making demands are clearly understood. Adults do not always recognize that conforming to social rules is a matter of learning, which sometimes takes a considerable period of time.

Developments in the Education and Treatment of Children with EBDs

Over the past sixty years or so, provision for the education and treatment of children with EBDs has substantially increased, even if progress has been uneven and gaps remain to be filled. In particular, there have been developments in (i) child guidance; (ii) support services; (iii) the training of teachers wishing to gain expertise in dealing with pupils presenting EBDs; and (iv) the provision of special classes, units and schools for such pupils. Here these developments will be discussed briefly; further reference to some of them will be made later on in the book, especially in chapters 8 and 9.

Child Guidance

Since the opening of the East London Child Guidance Clinic in 1927 by the Jewish Health Organization, inspired by pioneering establishments of this kind in the USA, the child guidance service in England and Wales has greatly expanded. The Underwood Committee (Ministry of Education, 1955) on the treatment of maladjusted children within the educational system recommended that there should be a comprehensive child guidance service available for each LEA area in England and Wales. This recommendation was endorsed by the government, and resulted in cooperation between education authorities and the hospital services in providing a pattern of child guidance. In 1974, the Department of Education and Science, together with the Department of Health and Social Security, recommended that the child guidance service should be based on a multi-professional team, providing diagnosis, consultation and help as required; also that more flexibility should be introduced into the arrangements for collaboration between the education, health and social services (DES/DHSS/WO, 1974). The Court Committee on Child Health Services (DHSS, 1976) and the Warnock Report (DES, 1978) endorsed the plea for more coordinated planning and working within child guidance services.

Child guidance clinics or centres, or child psychiatric clinics, are now widely available in England and Wales, under the aegis of the LEA or Health

Service, or under the joint auspices of both authorities. These clinics provide medical, psychological and social work help for disturbed children and their families; in some cases, paediatricians, speech therapists and psychotherapists work with psychiatrists, psychologists and social workers as members of the team.

The value of the child guidance clinic, particularly in its traditional form, has been called into question, particularly on the grounds that it focusses too much on the treatment of individuals rather than attempting to change the educational and social systems which give rise to many of the problems for which children are referred for help (Tizard, 1973). Gillham (1981) has criticized child guidance services for their long waiting lists, slow and cumbersome mode of action, physically remote context, and preoccupation with psychoanalytic explanation and protracted therapy. However, from the onset, the child guidance service has recognized the important contribution that parents and teachers can make to the treatment of children with EBDs, and acknowledged that the root causes of emotional and behavioural difficulties may lie in the home or school rather than in the child. In recent years members of child guidance teams have not only expanded their work with families (Campion, 1985; Barker, 1986) but often use schools rather than clinics as their working base, in order to strengthen their links with teachers (Callias and Rickett, 1986). Further, the help given by child guidance services to children with EBDs has undoubtedly contributed to many of them remaining in their ordinary schools and classes rather than being removed to special provision. Child guidance personnel have also promoted the understanding of emotional and behavioural difficulties and shaped much of the special educational treatment available to poorly adjusted children (Samson, 1980).

Support Services

The key support service relating to pupils with EBDs within the educational system is the School Psychological Service (SPS) (some LEAs have adopted other terminology for this agency, such as Educational Psychology Service). The increased establishment of educational psychologists employed by LEAs in England and Wales was recommended by the Summerfield Report (DES, 1968). By 1978 the Warnock Committee was able to report that almost all LEAs employed educational psychologists and that many had a well-developed psychological service. This service has a variety of functions relating to children in school, but has been increasingly concerned with emotional and behavioural difficulties. The Warnock Report acknowledged that educational psychologists play a central part in the discovery of children with EBDs and in helping them and their teachers in school.

The links between child guidance teams and the school psychological service are generally close. Educational psychologists tend to work as members of the child guidance team, or at least in collaboration with such personnel, as necessary. In some cases, however, the school psychological and child guidance services function as separate establishments. Some educational psychologists spend part or all of their time working within the Social Services Departments of local authorities, where they are likely to see a number of children with EBDs arising out of family upheaval or discord. The HMI Report (1990a) on Educational Psychology Services for the 1990s, while acknowledging that educational psychologists possess a unique range of specialist skills, stressed that, in view of the changes taking place in the education system, it was appropriate for school psychological services to consider carefully their future role. In particular, the Report highlights the need for educational psychologists to: evaluate the efficiency and effectiveness of their services; appraise the frequency and extent to which their specialist skills are used; negotiate their role with LEA officers, teachers and parents and those other professionals with whom they work; and publicize and promote their services to an extent that has not been usual hitherto.

Other LEA services concerned with pupils presenting EBDs include those set up to support pupils with special needs, and advisory staff directly concerned with helping children with EBDs. Because of the links between scholastic problems and poor adjustment, teachers of pupils with learning difficulties are likely to deal with many children both failing academically and causing concern because of their behaviour. Many different patterns exist of advisory services specifically established to help pupils with EBDs (Barnsley Special Education Team, 1981; Imich and Roberts, 1990), but there has been a growing tendency to focus on giving advice to class teachers rather than withdrawing children for special help (Smith, 1985; Bowers, 1987). This change of direction does not always commend itself to teachers, who may welcome the respite given by the withdrawal of difficult pupils even for a short period (Gipps *et al.*, 1987).

Teacher Training

The effective education of children with EBDs depends greatly on the skills of teachers. Universities and other establishments of higher education in Britain provide opportunities for experienced teachers to gain qualifications in special education. Many of the courses available, now mostly on a part-time basis because of funding difficulties, give teachers the option of specializing in the education of children with EBDs. In addition to courses leading to a degree or diploma, which involve a relatively small number of teachers, a variety of in-service courses (INSET) relating to EBDs are offered by colleges or LEAs designed to meet the needs of teachers of ordinary classes.

INSET courses are generally regarded by teachers as worthwhile if they have clear and realistic aims; involve participants in many different forms of learning but with the emphasis on problem-solving workshops; and require school-based work which takes account of the demands made upon teachers in busy classrooms (HMI, 1989a). INSET courses are not considered as being enough to satisfy all the needs of mainstream teachers (Gipps *et al.*, 1987). In the light of observations made by the Elton Committee (DES/WO, 1989) on disruptive behaviour, Hanko (1990) advocates the case discussion training approach, using group consultation. In this approach, an in-service coordinator arranges for staff to meet in their schools, pool their expertise and share experiences; training may be provided by an in-service day or a short sequence of weekly sessions stimulated by an outsider, then continued internally. In the USA, Kauffman *et al.* (1989), who surveyed teachers' attitudes towards the kind of help they wanted to deal with maladaptive behaviour, concluded that such help must be highly individualized: assistance in the form of typical workshops or in-service courses is apparently unlikely to meet most teachers' perceived needs.

Special Provision

Prior to the 1944 Education Act, there was little special educational provision for maladjusted children (the generally-used term at the time). Following the recognition of maladjusted children as a category of handicapped children in the School Health and Handicapped Pupils Regulations of 1945, and the stimulus given by the Underwood Report in 1955 to LEAs to make provision for this group of pupils, the number of special schools, both day and residential, steadily increased in England and Wales (Laslett, 1977). From the early 1970s, LEA special units providing education on a full-time or part-time basis for children with EBDs, within or separate from a mainstream school, proliferated. Although special schools and units for pupils presenting EBDs have tended to cater more for those of secondary school rather than primary school age, a considerable number of children in the 7–11+ age-group have been among their intake (Dawson, 1980; Lloyd-Smith, 1984; HMI, 1989b).

All but the more serious cases of emotional or behavioural disorder remain in their usual schools, and only a small proportion of children with EBDs are transferred to special provision segregated from the mainstream. However, since the 1970s there have been pressures in most countries with a well-developed educational system to reduce, if not abolish, separate provision for children with special educational needs of all kinds.

In the USA, the enactment of Public Law 94–142 (Education for All Handicapped Children,1975) has ensured that throughout the country, in spite of many variations among different states, significant developments have occurred in providing for children with special needs in the least restrictive environment. However, dissatisfaction with the progress made towards the mainstreaming of children with disabilities, not least those with behaviour disorders, has led to a vigorous debate on the extent to which emotionally disturbed pupils can and should be educated within the mainstream system. In relation to children with behaviour disorders, Braaten *et al.* (1988) contend that not all such children can be appropriately served in regular classes, and that a variety of options should be available for these pupils, many of whom require complex interventions. In opposition to this view the proponents of the recently established 'Regular Education Initiative' call for behaviour-disordered pupils to receive appropriate education and services through mainstream classes rather than through resource-room or withdrawal programmes (see, for instance, Algozzine *et al.*, 1990).

In England and Wales, the Report of the Warnock Committee of Enquiry into the Education of Handicapped Children and Young People (DES, 1978) encouraged the integration of children with special needs, but acknowledged that separate provision in special schools for some pupils with EBDs might be essential, particularly if boarding education was required (Chasty and Friel, 1991). The 1981 Education Act stipulated that children with special educational needs should be educated in ordinary schools, but only if their needs could be met with an efficient use of resources, without affecting adversely the education of the other pupils, and with the agreement of the parents. These provisos weakened the force of the Act in promoting integration, not least in the case of pupils with behaviour difficulties: an LEA could easily make out a case that these conditions were not being satisfied in respect of a disruptive or aggressive child. Pisano (1991), discussing children with EBDs in the primary school, argues that the availability of special provision alongside the mainstream school is essential, as some pupils have difficulties that mainstream schools cannot cope with. In support of this view, Pisano refers to official recognition of the need for some pupils to be withdrawn from primary schools (see the Elton Report, DES/WO, 1989 and DES Circular 23/89).

Goacher *et al.* (1988), surveying policy and provision for special educational needs since the 1981 Act in a sample of up to seventy-six English LEAs, found a widespread increase in the placement of primary-aged children with special needs in mainstream schools. However, the placement of pupils with EBDs was an exception, in that no clear trend was discerned. Seventeen per cent of sixty-six LEAs recorded a decrease in the use of special schools for these pupils, whereas 23 per cent reported an increase in such use, with a similar proportion recording a rise in unit provision for this group. Some countries, for example Italy (Lawrence *et al.*, 1985a), have dispensed with segregated schooling for pupils with special needs, while in others (the Netherlands, for instance — see Den Boer, 1990; and Rodbard, 1990) a heavy reliance on special schools has continued, especially for dealing with disruptive or so-called deviant pupils. Special school/unit provision for pupils with EBDs is discussed further later on in the book, particularly in chapter 8.

Effects of Recent Legislation in England and Wales on the Education and Welfare of Pupils with EBDs

The 1981 Education Act

Despite the 1988 Education Reform Act (DES, 1988), the 1981 Education Act (DES, 1981) remained the basis for dealing with children with special educational needs until the enactment of the 1993 Education Act (DFE, 1993a) which is being gradually enforced in 1994. The 1981 Act made it the duty of LEAs and school governors to identify, assess and meet the needs of children and adolescents up to 19 years of age who require special provision or help. Children with special educational needs were defined in the 1981 Act as those who have significantly greater difficulty in learning than the majority of children of the same age, and/or have a disability which makes it difficult for them to benefit from the educational facilities normally available to them (see Williams and Halliwell, 1992).

In the case of children with marked disabilities, the LEA is required to afford them the protection of a statement. The statement of needs is a composite account of a child's strengths and weaknesses, gathered from a variety of professional sources in addition to the parents. The statement, which is subject to annual review, also contains the LEA's proposals regarding the future placement and education of the child. In general, although local authority practice in interpreting the 1981 Act has varied greatly, LEAs have issued statements in the case of those children with the most serious disabilities (about 2 to 3 per cent of the school population), particularly those seen as likely to require special schooling, rather than in the case of the much larger number of children remaining in the mainstream who need assessment and help because of their special needs (up to about a further 15 per cent of the school enrolment). Indeed, statements are not needed where ordinary schools themselves make special provision from their own resources (DES/Dept. of Health Circular 22/89). Only a small proportion of children with EBDs are covered by statements, and many of the children in special units (as opposed to special schools) are placed in them without this degree of formality and support.

The Report of the Audit Commission and Her Majesty's Inspectorate (1992), reviewing the progress made in the decade since the 1981 Education Act, concluded that a great deal had been achieved by schools and LEAs on behalf of pupils with special educational needs over this period. In particular, LEAs have been placing a smaller proportion of pupils in special schools since the 1981 Act (though, as mentioned previously in this chapter, this has not been the case in a number of LEAs in regard to pupils with EBDs); and ordinary schools now match special schools in the quality of the learning experiences provided for pupils with special needs. However, the Report highlighted a number of deficiencies in the working of the Act. They drew especial attention to: (i) the lack of clarity in the definition of 'special educational needs' and about who should be given the protection of a formal statement; (ii) the lack of accountability of LEAs and schools in the way in which they put the Act into operation, especially in the excessive time taken to assess pupils and issue statements; and (iii) the lack of incentives for LEAs to remedy faults in procedures, as, for example, they stood to gain financially from delay in issuing statements that might well involve considerable expenditure (see Vevers, 1992).

The 1988 Education Reform Act

The key elements of the 1988 Education Reform Act were (i) the introduction of a National Curriculum, intended to give all pupils access to a broad, balanced and relevant curriculum (see Lewis, 1991 for a discussion of primary special needs and the National Curriculum); (ii) the assessment of all pupils at four stages (7, 11, 14 and 16 years [see Bartlett and Peacey, 1992]); and (iii) the Local Management of Schools (LMS), with schools being given control of their own budgets. LEAs retained the responsibility for the identification, assessment and determination of special educational needs, and since the Act have had to take into account the requirements of the National Curriculum. Otherwise, the 1988 Act did not have a great deal to say about children with special educational needs.

The 1988 Act has been seen as a challenge by some of these concerned with the education of children with special needs, but by others as having undesirable effects. On the positive side, Davies and Landman (1991) found that most headteachers of special schools for pupils with EBDs welcomed the introduction of the National Curriculum, as helping to achieve desirable developments within their schools, even if extra resources and better staff training were essential to bring this about. Acklaw (1991), looking at the 1988 Act from the point of view of an educational psychologist, asserts that the Act, supplemented by the circulars and regulations which have followed it, is radically changing the environment within which the school psychological service operates within England and Wales. In Acklaw's opinion, the Act could result in a curtailment of the service or offer increased scope for establishing the value of its work within the education system. For example, the National Curriculum assessment arrangements could result in teachers and psychologists working together at much higher levels of skill than may currently be the case; and psychologists could do much to help teachers identify the most appropriate methods for delivering the curriculum to particular pupils.

On the negative side, the implications of the 1988 Act with relevance to pupils with EBDs have been highlighted in recent publications (Stirling, 1991; Francis and Turkington, 1992; Travers, 1992; and Upton, 1992) and may be listed as follows.

1 The 1988 Act promotes educational values that discourage mainstream schools from admitting pupils with special needs, especially those likely to be a disturbing influence and to affect the school's public image. The Act stresses academic attainment as evidence of a school's efficiency, and since the school's finances under LMS depend upon the numbers of pupils admitted, the way in which the school is perceived by parents is important.

2 The introduction of the National Curriculum and the necessity to assess pupils at fixed times have resulted in increasing the stress on the teaching profession in addition to the strain and anxiety which dealing with difficult behaviour may cause them.

3   Separate provision for pupils with EBDs has been under far greater pressure in recent years, particularly as a result of the increased motivation for mainstream schools to exclude pupils for troublesome behaviour.
4   Many special schools and units for children with EBDs have considerable problems in providing a satisfactory curriculum and ensuring adequate standards of care and control. They tend to be small, and so to have a lack of specialist facilities and staff as well as limited space.
5   The 1988 Act has created considerable confusion about the future role of LEA support services, and there are fears that these services may not be viable as LEAs lose many of their existing functions.

The 1989 Children Act

Several sections of the 1989 Children Act, which is gradually being brought into operation, have relevance to children with special educational needs. Section 17, for example, makes it the duty of every local authority to safeguard and promote the welfare of children within their area who are 'in need' (now including children with disabilities) by providing adequate and appropriate services. The Act has provisions relating to medical and psychological assessment as well as to developmental screening; also to parental responsibility, which replaces the concept of parental rights in the context of the Act. The Act lays stress on family centres and services for under-8s, requiring cooperation between Education, Social Services and Health Departments in providing these and other services for children in need. Furthermore, under the Act, children's own views have to be taken into account in any decisions taken on their behalf; a range of new court orders is introduced to protect children who may be suffering or have suffered abuse in any form; and the welfare of children placed in independent schools must be safeguarded by the local authority (Bennett, 1992; Russell, 1992). As children with EBDs often have adverse family backgrounds, and some of them are placed in boarding schools, the Act is likely to result in increased support and protection for these children.

The 1993 Education Act

In an attempt to respond to widespread criticism of the operation of the 1981 and 1988 Education Acts in relation to children with special educational needs, the Government issued a consultation paper on *Special Education Needs: Access to the System* (DFE, June 1992a) proposing remedies for some of the existing causes for dissatisfaction. This paper was followed by a White Paper entitled *Choice and Diversity: A New Framework for Schools* (July, 1992), which makes reference to special education. In brief, the government proposed, through new legislation, to

(i) encourage the reduction in the number of special schools maintained by LEAs;

(ii) reduce the delays in issuing statements;

(iii) increase parental rights over choice of school; and

(iv) improve the appeal procedures available to parents dissatisfied with LEA decisions.

The 1993 Education Act, enacted in July 1993, gave force to these proposals and established a 'Code of Practice' which must be regarded when decisions are taken about which children need statements and special provision or other forms of help. The implications of the 1993 Act and the Code of Practice in relation to pupils with EBDs are considered in chapter 12 (pp. 193–5).

Overview

This chapter sets the scene for the discussion of emotional and behavioural difficulties (EBDs) in middle childhood (7–11+ years) with which this book is concerned. Most children in this age range are educated in primary or elementary schools spanning the years from 5, 6 or 7 to 11, 12 or even later. Their EBDs need to be considered in the context of normal development during the period in question, when a number of important tasks or challenges face every child. These include the acquisition of crucial physical skills, the achievement of a measure of personal independence, the mastery of the basic scholastic skills, competence in interacting with others and learning to conform to essential social rules.

Considerable progress has been made over the years in providing help and support for children with EBDs, mainly through child guidance clinics, the school psychological service and other support agencies, and special educational provision. Teachers in mainstream schools have become more knowledgeable about pupils with EBDs, and more responsive to their needs. There has been a general tendency recently to reduce segregated provision for children with special educational needs, but despite this, pressures have remained for maintaining or even increasing such provision for pupils with EBDs. Since the late 1980s, new educational legislation has aroused much debate about its effect on these pupils, and on the whole the reaction to it has been negative. Nevertheless, the 1988 and the 1993 Education Acts as well as the 1989 Children Act offer some hope of further progress in providing help for children with emotional and behavioural difficulties.

Part I

Discovering and Understanding Emotional and Behavioural Difficulties (EBDs) in Middle Childhood

Chapter 2

What are Emotional and Behavioural Difficulties in Middle Childhood?

As pointed out in chapter 1, 'emotional and behavioural difficulties' (EBDs) is a broad term, needing further amplification in any individual case. Children show that they are disturbed or that they cannot adapt to a particular situation in many different ways. Some demonstrate their feelings openly, by being disobedient, aggressive or destructive; in school these pupils are often referred to as 'antisocial' or 'disruptive'. In the literature, the term 'conduct disorder' is frequently used to refer to those children whose EBDs are 'externalized' or overreacting, that is when they display a persistent pattern of antisocial behaviour which interferes with their daily functioning, or when their behaviour is considered unmanageable by parents or teachers (for example, stealing, hitting, lying, non-compliance) (Webster-Stratton, 1991). A few children, even in middle childhood, become involved in serious delinquent acts such as arson (Kolko and Kazdin, 1991); or inflicting severe, even fatal, injury on others (Mouridsen and Tolstrup, 1988); or begin to take drugs or become addicted to other substance abuse (Farrell and Strang, 1991).

Some pupils stand out as being 'hyperactive', i.e. very restless, fidgety, unable to remain still for long and with a short attention span (Schachar, 1991). However, it is not always easy to distinguish such children from those with 'conduct disorders' (Soussignan *et al.*, 1992).

A number of children do not present disciplinary problems at home or at school, but show their lack of adjustment through 'internalized' or 'underreacting' EBDs. Such children may be persistently worried; tend to be solitary, unhappy or distressed; and are inclined to be timid and to cry easily (Tremblay *et al.*, 1987). They are referred to in the literature as 'socially withdrawn', 'anxious', 'highly introverted' or 'neurotic'. A small proportion of pre-adolescent children may have phobias which greatly affect their daily life, for example, school phobia (see chapter 11); or suffer from depression, shown mainly by a persistent sad mood over a period (Goodyer, 1993). Mainstream teachers may not have much contact with phobic or depressed children, because of the low prevalence of these problems; nor with autistic children, whose condition is characterized by extreme withdrawal, an unwillingness to communicate and often bizarre behaviour (Frith, 1989), and who usually need specialized placement.

Although the dichotomy between 'externalized' and 'internalized' EBDs is often stressed, a mixture of these types of difficulties is not uncommon; and most children with EBDs show some degree of failure in their interpersonal relationships. The following examples will serve to illustrate some of the varied ways in which children in the 7 to 11+ age group present EBDs in school.

Anti-social/Overreacting Behaviour

1 *Mark*, aged 10 years, an overweight boy of low average ability, terrorizes younger children at breaktimes. In school he generally conforms, both for his classteacher and the headteacher, but his compliance with discipline does not extend to other staff, and especially not to the ladies on duty at lunch-time. Mark uses verbal threats as well as his physical size, but is very selective about whom he bullies. He does not have a group of friends, though different boys attach themselves to him at different times.

2 *Andrew*, aged 10 years, leads a group of children into all kinds of trouble. There have been incidents of theft during the school day, truancy and vandalism in school premises during holidays and weekends. Andrew has given loyalty to some members of staff and has exempted them from his activities while focussing on others in terms of graffiti, classroom vandalism and theft.

3 *Gareth*, aged 8 years, has fits of very violent behaviour and frequent bouts of temper. He is prone to break anything within reach; likes to hurt others; and may throw himself on the floor or butt his head against the wall. He dislikes school, is very backward in the basic subjects and resents discipline.

Withdrawn/Underreacting Behaviour

1 *Kevin*, aged 7 years, a child with moderate learning difficulties, relates only to adults. Integration into a mainstream class has proved impossible despite all efforts, because Kevin communicates with no-one except his teacher. He understands language quite well, but his expressive language is marred by a slight speech defect. He sits passively in class, never shows aggression or unhappiness but will not respond to the efforts made by other children to involve him in their activities — efforts which are diminishing as a result of Kevin's lack of response. He rarely initiates any activity, even non-verbal, by himself.

2 *Ruth*, aged 11 years, attends school infrequently, seldom for more than three days at a time. This is a pattern set by her older sister. When in school, Ruth is an isolate, making little or no contact with

the other children in her class. Her mother colludes by always providing a reason for Ruth's absences.

3 *Jimmy*, aged 7 years, is above average in intelligence, but behind his peers in the basic subjects. He does not concentrate in class; is a poor mixer, with few friends; and has a number of nervous habits, such as an involuntary shaking of his head and clenching of his fists. He also has an occasional stammer, shown when under pressure.

A Mixed Pattern of 'Externalized' and 'Internalized' Behaviour Difficulties

1 *Margaret*, aged 8 years, is noticeably isolated from her peers. She seldom speaks unless spoken to directly, and always talks in an extremely quiet voice. She hangs back in every activity and is always alone at playtimes. Margaret has occasional outbursts of temper when she is physically aggressive to other children, but these tantrums are not frequent, and she quickly reverts to her withdrawn self.

2 *Ben*, 9 years of age, an attractive boy with a ready smile, has, for no apparent immediate reason, major tantrums which include storming out of the classroom, pushing past anyone in his way with total disregard for them and throwing himself down in a corridor. He then cries uncontrollably for a period before allowing himself to be coaxed back to the classroom. These outbursts can take half-an-hour to resolve, by which time the whole class has been upset.

3 *Emma*, aged 8 years, overreacts in any situation in which she feels herself to have been unfairly treated. She cannot line up unless she is at the front of the line, pushes and jostles until someone confronts her. Then she sulks and withdraws into herself, refusing to co-operate. Similarly, Emma cannot wait her turn in board games, which deteriorate into quarrels because she wants her 'go' immediately. She demands, and generally receives, a disproportionate amount of attention from her teacher.

As the above case-studies show, children may behave differently in different situations, at different times, and towards different individuals. EBDs may be relatively short-lived, or persist over a considerable time. The quiet, withdrawn child who is well-behaved in class but who has emotional problems may be overlooked to a greater extent than pupils with overt behaviour difficulties (Herbert, 1974). However, Moses (1982) considers that teachers do appear to be aware of the problems of withdrawn children, and seem to make a clear distinction between behaviour that is problematic to the child and behaviour that creates a discipline problem for the teacher. Merrett and Wheldall (1984) have suggested that teachers may find behaviour that is relatively trivial troublesome in class. In their study, teachers identified talking out of turn, disturbing others, a lack of attention and disobedience as the chief irritants.

The identification of children with EBDs in school will be considered later in this chapter. However, the above discussion and examples make it clear that it is not easy for teachers to be sure whether a child showing emotional and behavioural difficulties needs more than the usual disciplinary procedures employed in the classroom or a little extra attention. It is perhaps best to regard any display of behaviour or feeling which seems out of the ordinary, or does not respond to normal attention, as at least requiring further investigation, for example, by a teacher sharing thoughts on a child with colleagues or having an informal talk with the parents. In pursuing the matter, teaching staff should take care not to label, stereotype or stigmatize a child while he/she is under scrutiny.

Prevalence

Teachers of children aged 7–11+ will be interested in knowing how many pupils with EBDs are likely to be found in their classes. It is difficult to give a precise answer to this question, as so many factors affect estimates of the prevalence of EBDs. These factors are discussed below.

The Methods used to Obtain Estimates of Prevalence

Clearly, the method employed by researchers in attempts at discovering the extent of EBDs in schools will affect the estimate finally obtained. Teachers may be asked to nominate children presenting behaviour difficulties in class, without the use of a schedule or checklist. For example, Merrett and Wheldall (1984), who surveyed 119 junior (7–11 years) class teachers (average class size 30.5) in nineteen schools in the Midlands (UK), reported that 281 boys and 111 girls were nominated by the teachers as 'disruptive', and ninety-six boys and 121 girls as 'withdrawn'. The pupils nominated in this way represented about 17 per cent of the total sample of around 3600, that is an average of five to six pupils in a class of thirty.

In a wider survey involving 12,310 pupils aged 7–11+ in sixty-one schools in England, Croll and Moses (1985) found that 7.7 per cent of the sample were nominated by teachers as showing behavioural or emotional problems. Over twice as many boys as girls were seen by teachers as presenting EBDs. The researchers found that the teachers were quite good at identifying children with special needs of a variety of kinds in response to the simple question (for example, does the child have a behaviour problem?) without further prompting.

The use of a systematic screening schedule or checklist (see later in this chapter) may help to focus on those children who are unobtrusively disturbed as well as those showing more overt signs of poor adjustment. Further, having a two-tier approach (for example, screening by teachers followed by a clinical-type enquiry designed to obtain detailed information on those pupils picked out by the screening procedure) tends to lower the final estimate of prevalence of EBDs which require intervention of some kind. For instance, in the Isle of Wight study involving 2199 10 and 11-year-olds, Rutter *et al.* (1970) selected 172 boys (8 per cent of the sample) and ninety-nine girls (around 4.5 per cent of the sample) as showing 'deviant' behaviour on the basis of a screening schedule. After clinical enquiry, seventy-five boys (3.4 per cent) and forty-three girls (2 per cent) were considered to be presenting what the research team called 'a psychiatric disorder' warranting attention.

Who Does the Rating

Even in the same school, differences will be found between individual teachers in their perceptions of emotional and behavioural difficulties. Some teachers will be quick to detect early signs of such difficulties and to report them; others will be slower to notice indications of disturbance, or else will have a greater tolerance of, say, behaviour that some teachers might find disruptive. Long experience in the classroom could lead to earlier identification of EBDs, but also to greater skill in dealing with problems effectively. Harris *et al.* (1993) suggest that teacher differences within schools in rating EBDs in mainstream primary schools are more important than the differences existing between teachers working in different schools.

A number of studies have found that parents and teachers may have very different perceptions of the same children. The Isle of Wight Study (Rutter *et al.*, 1970 and 1975) reported that a schedule used with parents identified an almost totally different sample of 'deviant' children from that picked out by a schedule of similar format used with teachers. In a survey of behaviour problems in a sample of 951 7-year-old New Zealand children, 17.3 per cent were identified, by the parents only, as having a high level of problem behaviour, 8.9 per cent by the teacher only, and as few as 5.5 per cent by both parents and teachers (McGee *et al.*, 1984). Verhulst and Akkerhuis (1989), in a study of parents' and teachers' reports of behavioural and emotional problems in 1161 Dutch children aged 4–11 years, found only low to moderate agreement between the reports from the two sources, with parents identifying more problems than teachers. In children aged 6 to 12 years, the highest agreement was reached for externalized problems (see also Achenbach *et al.*, 1987 and Touliatos and Lindholm, 1981).

The above findings emphasize the need to obtain information on children from as many sources as possible within a school, and to consult parents whenever a pupil is considered to present EBDs in class.

The Location of the School

The location and catchment area of a school will affect the prevalence of EBDs, which tends to be related, at least to some extent, to the home background of the pupils. Individual schools in so-called disadvantaged areas, such as are found in many inner cities, do not necessarily contain large numbers of pupils with EBDs. However, in general very different rates of behaviour disorder are found in different types of area (whether inner city or suburban, socially disadvantaged or advantaged, urban or rural). For instance, the overall 'deviance' rate in a survey of 1689 Inner London 10-year-olds was 19.1 per cent, as compared with 10.6 per cent on the Isle of Wight, a relatively much more advantaged area (Rutter *et al.*, 1975). It is likely that the varying prevalence of behaviour difficulties according to location relates to differences in home, school and community environments.

Membership of certain ethnic minority groups has been associated with the prevalence of EBDs. For example, Rutter *et al.* (1974), in a total population survey of all 10-year-old children in an Inner London borough, found that teachers, using a rating schedule, reported more than twice as many pupils from families of West Indian origin as from 'non-immigrant' backgrounds to present EBDs. However, it is worthy of note that the difference between the samples was entirely confined to 'deviance' involving disturbances of conduct, and did not exist for emotional or mixed types of deviance; also that no differences were ascertained between West Indians and 'non-immigrants' in terms of disorder shown at home. Further, in interpreting the findings of studies such as that by Rutter and colleagues, it is necessary to take into account that some teachers have stereotypes of behaviour considered characteristic of certain ethnic minority groups (Swann Report, DES, 1985). For instance, Asian pupils are generally considered to be well-behaved in school, whereas West Indian pupils are seen by many teachers to be less well-motivated in school and more prone to behaviour problems than other children (Stone, 1981).

Sex Differences

By the age of 7, a clear-cut sex difference is found in the prevalence of EBDs overall, as a number of studies demonstrate. For example, Stevenson *et al.* (1985), using the Rutter Teachers' Child Behaviour Scale with a representative sample of 535 8-year-olds (270 boys, 265 girls) from an Outer London borough, reported 28 per cent of the boys as presenting 'deviant' behaviour, as compared to 15 per cent of the girls. This difference was the result of significantly more of the boys (17 per cent) showing 'anti-social' deviance than the girls (5 per cent), whereas there was little difference in the prevalence of 'neurotic' deviance between the sexes (11 per cent of boys, 10 per cent of girls). In general, other studies (for example, Rutter *et al.*, 1970 and 1975; Merrett and Wheldall, 1984; and McGee *et al.*, 1984) tend to confirm this pattern of sex differences in behaviour, though in some cases more girls than boys are rated as presenting internalized forms of EBDs.

There does not seem to be a completely convincing explanation for sex differences in respect of EBDs, but it is probable that constitutional, congenital and environmental factors are all involved (see chapter 3). Different levels of social expectancy and tolerance of misbehaviour are probably important factors (Peterson, 1961).

Cross-cultural Differences

There may be differences between different countries in the ways in which behaviour of various kinds is perceived. For instance, Weisz *et al* (1989), who compared behavioural and emotional problems of 6 to 11-year-old Thai and American children reported by teachers, found that Thai children were rated as having more problems in respect of both overcontrolled and undercontrolled behaviour. They suggest that Thai adults tend to be unusually intolerant of aggressive acts or disobedience in children. Vikan (1985), in a survey of 1510 10-year-olds in Norway, found that far more children were rated by teachers, parents and health nurses as 'neurotic' than as having 'conduct disorders' (ratio 2.33:1), unlike the picture given by many studies elsewhere. Vikan considers that a partial explanation of his findings may lie in the tendency of Scandinavian psychiatrists to prefer a 'neurotic' to an 'antisocial' diagnosis in dealing with children.

Continuity and Discontinuity

A question of considerable interest to both practitioners and researchers is the extent to which children presenting EBDs at a particular stage in their development continue to show such difficulties over time. This question is not easy to answer, since the issues involved in considering continuities and discontinuities in child development are complex (Rutter, 1989a). Upton (1981) stresses that there is continuity as well as discontinuity in children's development, while Clarke and Clarke (1984) assert that the major picture is of the inconsistency in the growth of human characteristics: most of the children who have an emotional or behavioural disorder either get better or worse — few stay the same.

Much, too, depends on whether intervention is tried, the timing of any action and the effectiveness of attempts to modify behaviour. It is possible, also, that teachers' perceptions of, and attitudes towards, deviance are important factors in the continuity of at least some behaviour problems. Teachers may feel strongly about any challenging behaviour shown by their pupils, and their attitudes towards troublesome children may not easily change (Safran and Safran, 1985). If a child is labelled 'disruptive' or 'anti-social' and becomes the target for persistent negative comment on the part of members of a school staff, it will be difficult for the label to be removed. Further, circumstances at home and at school which affect the child's emotional and social growth may change, for the better or for the worse. Marital difficulties, for instance, may be eased or become exacerbated over a period, while going into a different class at school may result in altered behaviour being shown by a child.

Looking Back

It would seem that while many problems arise for the first time in middle childhood, a sizeable proportion of children presenting EBDs at this stage have a history of behaviour disturbance going back to earlier years. Richman *et al.* (1982) followed up ninety-four children in London showing behaviour problems at 3 years of age and a control group of ninety-one children free from such problems at that stage of development. On the basis of all the available information, the research team concluded that 62 per cent of the problem group still displayed some degree of disturbance at 8 years of age. Among those who had shown evidence of disturbance at 3, the following variables were particularly predictive of continued problem behaviour:

(i)   *gender*: being male rather than female;
(ii) *degree of disturbance*: having moderate and severe rather than mild disorders;
(iii) *nature*: showing restlessness and hyperactivity.

Children not disturbed at 3 years were most likely to become so if:

(i)   they showed any problem behaviour, even to a minor degree;
(ii) they were restless and hyperactive; or
(iii) their family relationships were disharmonious.

Looking Forward

If a forward rather than a retrospective look is taken, longitudinal studies indicate that patterns of behaviour may well have become firmly established in some children by the age of 7 to 11+. In a follow-up at adolescence of the Isle of Wight 10 and 11-year-olds previously referred to in this chapter, Graham and Rutter (1973) found that, of the children diagnosed as showing conduct (externalized) disorders at that age, three-quarters were still presenting behaviour problems at 14 and 15 years. Children with 'emotional' or 'internalized' disorders did better, but as many as 46 per cent still had problems in adolescence, while 58 per cent of those who had shown 'mixed' disorders continued to present such symptoms. Robins (1966, 1972, 1978, 1981 and 1991), West and Farrington (1977), Osborn and West (1978) and Mitchell and Rosa (1981) all found that many adolescents and young adults who are persistent offenders or show other deviant behaviour had a previous history of emotional or behavioural problems in childhood.

Loeber (1982) stresses that it is important, for practical purposes, to identify at an early age, these children who are at risk because of chronic anti-social conduct and to distinguish them from those whose anti-social acts are more likely to be temporary. On the basis of a review of the literature, he suggests that children who initially display high rates of anti-social behaviour are more liable to persist in this behaviour than those who initially show such behaviour to a lesser degree. Further, Loeber asserts that chronic delinquents tend to have been children who were anti-social in more than one setting (family, school, community), who displayed a greater variety of anti-social acts, and who showed an early onset of such behaviour. Loeber observes that the number of youths who engage in overt anti-social acts (fighting, disobedience and so on) declines between the ages of 6 and 16, whereas during that period the number of youths who participate in covert acts such as theft and/or the use of drugs or alcohol increases.

The longitudinal study by Cox (1978) of a group of ninety-seven children from schools serving 'deprived' catchment areas confirms the need to focus attention on those children showing persistent behaviour problems. Teachers' ratings of the overall adjustment in school of the sample were obtained on four separate occasions over a six-year period up to age 12. Over the four occasions between 14 and 23 per cent of the children were judged to be poorly adjusted, but there was appreciable variation from one occasion to the next in terms of which children were so rated. A small group of six children showed persistent behaviour problems throughout the six-year period; this group also showed a high incidence of severe backwardness in reading.

Rutter (1989a), in considering the pathways from childhood to adult life, highlights the association between aggressiveness, hyperactivity and low peer acceptance shown in childhood and later disorder in adulthood. A Montreal study by Soussignan and others (1992) indicates that 6-year-old boys who show persistent signs of conduct disorder together with hyperactivity tend to have a worse prognosis for continued problem behaviour during the primary school years than boys who display conduct disorder but without hyperactivity.

Identification of EBDs

Teachers rely mainly on sensitive observation of the children in their classes to identify those who seem to need attention because of emotional or behavioural difficulties (Laing and Chazan, 1987). Although teachers should endeavour to look out for positive aspects of their pupils' behaviour, they may find it useful to bear in mind what are the signs of a child being disturbed. They may find it useful, also, to complete a behaviour schedule or checklist for the whole class (see later in this chapter); or, if this is too time-consuming, to do it only in the case of the pupils where the structuring of observations is likely to fill out a picture of behaviour perhaps hazily formed. Further, knowing something about the relationships between the pupils in a class, through the use of sociometric techniques, is likely to add to the teacher's awareness of which children are disliked, rejected or isolated.

Danger Signals

It is not easy, without reference to the specific context of a child's behaviour, to indicate what may be regarded as signs of significant difficulties, but the following may be considered as possible 'danger signals' in the primary school class, indicating that the child needs some help:

(i)   deterioration, sudden or gradual, in the standard of presentation of school work;

(ii)   restlessness, overactivity and an inability to sit still and concentrate — not explained by the inappropriateness of the tasks facing the pupil;

(iii)   a lack or loss of interest in school activities;

(iv)   a frequent loss or changing of friends; isolation in the playground;

(v)   detachment from, or a lack of interest in, other children; a lack of enjoyment in working and playing with others;

(vi)   uncalled-for aggressive acts; disproportionate anger when mildly reprimanded;

(vii)   bursting into tears for trivial causes or for no apparent reason;

(viii)   a speech defect, emerging or becoming worse in stressful situations; bizarre speech or refusal to communicate;

(ix)   indulgence in excessive fantasy: always seeming 'far away';

(x)   stealing, especially articles of little value, or to give away to others;

(xi)   repeated clowning in class; and/or

(xii)   excessive anxiety or fear in situations offering a possibility of failure, perhaps leading to the total avoidance of such situations.

This should not be taken as a complete list of behaviour indicative of a child's emotional disturbance, and it should be borne in mind that not all children who show some of these symptoms will need special attention. In deciding what action, if any, is necessary, the teacher should be guided by the degree and persistence of the behaviour as well as by his/her knowledge of individual children and their backgrounds.

Screening Schedules and Checklists

Teachers usually find that the completion of a behaviour schedule or checklist is valuable in systematizing their own thinking about a child. Screening schedules do not aim to probe into the causes of any EBDs which the pupils may present, but merely to provide a structured framework for the rater's impressions of the actual behaviour displayed, as an initial step in taking any action necessary. There are now available several schedules which focus on emotional and behavioural difficulties. The use of such schedules has the advantage of not involving the child at all directly, and enabling the rater to look at the results in the context of those obtained on other samples. They are best applied after observation over a month or two, as well as before and after a programme of intervention. They enable teachers to make comparisons of children's behaviour in different settings; and different teachers may compare their ratings of the same children (Scherer, 1990a). For a comprehensive review of measures of emotional and behavioural disorders in children, see Boyle and Jones (1985).

Listing a pupil's difficulties may have the disadvantage of encouraging a teacher to think in negative terms about that child. It is desirable, therefore, to use a schedule which elicits the child's strengths as well as weaknesses, or else to use additionally a more general scale which puts the emphasis on the child's total functioning in the classroom, and includes 'pro-social' or positive items (for example, Scherer's School Skills Checklist, 1988, discussed below). Examples of 'pro-social' behaviour are 'is calm and relaxed', 'is flexible in adapting to new situations' and 'is neat in school activities' (Roper and Hinde, 1979); and helping, sharing, comforting, praising and showing affection (Konstantareas and Homatidis, 1984).

Behaviour Schedules (Britain)

Two schedules have been widely used in Britain in the last two decades or so, namely the Bristol Social Adjustment Guides: the Child in School (BSAG) (Stott and Marston, 1971; Stott, 1975) and the Rutter Child Behaviour Scale, B (Rutter, 1967; Rutter *et al.*, 1970). A more recent checklist is that devised by Galvin and Singleton (1984), as a part of a system of management of behaviour problems in school. These three schedules will be described below.

1   The *BSAG*'s stated aim is to give a picture of the child's behaviour and to help in the detection of emotional instability. It is intended for the observation of children aged 5 to 16 years in day school, and provides a comprehensive variety of phrases (both positive and negative) describing a child's behaviour. The teacher has to underline those phrases which most nearly describe that behaviour. Examples of the format are as follows.
      Classroom behaviour: Too timid to be any trouble/too lethargic to be troublesome/generally well-behaved/misbehaves when teacher is engaged with others/openly does things he/she knows are wrong in front of teacher.

Ways with other children: Squabbles, makes insulting remarks/shows off (clowns, strikes silly attitudes, mimics)/gets on well with others; generally kind, helpful/spiteful to weaker children when he/she thinks he/she is unobserved/tells on others to try to gain teacher's favour/ nothing noticeable.

A diagnostic form is provided for recording those phrases under-lined which indicate 'under-reactive' or 'over-reactive' behaviour, and for scoring 'core syndromes'. The scores on the BSAG form the basis for identifying children with varying degrees of under-reactive or overreactive behaviour, in terms of categories ranging from 'stability' to 'severe maladjustment' (Stott, 1975). The five core syndromes are, in brief:

Underreaction

1	unforthcomingness	—	timidity: fear of new tasks or strange situations
2	withdrawal	—	various types of social unresponsive-ness
3	depression	—	lack of response to stimuli

Overreaction

4	inconsequence	—	unthinking, uninhibited behaviour
5	hostility	—	provocative or sullen avoidance of offers of friendship

The BSAG also makes provision for scoring items indicating underreaction or overreaction that do not fit clearly within any of the core syndromes.

The Guide takes fifteen to thirty minutes to complete for each child and may, therefore, be considered too time-consuming to use in the case of a large class. If this is so, it will be useful to answer the six adjustment pointers suggested by Stott (1963 and 1981), and then to employ the full guide in the case of those children who seem to present a problem. Baker *et al.* (1985) used a slightly modified version of Stott's adjustment problems in a survey of primary school children in North Wales. Teachers were required to tick the following statements if they were applicable to an individual pupil (the ticking of any item would indicate the need for further investigation):

(i) 'The child's behaviour is not as you would expect of a normal, alert child of his/her age'.

(ii) 'This child is exceptionally quiet, lethargic, depressed or very variable in energy'.

(iii) 'This child lacks concentration or is restless in a way that seriously hinders his/her learning'.

(iv) 'This child's behaviour seriously hinders the learning of others in class and/or makes teaching difficult'.

(v)   'This child in general does not get on with other children and/or teachers'.

(vi) 'There is something in this child's behaviour or appearance which makes you think he/she might be emotionally unstable or suffer from nervous trouble'.

Stott's approach to scoring, classification and the interpretation of the syndromes used in the Guide has not commanded universal support (see Buros, 1965; Chazan, 1970). However, the BSAG has undergone several revisions, and both researchers and classroom teachers have found it of use. A good overall picture of a child's behaviour in school emerges from the completion of the Guide, and a strong point in its favour lies in the fact that the adverse items are intermingled with positive ones. Thus, the rater is not disposed to take up a negative stance through the use of the schedule. For classroom use, therefore, it proves a very useful instrument, especially as a basis for discussion with a senior colleague or an educational psychologist.

2   The *Rutter Child Behaviour Scale B* consists of twenty-six statements of possible behaviour problems, the teacher having to check which statement — 'certainly applies', 'applies somewhat' or 'doesn't apply' — is appropriate for the pupil concerned. Examples of the items used are as follows:

1   Very restless. Often running about or jumping up and down. Hardly ever still.
5   Frequently fights with other children.
10 Often appears miserable, unhappy, tearful or distressed.
17 Tends to be fearful or afraid of new things or new situations.

The Rutter Scale has been carefully validated and widely used with children between 7 and 11+ years of age. Teachers find it straightforward to use and easy to complete (Chazan *et al.*, 1977), but its format (all negative items) may lead teachers to adopt a negative set towards particular children (Fitton, 1972). It should be used, therefore, together with a more positively-framed general schedule; and it should be kept in mind that the scale is intended to be a simple screening instrument to be followed up when necessary with a more detailed assessment. It should be used with caution in distinguishing between 'normal' and 'high risk' individuals (Venables *et al.*, 1983), as well as in allocating children to particular categories such as 'neurotic' or 'anti-social'.

3   The *Galvin and Singleton* (1984) behaviour checklist covers seven main areas: classroom conformity, task circulation, emotional control, acceptance of authority, self-worth, peer relationship and self-responsibility/problem solving. The teacher records his/her observations on the checklist to build up a profile of the child's behaviour and identify the

priority problem areas. Following the completion of the Checklist, a *Daily Record* is used to list priority behaviours each day and to develop goals and strategies.

A *Monthly Progress Chart* helps to monitor the effectiveness of the strategies employed. The *Manual* includes advice on the implementation of behaviour modification strategies (see chapter 5).

Behaviour Schedules (USA)

1 The *Achenbach and Edelbrock (1983, 1986) Child Behaviour Checklist Teacher's Report Form (CBCTRF)* has been used in a number of studies of children aged 6 to 11 years, including cross-cultural comparisons of the nature and prevalence of behaviour problems (Achenbach et al., 1987; Verhulst et al., 1988; Weisz et al., 1989; Auerbach and Lerner, 1991). This checklist includes 118 specific problems such as 'argues a lot', 'fears going to school', 'feels too guilty', 'can't concentrate'. On the basis of observations over two months, teachers score each item 0 'not true' of the child, 1 'somewhat or sometimes true' or 2 'very true' or 'often true'. Syndromes yielded by statistical analysis of the scale include aggressive, uncommunicative/social withdrawal, depressed, delinquent, hyperactive somatic complaints and anxious. A study carried out in Wales has confirmed that this is a reasonably valid scale for use in Britain (Harris et al., 1993).

2 The Conners (1973) Teacher's Rating Scale (CTRS) has also been employed in cross-cultural/studies of primary school children (Luk et al., 1988; Luk and Leung, 1989). This scale has thirty-nine items, each describing a problem behaviour to be rated by the teacher on a four-point scale (0–3), on the basis of observation over the previous month. Scores may be calculated on four sub-scales: (i) conduct problems; (ii) inattentive-passive; (iii) tension-anxiety; (iv) hyperactivity. Examples of the behaviour to be rated include 'fidgeting', 'restless', 'sensitive', 'disturbs' and 'destructive'.

3 Neeper and Lahey (1988) have devised a *Comprehensive Behaviour Rating Scale for Children* (CBRSC), intended for the age range 6 to 14 years. It contains eighty-one descriptive statements, with the analysis yielding seven scales relating to problems in school, namely: (i) inattention/disorganization; (ii) linguistic/information processing; (iii) conduct disorder; (iv) motor hyperactivity; (v) anxiety/depression; (vi) sluggish tempo; and (vii) social competence. Using a five-point scale, the teacher indicates how representative each item is of the child.

General Schedules

An example of a general schedule recording observations of the child's functioning in school, which might be used to put EBDs in a wider context, is

Scherer's (1988) School Skills Checklist (see Scherer *et al.*, 1990). This checklist, which is comprehensive and has a positive format, requires a rating on a five-point scale of applicability. It covers: A. Arriving at school/lesson; B. Physical abilities; C. Starting the lesson; D. Getting on with the lesson; E. Presentation of work; F. Peer interaction skills in class; G. Receiving and giving praise; H. Apologizing skills; I. Conversation skills, knowledge of school rules, home-work; J. At the end of lessons; what the pupil enjoys receiving in class; K. Social interaction in and out of class; L. Teasing and bullying; M. Showing feelings; N. Play and leisure activities.

Scherer suggests that checklists such as the above can be used to highlight a pupil's assets and deficits. Deficits should be listed in order of priority, and used to formulate goals for action to meet the pupil's needs.

Sociometric Techniques

Children who are ignored or actively rejected by their peers in school tend to be poorly adjusted and in need of help (Smith and Cowie, 1991). The use of sociometric techniques may be helpful to the teacher in identifying these pupils, particularly those who are 'isolates' in the classroom or playground groups. Each child in a class may be asked to name their three best friends, or to rate all the other children in the class in terms of 'like' or 'neutral'. A simple way of detecting 'isolates' is the 'Companionship Choice' approach. This requires the pupil to name three children, out of the whole class or other specified group, with whom he/she would like to associate on each of a number of criteria (usually three), for example, 'Which child in the class would you like to sit next to/play with /work with on a project?' Those children who receive no choices or no more than one or two might be regarded as 'isolates' or 'neglectees' and as warranting further investigation (for further information on sociometric techniques, see section 5, Cohen, 1976).

Asking children to state whom they do not like would be useful in identifying those children who are definitely rejected by their peers rather than just isolated from the group. However, it is undesirable for a teacher to invite such negative nominations, as this might draw increased but unwanted attention to children already out of favour. Bearing this in mind, teachers should still be on the look-out for rejected children, as it is children who are rejected by their peers who tend to be particularly at risk of continued maladaptive behaviour such as aggressiveness, disruption and hypersensitivity (Coie *et al.*, 1990; Dunn and McGuire, 1992). For example, Ladd (1983) found on the basis of observation of 8 and 9-year-olds in the playground, that rejected children spent more time in arguing and fighting than children who were of average social status or popular. Asher *et al.* (1990) assert that children in middle childhood who are disliked by their peers report more loneliness than those who are more acceptable to the group. Dunn and McGuire (1992) suggest that children may be rejected by their peers for a variety of reasons, including failure to abide by the rules of the group, being aggressive to an extent not sanctioned by the group or being withdrawn and aloof. Parker and Asher (1987) stress that it is necessary to distinguish between children who are actively disliked and rejected and those who are not liked but not specifically disliked. It is rejected children, not neglected children, who are most at risk of future failure in school, dropping out and delinquency.

Sociometric techniques should be used sensitively, and their results should be interpreted with caution. Pupils will be helped to understand why they are being asked questions about their peers if a sociometric enquiry is followed by practical action, for example, allowing children to sit next to chosen friends for some activities. It should be borne in mind that social status may change over time and in different settings, though it tends to become more stable with age, especially in the case of rejected children (Coie and Dodge, 1983; Hartup, 1983). Not all rejected children are aggressive or have low self-esteem (Boivin and Beigin, 1989); and socially withdrawn children may be unsociable or shy and timid but anxious to fit into the group (Asendorpf, 1990; Dygdon and Conger, 1990). However, many children who are ignored, neglected or rejected by their peers are unhappy and lacking in some social skills (Dodge *et al.*, 1986); it is important to identify these children as early as possible.

Overview

Children in the 7–11+ age range may present emotional and behavioural difficulties (EBDs) in a variety of ways, through anti-social conduct, hyperactivity or withdrawal, or through a mixture of externalized and internalized behaviour symptoms. The prevalence of EBDs in a school will depend on the methods used to identify such difficulties, the attitudes and perceptions of the raters and the make-up of the school population in terms of social background, gender and ethnicity. While some teachers will have only one or even no pupil in their classes needing help on account of emotional or behavioural disturbance, others particularly in socially disadvantaged areas, may have three or more children in a class of thirty who appear to be poorly adjusted.

Some children show EBDs for the first time in middle childhood, having no history of previous disturbance; but others have already caused concern at an earlier stage. Whether EBDs exhibited in middle childhood persist or not will depend on a variety of factors, including the timing, nature and effectiveness of any action taken. Children who are persistently and severely anti-social, hyperactive and/or rejected by their peers are the ones who seem to be most resistant to modification of their behaviour, and such children may continue to show deviant behaviour, into adulthood. It is important to identify EBDs in school as early as possible, but with sensitivity and avoiding negative labelling. Identification may be carried out through observation, with or without the aid of systematic schedules or checklists, and through the use of sociometric techniques.

Chapter 3

Assessment in Context

The identification of children with EBDs in the classroom is the first step in the teacher's attempt to understand the reasons for the difficulties and to take appropriate action to remedy the situation. Next, the teacher needs to make as complete an assessment of the problem as he/she can, bearing in mind that spending time on assessment is worthwhile only when it is linked to measures to be taken to help the children involved. A comprehensive assessment includes (a) describing in precise terms both the nature of the difficulties presented and the various contexts in which these do or do not occur; (b) drawing up a profile of the many aspects of the child's development and scholastic progress, highlighting strengths as well as weaknesses; (c) getting to know, as far as proves possible and desirable, relevant details of the child's home background; (d) selecting those factors, including school and classroom variables, which seem to be associated with the child's behaviour; and (e) trying, from what is known about the child and his/her background, to hypothesize what the child's needs are and to plan a programme of action which will lead to better adjustment.

A full assessment of a child's emotional and social needs is a complex matter, and in many cases, particularly of the more serious EBDs, a teacher will require help from senior colleagues or outside professionals such as those working in the school psychological service. The Draft Code of Practice on the Identification and Assessment of Special Educational Needs (DEF/WO, 1993), established by the 1993 Education Act, recommends the adoption of a model of assessment and provision involving five stages. The first three stages are school-based, with the school's SEN Coordinator and the teacher taking the main responsibility; at the fourth and fifth stages, if these prove necessary, the school shares responsibility with the LEA, with a statutory assessment and a statement of possible outcomes. The Code goes into detail concerning the action that should be taken at each stage. It advises that, as early as at the first stage, the teacher should collect information from the parents and the child himself/herself as well as from observation and school records. If appropriate, external specialists should be consulted.

Whoever is involved, the assessment of EBDs is always a matter for team-work, with each member of the team taking a broad view of the situation while making a contribution from a particular standpoint. It is always necessary to avoid being dogmatic in reaching conclusions about the causes of a child's behaviour, as there are so many factors possibly associated with behaviour problems in children. These factors will be discussed below, after which assessment techniques will be considered.

Factors Associated with EBDs in Middle Childhood

It is rarely possible to state with precision what has caused a child to behave in a particular way at any time. Even in cases which seem, on the surface, to be clear-cut, careful enquiry often shows that a combination of factors is at work rather than a single factor. The 'precipitating' factors which appear to have been directly responsible for a problem may be less important than other 'predisposing' factors which have helped to bring about an explosive situation. For example, mild reproofs in class provoked a boy of 8 to outbursts of temper tantrums, but it turned out that the child was reacting to a prolonged experience of stress at home rather than to being told off in school. Further, it is often difficult to sort out cause and effect: for example, a speech problem such as stammering may cause a child to feel under strain, or pressures at home or at school may contribute to the speech impediment.

It is important to avoid expecting all EBDs to be the result of extremely adverse or unusual circumstances in the life of the pupil presenting such difficulties. As pointed out in chapter 1, children have to face many 'normal' tasks in everyday life which may cause them stress and strain, and many 'normal' events in the life of a family, such as illness or moving house, may cause a child short-term or more lasting distress.

The case of *Gareth* (aged 8 years) mentioned in chapter 2 (see p. 20) provides a good illustration of the many factors involved in a single instance of EBDs. Assessment by a child guidance team showed that the boy's highly aggressive behaviour was related to a variety of factors.

1 *Medical/physical*: Although Gareth did not have epileptic fits as such, his outbursts of violent temper seemed to be related to a neurological problem: an electroencephalograph revealed brain patterns of an epileptic type, and it was considered that his outbursts could be regarded as 'epileptic equivalent'.

   Gareth also had a squint and suffered from being called 'Squinty', which led to low self-esteem.

2 *Home background*: The home background was not harsh or rejecting, and the parents were cooperative and sympathetic to the boy. However, the mother had a history of depression, and the father had had two nervous breakdowns. The home was clean and pleasant, but small and overcrowded. Overall, therefore, family life was stressful and provided persistent models of tension, adding to the pressures on Gareth.

3 *Intellectual*: Gareth was slightly below average in measured intelligence.

This may have been a partial explanation of his educational retardation, but did not account for his extreme lack of basic attainments.

4 *School background*: The school was not hostile to Gareth in spite of his provocative behaviour, but they were unable to offer him much direct specialized help for his school failure.

The multi-faceted assessment of Gareth's problems led to intervention of varied kinds — medical, educational, therapeutic and social. Over a period, the boy improved greatly, remained in his usual class and was able to enter secondary school without presenting undue problems.

Temperament

From early infancy, considerable individual differences are apparent in temperamental characteristics such as adaptability, intensity of reaction, quality of mood and distractibility. By middle childhood, this individual variability in temperament is still obvious to parents and teachers. At this stage, some children will seem to be natural 'copers' in the face of difficulties, while others will find life burdensome or present themselves as lethargic and unresponsive. Some children are very placid and seem to react to adversity without turmoil; others are easily excited and overreact to everyday occurrences. Some are readily distracted from tasks in hand, and put off by the slightest obstacle; others show much persistence, even when faced with difficulties.

Temperamental factors tend to receive less attention than environmental factors in any consideration of EBDs in childhood, probably because the former seem to be genetically determined to quite an extent and therefore less amenable to intervention. However, Carey and McDevitt (1989) argue that greater sensitivity to children's individual differences in temperament will improve the understanding and treatment of children with emotional and behavioural disorders. Studies have suggested that temperamental features do play a significant role in the origin of behaviour problems in children, even if it is the interaction between temperament and environment which determines the development of such problems (Thomas and Chess, 1977; Dunn, 1980; Rutter, 1981).

From the practical point of view, it is helpful for parents and teachers to recognize the importance of temperamental characteristics in their relationship with children, which need to be considered as a two-way process rather than in terms of the child merely responding to his/her environment. St. James-Roberts and Wolke (1984) stress that ratings of temperamental characteristics by mothers reflect the mother's own psychological state and how she understands her child's behaviour. Teachers of 7–11-year-olds, who spend much of their time with the same class, will find that they get on better with some children than with others. Occasionally there may be a clash between the teacher's own temperament and that of a pupil. Recognition of such a situation may help to prevent conflicts from arising which could lead to outbursts of temper or withdrawal on the part of the child. As Rutter (1981) points out, children with adverse temperamental characteristics are much more likely to be the target of criticism from others: a child's temperament may protect him/ her or put him/her at risk because of its effect on interaction with adults.

Medical/physical Factors

Recurrent illness or a marked physical or sensory disability may be factors in the causation of EBDs. Poor physical condition may reduce a child's resistance to everyday stresses, or lead to frequent or prolonged absences from school. Missing school may result in the child feeling unsettled when he/she is present and suffering from a lack of continuity in school work, perhaps leading to some degree of retardation in all or some aspects of the curriculum. An awareness on the part of the teacher of possible difficulties arising out of frequent absences due to illness may well help to minimize the consequences of absenteeism. Some pupils who are vulnerable to ill-health may be kept at home without justification by parents who are over-protective. The mother of *Ruth*, mentioned in chapter 2, seemed to enjoy having the girl at home, and Ruth's work and behaviour suffered greatly as a result of poor attendance at school over a number of years. Effective action in such cases is limited, especially if the parents go out of their way to justify the absences.

Chronic physical disorders

Children with a marked physical or sensory defect or disability do not always present EBDs. Anderson (1973), for example, found that about three-quarters of a sample of seventy-four physically disabled children aged 7–11+ in ordinary junior schools in Britain were making a good adjustment to their disabilities. However, children with chronic physical disorders (for example, asthma, cancer, anaemia, renal failure) are more likely than healthy children to show evidence of emotional disturbance (Eiser, 1990; Pless and Nolan, 1991). Eiser, in a review of the literature, concludes that children with disorders of the central nervous system and those with birth defects (for example, cardiac disorder, hearing impairment) are particularly at risk; also, that younger children are more affected in terms of school achievement, while older children tend to show a lack of social adjustment.

Thomas (1978) stresses that physically disabled pupils are often susceptible to emotional disturbance because of their feeling of being different from others and because of the attitudes of peers and society generally. Children with disabilities will often be frustrated at not being able to do what others can achieve with ease. Pless and Nolan (1991) find that chronically ill or disabled children are especially at risk of social isolation, low self-image, attention-deficit disorders and internalized/neurotic behaviour difficulties.

Brain damage

Children whose disability has a definite neurological basis tend to present EBDs to a greater extent than physically disabled children where there is no evidence of brain damage (Anderson, 1973; Rutter, 1989b; Taylor, 1991). As the case of Gareth illustrated (see chapter 2), symptoms of epileptic activity may be associated with behaviour disturbance, and the discovery of abnormal brain rhythms may lead to the helpful use of medication in the control of aggressive behaviour. However, there are often difficulties in the interpretation of brain patterns charted by electroencephalography (Deonna, 1993). Certain kinds of behaviour such as extreme restlessness/hyperactivity and distractibility tend to be regarded as associated with indices of brain-damage, and children displaying such behaviour are often diagnosed as having 'minimal brain damage' (Schachar, 1991). While the concept of 'minimal brain damage' (MBD) is not altogether unmeaningful, Schmidt *et al.* (1987), for example, are unable to support the basic assumptions of the clinical MBD concept, namely the existence of a well-defined, homogeneous syndrome; linkage with specific emotional or behavioural disorders; and evidence of increased perinatal risk. The link between brain damage and EBDs in children is still not fully understood (Werry, 1972; Rutter, 1977; Schachar, 1991).

Inconsequential behaviour

Of particular interest to teachers is the concept of 'inconsequential' behaviour developed by Marston and Stott (1970), and regarded by them as of a neurological and probably congenital origin. 'Inconsequential' pupils are those who are easily distracted and who often provoke or interfere with others. They are frequently the focus of disturbance within the classroom, playing the clown and shouting out regardless of the normal conventions; they tend not to be responsive to discipline and generally act very impulsively and foolishly. While behaviour of this kind will be familiar to teachers, it is questionable whether in many cases 'inconsequential' pupils can be clearly distinguished from those with 'conduct disorders' in general.

Exposure to lead

In recent years, a number of studies have been carried out to determine the association between behaviour disorder in childhood and exposure to lead. A link between blood-lead levels and children's behaviour has been found by Yule *et al.* (1984), Silva *et al.* (1988), and Thomson *et al.* (1989). In particular, exposure to lead seems to lead to hyperactivity, distractibility and aggressive behaviour. However, Taylor (1991) cautions that it is difficult to know whether the relationship between lead and behaviour is independent of other adverse features of the child's environment such as a discordant family atmosphere.

Diet, food additives and allergies

Teachers, especially those working in socially disadvantaged areas, will readily acknowledge that malnutrition or a poor diet may well result in a child being inattentive and sluggish in school. Further links between diet and behaviour problems have been claimed, particularly since Feingold (1975a and 1975b) asserted that hyperactivity is often caused by an intolerance of food additives such as artificial colours and flavourings and antioxidant preservatives. These claims have aroused much public interest and concern, but subsequent appraisal has not given them a great deal of support. While acknowledging that a small proportion of children with behaviour disorders may be helped by eliminating food additives from their diet, Taylor (1979) and Graham (1987), for example, argue that there is no conclusive evidence which supports a strong connection between being allergic to food additives and behaviour problems in children. An objective judgment on this issue awaits further controlled experimental research (see Connor, 1991).

Although physical factors related to EBDs in childhood may be largely outside the teacher's control, the adjustment of physically ill or disabled pupils is affected by the attitudes of teachers to them, and by the opportunities given to them for experience of achievement and success in school. The adjustment of some of these pupils is also related to the way in which their parents adapt to the stress that results from having to care for a severely physically disabled child (Sloper and Turner, 1993).

Home Background

A high proportion of children with EBDs are significantly affected by an adverse or disturbed family background, whatever other factors are additionally involved (Blanz *et al.*, 1991). Among the cases mentioned in chapter 2, there was a history of child abuse in *Margaret's* family; and *Andrew's* mother had little control over him and was not cooperative with the school's efforts to help him. *Gareth* was helped by his mother's sympathetic attitude towards him, but was undoubtedly disturbed by his parents' mental ill-health, while the overcrowded atmosphere at home added to his problems. *Jimmy* had a very good home materially, but his stammer and nervous habits were particularly in evidence when his parents applied undue pressure on him at home, as they often did.

Familial adversities

A variety of familial adversities have been found to increase the risk of a child having EBDs at home or at school. Among these, low socioeconomic status associated with a low income; mental illness of the parents; overcrowding, especially in the case of a large family; marital disharmony and violence; the child having to go into care; and models of delinquent behaviour presented by either parent have been emphasized (Rutter and Quinton, 1977; Wolfe *et al.*, 1988; Blanz *et al.*, 1991). Fergusson *et al.* (1990), in a study of children up to 11 years of age in New Zealand, found that collectively, life events, social position and living standards act as relatively strong determinants of vulnerability to problems in the areas of health, education, behaviour and delinquency.

Relationships

While adverse material conditions in the home add to the pressures on a family, it is probable that the most important factors among those relating to the home in the causation of EBDs concern the relationships within the family. Rutter (1981) points out that children can be helped to cope if the relationships between the parents are supportive, and if they have a good relationship with at least one parent. Among factors most frequently present in cases of children with EBDs are rejection by parents or a lack of warmth in the parent-child relationship, inadequate or distorted intrafamilial communication, inadequate parental supervision and control, over-protection and the loss of a love relationship (Steinhausen and Erdin, 1992). Anti-social, over-reacting behaviour is, in particular, the outcome of parental discord and erratic or severe discipline (McCord, 1990). The strength of the association between poor parental disciplinary practices and EBDs in children seems to lie in their creation of a vicious circle. A difficult child easily irritates the parents, and proves unrewarding to them; they then alternate between trying to avoid the child and treating him/her harshly. This treatment in turn only increases the child's hostile and unrewarding behaviour (Patterson, 1982; Robins, 1991). Criminal, alcoholic or aggressive parents also provide unsatisfactory models of behaviour for their children (Rutter, 1985). Particularly vulnerable families are those where the mother is young or of low ability (McGee *et al.*, 1984).

Child abuse

The physical abuse of children at home often goes undetected, sexual interference being particularly difficult to uncover. Teachers need to cooperate with the appropriate agencies, as far as they can, in the identification of abuse within the family. While some children show a remarkable resilience even in the face of considerable ill-treatment (Frude, 1989), abused children may not be able to give their full attention to their school work. Reported effects of child abuse in the home include emotional, behavioural and bodily disturbance, as well as low self-esteem (Walford, 1989).

It is important for teachers and other professionals not to regard children as necessarily the victims of particular social and familial circumstances, and not to be over-ready to cast blame on parents. The parents may be doing their best to cope in most difficult conditions, and the possible negative effect of a child's behaviour disorder on a family's functioning should always be taken into account (Blanz *et al.*, 1991). Children's own perceptions of the family situation should also be considered whenever practicable: Rossman and Rosenberg (1992) assert that children's beliefs that they have some measure of control over their parents' conflicts help them to cope with these conflicts.

Positive parental attitudes and behaviour can help to reduce children's behaviour problems (Patterson, 1982). It is, therefore, desirable for schools to involve the parents in the early assessment of a child's EBDs, and to seek advice from support agencies when this is considered appropriate. The part played by the parents in relation to EBDs and cooperation between home and school are discussed further in chapter 6.

The School Environment

Until recently, school factors have not been as readily acknowledged as possibly contributing to the causation of EBDs as factors relating to the home. Schools have perhaps tended to attribute EBDs, even those occurring in the classroom, to parental deficiencies rather than examine their own policies, attitudes and practices. It is true that, in general, primary schools offer a secure and congenial environment to their pupils, who are for the most part treated sensitively in the classroom. However, when behaviour difficulties occur in school, it is not sufficient to regard within-child or within-family factors as the only ones of importance. Rutter (1981 and 1983) stresses that the mechanisms which are operating in producing problem behaviour in the home probably apply as much to school influences as to family effects. These mechanisms include emotionally discordant patterns of social interaction, unsatisfactory relationships, inefficient supervision and discipline, and deviant models of behaviour. It is always worthwhile, therefore, for school staffs to consider whether their attitudes, management practices or other within-school factors have any bearing on the general occurrence of EBDs in the school as well as on individual cases. The links between EBDs and learning difficulties and between EBDs and school absenteeism also need to be taken into account.

School policies and practices

The role of the school in relation to pupils with EBDs is discussed in detail in chapter 4. Here it will suffice to refer to a project developed by Gersch (1990a) in primary school. Gersch emphasizes the need for schools to assess individual roles, procedures, staff organization, hierarchies and the pastoral care system. He describes a behavioural systems project in which two educational psychologists worked with a primary school staff in carrying out a programme which aimed at (i) clearly understanding the behaviour required of the pupils; (ii) helping to encourage that behaviour; (iii) discussing and sharing new systems of behaviour management; and (iv) arriving at a clear and agreed system of management.

School staff were able to produce a list of pupil behaviours which were causing concern, under three main headings (i) school work and working on-task; (ii) anti-social behaviour/social behaviour; and (iii) following school rules. Working parties were set up to focus on these areas of concern, and the staff finally produced a number of recommendations for action on their part, including a reorganization of the school day, publishing a new set of school rules, a review of the curriculum, and agreed procedures for teachers dealing with disruptive behaviour. Gersch emphasizes the value of a whole school staff working together, analyzing problems, brainstorming ideas and suggestions, making decisions together and evaluating outcomes of any changes made.

Chapter 4 considers the sense of collective purpose needed in the complex organization of the school; the importance of a 'whole school' policy; lines of communication within the school; and decision-making involving the governing body and school staff.

Teachers' attitudes and classroom management
Teachers' attitudes are a major factor in the placement, management and treatment of pupils with EBDs (Ritter, 1989). Studies have shown that many mainstream teachers have negative perceptions of, and limited tolerance for, problem behaviour in the classroom, particularly if this amounts to disruption of the class (Cooper, 1989; Semmel *et al.*, 1992). This is not surprising, as increasing pressures on teachers have caused them considerable stress, quite apart from that resulting from having to deal with pupils who interfere with the conduct of classes (Travers, 1992).

It is, indeed, easy for the relationship between a teacher and a troublesome pupil to deteriorate rapidly. As in the case of relationships between parents and difficult children referred to above (p. 41), a vicious circle may be created. A troublesome pupil may provoke and challenge the teacher deliberately; a teacher feels threatened and shouts at or punishes the child; the child may feel picked on or think that the teacher is being over-severe, and may try to retaliate by even worse behaviour than before. However positive the teacher may wish to be, it is admittedly difficult to sustain a positive attitude in the face of persistently hostile and disruptive behaviour on the part of a pupil who is undermining the teacher's authority and self-image. It is essential, therefore, for teachers to be involved in a calm examination of their attitudes and relationships as a part of a school's self-assessment.

Many teachers successfully manage their classes without a deep examination of their techniques. However, it is useful, particularly for less experienced teachers, to have a framework for the analysis of those aspects of lesson planning and management which contribute to a smooth partnership in learning between teacher and pupil and which help to prevent behaviour difficulties from arising (Smith, 1990). Apart from the relationships which they develop with pupils, teachers need to think about the rules they set up and the routines they follow; also the system of reward and punishment which they employ, and their recourse to grouping within the class. The design of the classroom and the seating arrangements are also of relevance in the maintenance of class control (Hewett and Taylor, 1980; Wheldall, 1989).

Teacher's attitudes and expectations, as well as classroom management skills, are discussed further in chapter 5.

Learning difficulties
Emotional and behaviour difficulties often occur together with learning difficulties, especially in reading (Chazan, 1985). For example, 7.7 per cent of a sample of 12,310 pupils in English primary schools were identified by their teachers as having behaviour problems in the study carried out by Croll and

Moses (1985): more than two-thirds of the children with EBDs had associated learning difficulties. In the cases of EBDs presented in chapter 2, a number (including *Gareth*, *Kevin*, *Ruth* and *Jimmy*) had serious learning difficulties that needed special attention.

It is difficult to establish whether learning difficulties are the result or cause of EBDs, or whether both learning failure and poor adjustment are related to a common cause, such as social disadvantage. Some studies have indicated that more often behavioural difficulties, especially of the anti-social type, develop as a secondary reaction following educational failure (Davie *et al.*, 1972). Failure in an important area of learning is likely to lead to frustration; compensatory acting-out; and/or anxiety and possibly withdrawal. Failure in the basic subjects may result in an attitude of seeming not to care about people or scholastic progress, truancy perhaps combined with delinquency, or school refusal. Learning difficulties often produce a poor self-image, especially when the child has to face the disappointment of parents, the mockery of fellow-pupils, or perhaps even the disapproval of teachers, who may interpret the pupil's failure to learn as due to 'laziness' rather than to other factors beyond the child's control. Children at about the age of 7+ are particularly vulnerable: they are no longer regarded as 'infants', they are expected to have made significant progress in school, and they are less likely to receive direct instruction in the elements of reading, writing and mathematics once they have left the infant school. Even intelligent children with learning difficulties may see themselves, or be seen by others, as slow learners generally.

Other studies stress that it is poor adjustment which causes learning difficulties rather than the other way around (McMichael, 1979; Chazan *et al.*, 1977; Stott, 1981). According to this view, EBDs are often likely to lead to a learning blockage. Children may be hampered in learning by a primary lack of confidence, insecurity, lack of motivation, anxiety or excessive timidity — all impeding progress in class. Some young children bring to school EBDs which affect their self-perceptions, the perceptions of themselves by others and their progress in class. Bale (1981) concludes that a chain reaction often sets in: hyperactive, restless behaviour before entry to school leads to difficulties in learning which result in anti-social tendencies after two or three years in school. Stott (1981) also found that hyperactivity as well as lethargy (unresponsiveness) at 5+ years of age were closely associated with poor attainment, both in reading and number, three years later.

Sturge (1982) suggests that there may not be a simple causal relationship between reading problems and behaviour disorder. Rather, the link between reading retardation and anti-social behaviour which is often found could be the result of associated background factors, particularly those common in inner city areas — disadvantaged and broken homes, large families and perhaps less effective schools. Or else, those children who have both behaviour and learning difficulties form a very mixed group, to which a variety of explanations could be applied.

The close association between poor adjustment and learning difficulties means that in the assessment of individual pupils with EBDs attention should be given to the nature of any learning problems that may be present, with a view to appropriate remedial measures. Helping the child to make better progress with school work is likely to improve motivation and self-concept (see chapter 5 for a further discussion of learning difficulties in relation to pupils with EBDs).

School absenteeism

The child's school attendance history may well be of relevance in the assessment of EBDs. Children who are frequently and persistently absent from school, whatever the reason, tend to present behaviour problems when they are in class (Reid, 1982). Research studies have shown an association between poor school attendance, low basic attainments and delinquency (Carroll, 1977; West, 1982; Reid, 1985). Fogelman (1978) found that pupils as young as 7 years of age with poor attendance records obtained lower scores on average in basic attainments than children with satisfactory attendance, and were more often rated by their teachers as deviant in their behaviour.

Non-attendance in the early years of schooling is a predictor of poor attendance in the secondary school as well as of continued low attainment (Fogelman, 1978). Hibbett and Fogelman (1990), and Hibbett *et al.* (1990), in a follow-up into early adulthood of children truanting at school, found that truancy was associated with lower status occupations, less stable career patterns and more unemployment. Truancy also seemed to be linked with subsequent marital and psychological problems in early adult life.

The causal relationship between school absenteeism and EBDs is not a simple one. Persistent absence from school, as previously mentioned (p. 38) may lead to unsettled behaviour on return to school, hurtful comments from classmates and perhaps critical remarks from teachers. Or else being far behind others in school work and being often reprimanded in class for troublesome behaviour may result in a child being reluctant to go to school. As truants often find themselves with little to do when not at school, it is not surprising that they are susceptible to becoming involved in delinquent acts, especially if a number of children truant together (Farrington, 1980). In many, though not all, cases of poor school attendance, there is a background of disadvantage in the home and community (Hersov and Berg, 1980; Galloway, 1985a; Reid, 1986; Fogelman, 1992).

Peer Influences

Although peer influences in the causation of EBDs are probably less powerful in middle childhood than they are later on during adolescence, it has already been pointed out in chapter 1 (pp. 5–6) that children at this stage may react badly to being rejected by their peers. Rejection may lead to social withdrawal and undue submissiveness, or else aggressive behaviour (Dunn and McGuire,

1992). If a child fails to respond to overtures made by others, classmates will give up trying to be friendly. For example, other children soon began avoiding *Margaret* (see chapter 2) when their initial attempts at approaching her amicably were not welcomed, and this avoidance was exacerbated by Margaret's rare but dramatic outbursts of temper. In the case of *Kevin*, the boy would sit passively amongst other children. He never showed aggression or unhappiness but would not respond to their efforts to involve him in their activities — efforts which decreased as a result of his passivity.

Children who have a tendency towards various forms of troublesome behaviour in class — for example, clowning, bullying or defying a teacher — may be encouraged in this behaviour by one or more of their classmates. *Mark*, who bullied other children selectively, did not have any friends who were consistently loyal to him, but was supported in his misbehaviour by different boys who attached themselves to him at different times. Some children may be easily attracted to models of deviant behaviour shown by other members of the class, or take pleasure in being the leader of gangs: *Andrew* was a skilful leader of a group of younger children, whom he led into all kinds of trouble. Further, children who are the victims of bullying may react with symptoms of stress (see chapter 10 for a detailed discussion of bullies and their victims).

Exposure to Television Models of Anti-social Behaviour

During the past three decades or so, the influence of the mass media on the behaviour of children has been much debated. In view of the attractiveness of the visual medium to children from an early age, the controversy has in particular centred around the effects of models of violence, vandalism and other forms of anti-social activity shown on television. Reviews of the relevant research have reached differing conclusions (see Smith and Cowie, 1991, pp. 155–162). Some writers, like Howe (1977), assert that exposure to violence on the screen does contribute to aggressive behaviour and imitative anti-social acts; some are sceptical about blaming television for deviant behaviour in children (Howitt, 1982; Cullingford, 1984a); while others, such as Greenfield (1984), stress that although television violence can result in a desensitizing of feeling, the medium can also help in the education of the emotions.

Recently, the easy availability of videos showing acts of extreme violence ('video nasties') has increased public concern and has led to action by the Government intended to reduce children's access to such videos. Disagreement persists about the effects on children of viewing such undesirable models of behaviour as well as about what effective action, if any, can be taken to prevent children from watching unsuitable television broadcasts and videos (Coughlan, 1994). No aspect of television content should be seen as an independent cause with consistent effects irrespective of the social, emotional and cognitive conditions of the viewer (Hodge and Tripp, 1986). However, the issue remains an important one watching as television plays a large part in most children's daily activities. Quite apart from 'video nasties', some of the programmes shown as part of regular broadcasts for children are unduly frightening and violent. Even if they do not have a permanent effect on the behaviour of the majority of child viewers, these programmes may cause even well-adjusted children to develop fears and to suffer nightmares; and they may add to emotional disturbance in the case of more vulnerable children, as suggested by an early study by Himmelweit *et al.* (1958). Children in middle childhood are at a sensitive stage, and it is advisable, therefore, that their parents should accept the responsibility for exercising a degree of control over their children's viewing habits. Schools should discuss television viewing with parents generally, and be ready to offer support and guidance on an individual basis to parents needing help in this connection.

Assessment Techniques

Whether or not a child with EBDs is assessed by the School Psychological Service or other agencies such as a hospital clinic, the teacher's report on the child is an essential part of the assessment. In recent years, there has been an increasing tendency to ask children themselves about their behaviour and their situation (Robins, 1991); and, as previously emphasized, it is important to obtain the parents' views, especially as they may provide a different perspective on the child's problems. Peers may also be involved in the assessment of behaviour disorders (Achenbach *et al.*, 1987).

The Role of the Teacher in Assessment

Teachers have to rely mainly on observation in making judgments about their pupils (see Wragg, 1994). It is not easy for a teacher in charge of a whole class to make planned and systematic observations on an individual child or a small group, and so teachers' observations tend to be informal and relatively unstructured. Yet precise observation of a child's behaviour in a variety of situations may well alter a teacher's initial judgments. For example, a teacher viewing a child negatively because of troublesome behaviour in class may find that, over a period, the pupil engages in a good deal of positive or 'pro-social' behaviour (for example, helping others, paying attention to tasks, sharing with classmates). Many periods of watching may be required before full insight is gained into a child's behaviour (Tyler, 1984). The use of schedules such as the Bristol Social Adjustment Guides and the Rutter Child Behaviour Scale as a first step in recording observations has been discussed in chapter 2.

In spite of all the difficulties, teachers should try to make their observations of pupils with EBDs as objective, accurate and informative as possible. It is not sufficient merely to label a child as 'aggressive' or 'timid' in school.

It is helpful to record exactly how a child behaves in specific circumstances in a variety of contexts. Questions a teacher might bear in mind include:

Where does the behaviour occur?
At what time(s) of day . . . ?
How often and for how long does the behaviour last?
When does the child behave normally and positively?
What activities hold the child's attention?
With which children does the child play cooperatively?

In the case of a child being aggressive in class or playground, the teacher might attempt to ascertain:

What form does the aggression take (for example, hitting, scratching, kicking)?
Against what or whom are the aggressive acts aimed?
Are the aggressive acts carried out by the child alone or with others?
What happens beforehand/afterwards?
In what circumstances does the child quieten down?

With a timid, inhibited child, the teacher might want to know:

In what particular circumstances is the child particularly timid or withdrawn?
What does the child do in the face of stress? (for example, covering face, sucking thumb, refusing to answer).

The use of a schedule for recording critical incidents, that is incidents which seem to be of significance, may help the teacher to monitor a child's behaviour over a period of time. Steed and Lawrence (1990) describe the use of an Incident Report Form in a survey of disruptive behaviour in primary schools. This form asks a number of factual questions, for example, about place, time, participants and activities, and provides a list of possible descriptions of the incident to be ticked by the teacher. Steed and Lawrence have also developed a more detailed form which aims at obtaining an immediate picture of the incident, as well as a description of the events which led up to the incident and its consequences. The form also includes sections for recording recommended action and strategies actually implemented.

If a behaviour modification programme is initiated in school (see p. 80–1) a chart of the child's behaviour is needed to establish a baseline and to record the course of the child's actions over a period. For example, the number of 'disruptive' incidents involving a pupil in class may form the basis of a graph: or sample observations may be taken at specific times each day for a few minutes in each hour. The aim, say in the case of a 'hyperactive' child, might be to find out when the child is more restless and distractible than usual and what conditions seem to trigger off this overactivity. The child's less restless periods should be noted, and the situations in which he/she seems to quieten down (Wheldall and Merrett, 1984; Scherer, 1990a).

Obtaining a baseline will help teachers to decide on the objectives of any help they plan; in what circumstances giving reward might be most effective; and what kinds of rewards might be given. The baseline will also be invaluable in monitoring the success of any strategies of intervention carried out.

Ascertaining the Child's Point of View

The 1989 Children Act, relating mainly to the work of Social Services Departments (see Department of Health, 1990; Russell, 1990 and 1991), stressed the importance of having regard to children's rights, but in the past children's own views about their situation have been given little attention in educational legislation (see also chapter 5, pp. 86–7 and chapter 9, p. 144). The Code of Practice established by the 1993 Education Act puts a new emphasis on taking into account, in an assessment of pupils with SENs, the opinions and wishes of the children themselves. The Code recognizes that the effectiveness of any assessment or intervention will be influenced by the involvement of the child concerned. It recommends that schools should consider how they should involve pupils in decision-making processes and record pupils' views in identifying their difficulties, setting goals and monitoring progress.

It is not easy to put into practice the principle of taking into account the right of children to be heard. As the Code points out, due regard must be paid to the child's age, ability and past experiences. Questioning children has to be carried out with sensitivity, and sympathetic encouragement will always be required to help pupils respond fully. Teachers should strive to find time to have a relaxed discussion, away from other children, with a child in any kind of difficulty. The scope of the discussion will be determined by the teacher's discretion in each case, and guided by the need to avoid over-sensitive areas, at least in the early stages. Gersch (1990b) has developed a Child's Report Form for use with adolescent pupils. This could well be adapted for use with younger children, with adult help in writing the answers where necessary. The form includes questions relating to (i) school background; (ii) present school; (iii) special needs; (iv) friends; (v) hobbies, interests and out-of-school activities; (vi) the future; and (vii) additional comments.

Gersch stresses that there would appear to be much merit in inviting pupils to discuss their perception of problem behaviour more openly, to listen to what children have to say about what triggers off such behaviour, and to ascertain what the significance is of the behaviour to them. It seems sensible to do this in the context of obtaining general information of the kinds asked for in the Child's Report Form.

Obtaining Information from Peers

As previously emphasized (see pp. 45–6), unsatisfactory relationships with peers in the classroom, playground and out-of-school settings are often found in cases of EBDs in middle childhood. Information from peers can, therefore, form a valuable part of the assessment of EBDs (Coie and Dodge, 1983), though in general it is not desirable to confront pupils directly with questions about their peers. It is essential to obtain the points of view of both victim and aggressor in cases of 'bullying' and to involve all members of a group cooperating in anti-social behaviour (see chapter 10). The use of sociometric techniques to alert teachers to some of the group dynamics in a classroom, and to help in the identification of isolated and rejected children, has been discussed in chapter 2 (pp. 33–4). The application of such techniques as these is unlikely to meet with resistance from most teachers, but there may justifiably be a reluctance to go further in gathering information by questioning children not directly affected, about a fellow-pupil's behaviour. Thus a child's peers may, for good reasons, not be fully utilized as a source of information in the assessment of EBDs.

The Contribution of Parents to Assessment

It has already been stressed that whenever a school is concerned about a pupil's behaviour or emotional development, it is desirable to call in the parents at an early stage (pp. 41–2). This needs to be done with sensitivity, avoiding causing undue alarm or appearing to attribute blame to the parents for the problems the child may be presenting or experiencing in school. The class-teacher as well as the headteacher should be involved in a calm talk with the parents, sharing facts about the child's general progress and development as well as perceptions of his/her behaviour.

Chazan *et al.* (1983) have listed a number of points which might be borne in mind by teachers in their talks with parents of young children. Many of these points apply equally to parents of older pupils including the desirability of:

(i) having a clear idea about what information is needed, and preparing some basic questions beforehand;

(ii) establishing rapport, which will be helped by the teacher's positive attitude to the child and by imparting information as well as seeking it;

(iii) being ready to listen;

(iv) starting off by trying to obtain factual information about the child and family which is not likely to arouse resistance on the part of the parent;

(v) discussing matters of delicacy only when the parents are receptive and willing to talk about them.

Teachers should keep in mind that their own perceptions of a child's behaviour may often differ from those of the parents (Touliatos and Linholm, 1981). This may be the result of different standards of tolerance or show that the child behaves differently at home and at school. Too much should not be attempted in an initial discussion with the parents, and further talks may be needed. It may be advisable in some cases to leave exploration of family concerns and relationships in depth to specialist agencies, such as the psychological or social services. At a suitable stage, when the problem has been assessed sufficiently to warrant it, the discussion should focus on what strategies might be adopted to modify the child's behaviour, possibly involving the school and the parents as well as the child (see chapter 6 for a further consideration of the role of the parents).

The Role of the School Psychological Service in Assessment

A number of support services, including the health and social services as well as voluntary bodies, may be in a position to contribute to the assessment of pupils presenting EBDs in school (see chapter 6, pp. 100–3). However, it is the School Psychological Service, often working closely with a Child Guidance Centre providing psychiatric advice, which has the key role in the assessment of EBDs. Educational psychologists work in a variety of ways, but their functions usually include making an objective assessment of the child's abilities, school progress, strengths, weaknesses and needs. They will seek to put the child's behaviour in the context of his/her school and home environment. They do this through direct observation, tests, interviews and/or discussions with the child, parents and teachers (see Wood *et al.*, 1993; McCall and Farrell, 1993).

Educational psychologists will also advise on the extent to which the school appears to be dealing appropriately with the child and whether further investigations or special provision are required. Some will wish to work with the teacher in making precise sample observations in order to establish a baseline for further action, perhaps leading into a behaviour modification programme, as discussed earlier in this chapter (pp. 48–9); others may focus on obtaining the child's own perceptions of his/her situation. Psychologists are well placed to monitor the effects of any intervention programmes undertaken in school, and to decide whether a reassessment of the situation would be appropriate.

Increasingly, educational psychologists prefer to work in the realistic context of the school rather than from a clinical base often remote from the school. They are also ready to co-operate with staffs in assessing the needs of schools as well as those of individual pupils, and to set up in-service courses for teachers which provide guidance in the assessment of EBDs (see Pearson and Lindsay, 1986; Burden and Hornby, 1989; Frederickson *et al.*, 1991).

Recording

It has been stressed that the assessment of a child's emotional and social progress is a continuous process, and should be recorded as a part of a child's educational profile. In cases where EBDs are involved, detailed and systematic records need to be kept by a school, to include any checklists, schedules or other forms used, the class teacher's observations and accounts of significant incidents. A note should be kept of the positive aspects of the child's behaviour, and a record of discussions with the child, the parents and support agencies. Apart from the importance of having such records in writing rather than relying on memory, teachers tend to find that collating written information helps to clarify their thoughts and enables them to form a more coherent and objective picture of the child. To save time and to encourage a consistent approach throughout a school, agreed and prepared forms for use by teachers may be of value. Teachers can record much information through ticks or underlining, but it is always desirable to leave plenty of space for free comment and longer accounts of incidents when these seem necessary.

It is difficult to decide for how long records of a child's behaviour should be kept. It is useful to keep records as long as a behaviour difficulty continues, and it is clearly an advantage to be able to look back at a child's history when new concern arises about his/her behaviour. It is also helpful to be able to pass records on from the primary to the secondary stage or if the child moves school. However, to regard behaviour records as permanent documents may result in a child retaining the label of being 'a problem' when he/she has long ago achieved a successful readjustment. Schools need to consider their policy on this issue carefully.

Schools are now required to give details of a pupil's general progress, which should include information about his/her behaviour, as part of a written report to be provided at least annually to the parents (DFE, 1992c; Education Circular No. 14/92). The Draft Code of Practice on SENs recommends that schools should keep records of all children with SENs and of the steps taken to meet those needs. For practical advice about record-keeping in the primary school, see Ritchie, 1991; Lawson, 1992; Mitchell and Koshy, 1993; and Johnson *et al.*, 1992.

Overview

A comprehensive assessment of a child's emotional and social difficulties and needs is a complex matter. Many interacting factors are associated with EBDs in middle childhood, including temperament, medical/physical factors, home background and family relationships, the school environment, learning difficulties and peer influences. Teachers, by virtue of their direct contact with their pupils in a variety of circumstances, always have a very important contribution to make to the assessment of EBDs. The more precise the information they can provide the more valuable this contribution will be. It is also desirable to obtain the child's own point of view and, as far as is practicable, that of his/her peers. Parents need to be involved at an early stage whenever a school is concerned about a child's behaviour or emotional development; and it may be advisable to call in one or more of the support agencies, especially the School Psychological Service, to assist in the assessment of the more serious cases. Accurate and up-to-date records of significant aspects of children's behaviour and critical incidents should be kept by the school.

Part II

Helping Children with EBDs

How Schools can Help

Disaffection with school may not be so common among younger pupils as it is among older ones but, as previous chapters have shown, behavioural and emotional difficulties certainly exist in the primary school. There are children who, from an early age, cause concern to their teachers because it is felt that their response to what school is offering is not what it might be. Such children may be apathetic, disruptive, uninterested, aggressive, timid, cheeky or sullen. They may show more than one of these behaviours at the same, or different, times and may also show other types of negative behavioural response.

Response is not one-way. Children interact with what is happening to them and around them and, by interacting, change what happens next. What goes on both inside and outside classrooms reflects many contributing factors. To focus on pupils as the sole source of uncooperative behaviour is to consider only part of the situation, just as it is if only the classroom is considered. All those involved bring into the school with them what has happened to them outside it. The following case study illustrates the complex interrelations involved which, in this instance, led to a complete break-down in the educational process.

Andrew, who is 10 years of age, has shown difficult behaviour for a number of years. His twin sister, Alison, has learning difficulties but cooperates well with the school. Andrew is disruptive within the classroom, particularly so with some teachers. He has indulged in pilfering on several occasions, often truants and, over the holidays and weekends, has been involved in vandalism of school property, including daubing graffiti on the walls. He is often discussed in the staffroom, his reputation going before him even into the secondary school he is likely to enter. He is known to be the leader of a group of younger boys who eagerly do his bidding. Over the years, different members of staff have tried to cope with Andrew in a variety of ways, some more successfully than others. He is completely beyond the control of his mother and there is no father at home. Andrew has never been referred to anyone outside school and the full extent of his problems only became known when, after a number of serious incidents, he was excluded from school.

Would a systematic programme of help, offered when his behaviour first gave cause for concern, have prevented the escalation of Andrew's problems? Who should have been helped — Andrew, his mother, his teachers? Who should have provided the help — his teacher, his headteacher, a social worker, the educational welfare officer, an educational psychologist? What help could have been given? Perhaps some guidelines towards the answering of these questions will emerge from the discussion in this and subsequent chapters.

School Policy

It is not easy to carry out research on how schools can be effective in helping children with behavioural problems. Yet, general observation of primary schools seems to reveal considerable differences between schools and between teachers in the extent to which their pupils appear cooperative and motivated in their response to the educational programme offered. There is no simple way of accounting for these differences, although some studies have tackled the problem (for example, Mortimore *et al.*, 1988). Effective schools would seem to have positive expectations of their pupils, a sense of collective purpose in what they are doing and easy communication at all levels both inside and outside the school. Adult and pupil expectations will be discussed later in this chapter; the other two areas will now be looked at a little more closely.

A Sense of Collective Purpose

Schools are very complex organizations which have to be managed, as does every organization, but with the added complication that there is little time left over from teaching to allocate to management. Yet if schools are run on purely autocratic lines, with headteachers taking all decisions, staff may well lack any sense of collective purpose and may, in turn, act autocratically in their own sphere of influence. The management task is certainly simplified when one person decides what will be done and the other adults involved implement the decisions without question. But with no easy means of influencing these decisions, many staff may lack commitment to them and may come to feel apathetic towards them or even resentful of them. Pupils may also have similar feelings in like circumstances.

To try to involve all concerned in the decision-making process is, of course, extremely time-consuming. Construction of a 'whole school' policy (i.e., a policy agreed through discussion with all school members concerned) with regard to the teaching of reading, for example, can become a nightmare undertaking, usually only resolved by compromise. A 'whole school' policy for pupil behaviour is likely to be even more complex because of the many aspects which have to be considered. Some of these aspects are:

(i)   the age and sex of the pupils;
(ii) the age and sex of the members of staff;
(iii) parental views on child-rearing;

(iv)   personality variables in all concerned;
(v)   staff competence;
(vi)   ethnic, intellectual and cultural differences.

There are many others.

Without a 'whole school' policy, however, discipline may become confused, approved behaviour may not be clearly indicated and children may learn how to dissemble or even rebel instead of how to cooperate. Punishments can also be erratic. There would seem, therefore, to be a strong case for at least attempting collective decisions on pupil behaviour so that everyone in the school feels that they know what is expected of them and what will happen if reasonable standards are not maintained. Total conformity will never be achieved and, indeed, may not be desirable but consistency should be possible.

What specific areas should a 'whole school' policy on behaviour address? They must surely include:

(i)   the importance of respect and concern for others and for their belongings;
(ii)   the degree of noise and movement that is acceptable;
(iii) what is to be done with those that need help;
(iv)   how communication between all concerned can best be achieved.

Docking (1990a) suggests that staff should consider a number of topics when working out a 'whole school' policy. These include management styles; behaviour during play-times and lunch-times; rewards and punishments; liaison with parents; curricular content and classroom organization; support for teachers; and strategies for monitoring behaviour standards. How these can be tackled and how other people (including pupils, parents and lunch-time supervisors) can be involved are discussed further in Docking's book.

While individual schools will decide on different guidelines, the success of any agreed policy depends in no small degree on the involvement of the headteacher in the discussion on, and the implementation of, that policy. This is not only because the headteacher may be the ultimate sanction but because only his/her overt support of any decisions taken can ensure that they will become established and identified as part of the school ethos.

Lines of Communication

In primary schools, where numbers are reasonably small, most school members are known to each other by name. Communication would seem to be easy. This apparent ease can, however, be deceptive. As Docking (1990a) points out, if a teacher refers in the staffroom to a child as being particularly naughty or a 'troublemaker', the others may chorus agreement, thereby confirming that pupil's status in the eyes of the teacher and, indeed, of his/her colleagues, or they may express surprise or disbelief with the view expressed, thereby causing the teacher to think again about the problem. The staffroom, therefore, provides a central area for the dissemination of information but also encourages almost unthinking acceptance of prevailing opinions. If a teacher's views on behaviour coincide with those of most of the other teachers, there is an encouraging feeling of solidarity ('we can't all be wrong'). On the other hand, a teacher who holds different views on the children mentioned may be influenced towards the majority view ('they can't all be wrong'), may be frustrated by or unhappy with the others' easy acceptance of a label, or may feel that the child in question presents a threat to his/her competence as a teacher. An understandable expression of annoyance or anger at a child's behaviour may not lead to teachers reconsidering their approach to him/her but may instead have other undesirable effects.

Even in relatively small schools, therefore, there need to be lines of communication which enable a problem to be tackled constructively. Agreement on the existence of 'troublemakers' does not help anyone and disagreement clearly indicates the need for further discussion. Teachers and others (for example, the caretaker, the dinner ladies, the 'lollipop' person) should know who has to be contacted about their concerns. Part of the 'whole school' policy on behaviour is the delineation of a hierarchy of support for staff which is more formal than a casual remark in the staffroom but not so formal as to make those in question feel reluctant to make their concerns known.

As so often, headteachers are central to ensuring easy and useful communication. They can offer advice and information, can arrange for the whole staff to talk around the specific problem while relating it to pupil behaviour in general and can call in others, such as parents or psychologists, if required. In other words, the 'whole school' policy is implemented. As part of that policy is a general concern about the welfare and behaviour of all school members, no teacher should feel that a behaviour difficulty is his/her sole responsibility. Rather it should be seen as an indication that something is going wrong with the policy which, therefore, needs some fine tuning.

Lines of communication which are well-established and easy to access are fundamental to establishing acceptable behavioural standards. They must encompass all those involved with any aspect of life in school. It is clear that a behavioural policy links into the school's policy on parental involvement. It also links into policies on communication with other interested outside parties (such as therapists) and with the governors (see later).

It might be interesting to reconsider the case of *Andrew* in the light of what has just been said. First, it must be admitted that the school was largely concentrating on containing Andrew and was eventually unsuccessful in this. It is also the case that no-one else had been approached for advice (for example, advisory teachers, educational psychologists), and so no considered statement of Andrew's needs had been drawn up and no supportive help offered to his classteacher. With an agreed policy on behaviour, it is unlikely that the situation would have been allowed to deteriorate until Andrew was excluded. These points may seem unduly critical of the way in which Andrew's behaviour was handled but this is not intended. The staff were aware of what was going on, were concerned about Andrew and his mother, and were doing their best to manage his behaviour within their own classrooms. It does seem, however, that a more unified approach, with everyone (including the dinner ladies who had a bad time with Andrew and his followers) pulling in the same direction and with realistic objectives in mind as regards acceptable behaviour, might have been more productive.

The Role of the Governors

Since the Education Act of 1986, the school governing body, which includes representatives of the parents, the staff and the community, as well as members co-opted for some special expertise, has a general responsibility for the discipline and well-being of the school. To a large extent, this responsibility is devolved to the headteacher and staff of the school but they remain accountable to the governors for their actions with regard to pupils with behaviour difficulties and are expected to report to the governors any problems which arise with regard to behaviour.

Governors also have responsibilities with regard to the financial management of their schools. In so far as this affects class size, they have a considerable input into class management strategies, an area in which disruptive children are often seen as a considerable threat. More will be said about class management in the next section but meantime it could be noted that teachers report stress as arising, among other factors, from poor working conditions, including 'large size schools and classes and high noise levels' (Dunham, 1986). Financial restraints could also lead to inadequate classroom resources (for example, the use of out-dated textbooks or insufficient books for class demands), an absence of support teachers to help with pupils showing emotional or behavioural difficulties, and premises which are showing deterioration. Certainly no-one would suggest that governors are deliberately creating teaching conditions which make for behaviour difficulties in the classroom. At the same time, it must be recognized that circumstances do not always conspire towards producing the best possible conditions for teachers and pupils. The decisions of the governing body have long-reaching effects on what happens in schools and it is perhaps only fair that the ultimate responsibility for creating conditions in which schools can work efficiently and effectively lies with them.

Ease of communication is, however, often lacking in just this area of accountability and responsibility. Staff may feel that to indicate to the governors (who have the right to 'hire and fire' staff) that they are finding some children exceptionally hard to motivate towards learning, may reflect on their ability as teachers. In a small scale study of teachers and pupils in first year

(Y3) junior classes (Laing and Chazan, 1987), many of the teachers concerned felt 'somewhat uneasy' about asking for help with behaviour difficulties from their colleagues or friends. They would have been even less happy about reporting them to the governing body.

Confrontations with pupils should not be allowed to escalate until the need for exclusion is brought to the notice of the governing body. Unless there is close and frequent contact between governors and staff, such a situation can well arise (consider the case of Andrew who was discussed earlier in this chapter). It would seem that, if a 'whole school' policy on behaviour is to be established and successfully implemented, governors must be involved throughout. Their contribution must be more than simply receiving the occasional report or confirming the removal of a pupil from school and must be seen by all concerned as supportive, not judgmental.

Classroom Management

Pupils, parents, teachers, governors and indeed the general public all have views as to what constitutes an 'ideal' classroom. The problem is, however, that these views frequently differ and consensus is reached on remarkably few points. No-one, for example, would endorse the infliction of physical cruelty on children although this has not always been the case. Looking at management more positively, there might also be considerable agreement that to prevent behavioural difficulties from ever arising is probably more effective than trying to deal with them once they have occurred.

The Teacher as Manager

The Elton Report (DES/WO, 1989), which contains the findings of a Committee of Enquiry set up to examine discipline in schools, comments: 'Group management skills are probably the single most important factor in achieving good standards of classroom behaviour' (p. 70). Handy and Aitken (1986) emphasize this point when they say: 'Each and every primary teacher, therefore, has to be a manager'. They go on to point out that it is effective functioning as a manager which creates the conditions in which pupils can respond positively to educational opportunities. Even knowledge of the subject, although clearly important, is not enough if the teacher's management skills are inadequate.

First of all, the question of what has to be managed can be posed. Obviously, the nature of the teaching/learning activity is of prime importance. By this is meant the teacher's intentions as to what the children should be doing at that time, what they should be learning and how they should be learning it. Classroom learning experiences have to be designed, implemented and maintained (Calderhead, 1984). But, in addition, the teacher has to manage the allocation of time, space, resources and the people involved in the activity (Haigh, 1990).

It is not appropriate here to examine class management skills in general. There are many books which can be consulted in addition to those already mentioned (for example, Craig, 1990; Bull and Solity, 1987). Laslett and Smith (1984) suggest that effectiveness in the classroom depends on the extent to which teachers develop skills in getting pupils into classrooms; getting pupils out; getting them involved; and getting on with them. If teachers are not skilful in these areas, the classroom may well become a source of stress and unhappiness for all involved.

Each teacher has a unique approach to management and so to the decisions which are taken. It goes without saying that the contribution of the class to the effectiveness of the teacher's management skills is not insignificant. If, for whatever reason, class management comes under threat or even breaks down, positive learning is at risk. 'A successful school is one in which the relationships and interactions are facilitated and coordinated in order that the people involved can achieve their common mission' (Ainscow, 1991).

Pupils with emotional and behavioural difficulties of whatever nature or degree of severity often do not facilitate relationships with staff or promote coordinated interactions with them. In fact, it is because they do not do so that they are seen as presenting difficulties. They involve teachers in classroom incidents which throw doubt on the success of the management skills being employed. Take, for example, *Lucy*, aged 7 years, a very quiet girl in Y3 who, to everyone's astonishment, suddenly burst into tears. It transpired that she was not understanding the work being done in mathematics and, as far as she was concerned, did not feel she had any means of overcoming her difficulties. Being aware at all times of what is happening in the classroom is usually cited as a basic management skill for any teacher. How did Lucy's action reflect on this? Furthermore, what does it say about Lucy's view of herself as a class and school member that she could not indicate her problem in a more constructive way than she did?

The Teacher as Model

To suggest that teachers are, or should be, models for pupils' classroom behaviour may seem to be viewing them in an old-fashioned way. Yet, however much teachers may be wary of imposing their standards of behaviour on others, the fact remains that, at the primary stage, the classteacher is the principal adult with whom the pupils interact for considerable periods of time. Rudeness to teachers can be taken as an example. Children are often 'cheeky' to teachers, sometimes inadvertently, sometimes deliberately. Teachers' reactions are vital. If teachers respond with rudeness, anger or sarcasm, children receive a clear message as to behavioural expectations. They may also resent that the adult can display the very behaviour which is being challenged in themselves. When adults defuse the situation and, if appropriate, discuss it later in a relaxed and supportive way, pupils have been shown strategies which could be helpful to them in similar situations. The same could be said with regard to neatness, care of equipment, use of books and general appearance, to name only a few.

Adults' interactions with each other are also observed. Tone of voice, fleeting expressions and body language are easily read, even by young children, and certainly are observed at the 7 to 11 stage, when pupils are developing an active interest in social relationships and are experimenting with different roles. Erikson (in Evans, 1969) points out that pupils in the primary school have 'increased cognitive capacities and a much greater ability to interact with a much wider range of people' (p. 26). The models of behaviour presented by teachers in their dealings with other members of staff, headteachers, parents and visitors to the school are rapidly noted and considered.

The Teacher as Rule Enforcer

Teachers' aims in managing their classrooms are in the main concerned with achieving effective delivery of educational topics in a social context which will allow that effective delivery. Horbury (1990) suggests that 'socialization is a rule-based process of cultural induction where certain interactional requisites are assimilated' (p. 227). Socialization in this sense becomes a question of tension between opposites, for example between the teacher's desire for control and his/her acceptance of the importance of individual freedom in learning; or between the pupils' demands for individual attention and the recognition of the existence of a whole group to be catered for. Procedural rules are intended to ease the tensions by indicating how teachers and pupils can interact to the benefit of all. That they do not always succeed serves to emphasize the importance of this aspect of school organization.

The mismatch between outcome and intention can be seen in what happened to *David*. From entry to the reception class, David was not an easy child for his teachers to manage. At that time, and over the next few years, he had temper tantrums of considerable intensity when he was thwarted. These extreme reactions modified somewhat as he grew older but his emotional control remained fragile and he would lash out at other children if he did not get his own way. He was a bully in the playground, pushing and shoving younger children and twisting arms to get what he wanted. David had it all his own way at home, his parents making little attempt at discipline for the sake of relative peace and quiet. He always had money, wherever he got it from, and he had been known to help himself to other children's property in school.

David was not the only bully in school and, in an attempt to protect pupils, a rule was made that any pupil who physically attacked another must be sent to the headteacher. When David was just over 10 years of age, money went missing from the pocket of a member of his class. David in fact had not taken it but the finger was pointed at him. Incensed by this, David hit out at one of his accusers and was sent by his teacher to the headmaster. There David lost his temper completely and, when the headteacher approached him to try to calm him down, he kicked and punched the headteacher and was excluded from school. It should be noted that, whatever the rights and wrongs of this incident, the rule with regard to physical aggression between pupils was correctly implemented.

The above illustration reveals the moral dilemmas which surround many, if not all, procedural rules and which make it difficult for class teachers to maintain the consistency of approach and fairness of judgment essential to productive relationships with their pupils. Merrett and Wheldall (1990) suggest that teachers should establish, in negotiation with their pupils, three or four short rules only and that these should be positively, rather than negatively, phrased. These act as 'a form of prompt or cue for appropriate behaviour' rather than an immutable statement of what should not be done.

Ashton (1981) carried out an interesting piece of research with a group of primary teachers in which she endeavoured to find out what they did in order to promote the social and personal development of their pupils. While the teachers put social and personal development high on their list of aims (see also Ashton *et al.*, 1975), their strategies and objectives in pursuit of this aim were not always clearly thought out. The demands of the National Curriculum in this area may have led teachers to consider more carefully than previously how personal and social development is taking place in their classroom, as may the 'whole school' policy on behaviour discussed earlier in this chapter. On the whole, however, it would seem that teachers hope that by example, by indicating approved behaviour, by the setting of rules, and by checking undesirable behaviour in some way after it has occurred, they will promote the kind of behaviour they wish their pupils to exhibit.

Teachers' strategies in dealing with behaviour they find unacceptable are also not clearly thought out in some cases. Teachers tend to be reactive, not proactive, that is they attempt to deal with the behaviour once it has occurred rather than planning in advance to prevent the behavioural difficulties arising. In the Ashton study, it was also shown that teachers' reactions varied according to which child was involved. Teachers dealt with misdemeanours differently and with different consequences to the pupil. David may be a case in point. There are similar findings to Ashton's in the study of seven-year-old pupils carried out by Laing and Chazan (1987). 'While it can be assumed that teachers hope for long-term improvement, the coping strategies they described seemed directed towards the short term' (p. 67). These strategies, as in Ashton's study, involved either talking to the child in question, the nature of the conversation depending on which child was involved, or altering the organization of the classroom or the method of presenting the educational content. For example, they might move a child to a different part of the classroom, send a child out of the room, offer further or different examples for certain children or change the direction of their questioning.

Adopting short-term strategies within an over-developed framework of rules can provoke confrontation rather than prevent it. If there are too many rules, feelings of coercion grow and pupils resent the restrictions on their behaviour. This resentment will be even more pronounced if the rules are applied inconsistently. Yet a rigid adherence to rules may be equally unproductive. For personal and social development to occur, there must be opportunities for children to discuss their difficulties, to listen to one another and to become aware of the consequences of their behaviour for others as well as themselves. More will be said about these points in the next chapter. On the question of procedural rules, the aim would appear to be, as has been said before, to establish after discussion with all involved a few agreed and accepted guidelines to classroom behaviour which indicate clearly what behaviour is acceptable. These rules need not be hedged round with threats if they are reasonable and effective.

Attempts have been made (e.g., Galton and Simon, 1980) to classify teachers and pupils into a number of categories based on their typical approach or reaction to teaching. While it could well be that teachers and pupils have preferred patterns of behaviour, it may be dangerous to think of these patterns as fixed. It is much more likely that teachers and pupils alter aspects of their behaviour according to their perception of the situation. Personalities may clash within a classroom; stresses from outside the classroom lead to atypical behaviours inside it; preferences or dislike of certain aspects of the curriculum affect how they are dealt with; and frustration at lack of resources or space upset normal procedures. It is also dangerous if those concerned with education develop fixed expectations of others involved. The next section will consider this aspect.

Expectations and Attitudes

In almost all relationships, the different parties involved hold expectations of how the others in these relationships will behave. Expectations are influenced by the attitudes of the various parties and, in their turn, influence these attitudes. Impartiality is very difficult to achieve, even in the judicial system, as people may not be fully aware of the attitudes and expectations they hold. Relationships between home and school are far from unaffected by the expectations and attitudes of all involved and the same could be said for relationships within schools. This section will look fairly briefly at this topic as more will be found about it, especially with regard to home–school relationships, in chapter 6.

Parents' Expectations of Schools

Perhaps because for so long parents were seen more as a threat to the school their children attended than as a support, not a great deal is known about what parents expect of schools. Since the Plowden Report (DES, 1967), schools have been urged to encourage the involvement of parents in schools and there are many instances recorded of the variety of ways in which this has been done (see, for example, Jowett *et al.*, 1991). Whilst involvement in school may well alter parents' expectations and attitudes, little is known for sure about the extent to which this happens.

In a study of pre-school children, Chazan *et al.* (1971) found parents optimistic about their children's educational future, many commenting that they hoped their children would do better at school than they had done. They affirmed their support of the school, provided that the children had settled in well and appeared happy there. Early goodwill may not persist, however. A study of pupils at the secondary stage (Bynner, 1972) showed that, on average, only just over half of the parents questioned were satisfied with their children's present school. There were far fewer contacts between parents and schools at the secondary stage, so that dissatisfactions were probably not being discussed. The impression is given that, to many parents, schools become rather remote places. The expectation is that teachers, as professionals, know best and that querying decisions, even although these may be felt to be wrong, is not going to help.

More recent information shows that parental attitudes and expectations have not changed radically since the publication of the Taylor Report (DES, 1977) which set out to strengthen and extend relationships between parents and schools. Parents still show a rather higher level of satisfaction with primary schools than with secondary, although what is meant by 'satisfaction' probably varies widely from parent to parent. Social class, ethnic group, personal experiences of education and children's individual differences all affect parents' views (Docking, 1990b). The fact that one of the major criticisms of schools voiced by the parents concerns what they see as a lack of communication (Tizard *et al.*, 1988) seems to indicate that parents would appreciate more involvement than at present. Docking (1990b) points out that parents can be seen as problems, customers or partners. Primary schools are ideally suited to involving parents in a joint endeavour, especially with regard to pupils' emotional needs and behaviour. More will be said about this in chapter 6. Greater involvement can only increase understanding of what schools are striving to achieve and it is to be hoped that understanding will promote cooperation and realistic expectations on all sides.

To what extent may the current changes in the educational scene, brought about by the 1988 Education Act, change attitudes and expectations? Parents are now going to have information on educational progress and be able to compare this information within classes and between schools. At the primary stage, however, it may well be that parental views of school will be influenced, as they have been in the past, by intangibles such as a school's reputation (not necessarily for high academic prowess), the accessibility of staff, the ethos of the school and the atmosphere generated on formal and informal occasions.

When children show behavioural difficulties, their parents may feel particularly vulnerable *vis à vis* school. It may be suggested to them in any number of ways that they are to blame for what has happened. If they are sent for to discuss their child's behaviour and this is not part of the school's normal policy of parental contact, they may feel singled out; if they are not sent for, they may feel overlooked and inadequate. Attitudes and expectations are affected adversely. On the other hand, if contact with school has been routinely established for all parents, discussion of behaviour problems and an indication of strategies that could be tried out inside and outside school can be accepted as genuine attempts to find a way forward which involve everyone (child, school and parents). 'My mum says he is the only teacher who ever takes any trouble with her' (Lane, 1990, p. 94).

There probably always will be mismatches between the teachers' and parents' views of what school is for (Cullingford, 1984b). Parents often cannot understand how learning can take place in informal, child-centred classrooms. Some cannot see the point of play, exploration or discussion, feeling that a traditional, formal, autocratic approach is more likely to promote the inculcation of knowledge. Cullingford points out that while both teachers and parents see the basic skills as central to the primary curriculum, they justify this belief on different grounds. Parents see the acquisition of the basic skills as essential for their child's future at and beyond school; teachers see them as essential for developing immediate social skills, including decision-making and self-dependence in learning. While these aims may not be dissimilar, they do at times lead to differences in expectations.

Pupils' Expectations of Schools

As Nash (1976) remarks, 'No-one is going to win a Nobel Prize for discovering that pupils prefer their teachers to be knowledgeable and helpful rather than ignorant and unfair' (p. 65). He adds that even pupils whose behaviour is causing concern to their teachers subscribe to that view; indeed they may subscribe to it even more strongly than the rest of their peers (Davies, 1984). Pupils, certainly at the primary stage, expect teachers to be able to control them and to show tolerance, humour and flexibility in managing their classroom (Fontana, 1985).

The effect of teacher behaviour was seen as a crucial factor in pupil or class misbehaviour at the secondary stage when pupils in each of the first five years were invited to write essays on behaviour in their classroom (Badger, 1992). They cited teachers coming late to lessons, being out of the room, 'doing nothing', being inconsistent or 'too soft', shouting too much and 'not listening' as among the main causes of classroom disruption. Similar factors are probably at work in the primary school when misbehaviour and inattention are found, both contributing greatly to 'teacher stress and low staff morale' (Rumbold, 1992).

Looking particularly at children in the primary school, Mortimore *et al.* (1988) showed that, in general, they viewed school activities favourably although, as they grew older, they tended to become more neutral in their views (but not more unfavourable). Most also claimed to find their teachers approachable, only a fairly small percentage admitting that they would not be keen to ask for help or to show their work. It should be remembered, however, that it is precisely this small minority (of which presumably Lucy would be one) that may be experiencing behavioural or emotional difficulties. It is also interesting that just under half of the pupils in the study said that they were 'happy and contented' at school and only 38 per cent thought their teachers saw them as well-behaved.

Mortimore *et al.* (*ibid*) also looked at the relationships between attitudes to school in general and behaviour in school. The relationships found were rather complex. The authors conclude, however, that in their sample aggressive children were poor at assessing their own behaviour. These children also felt that their teachers viewed them more negatively than the teachers themselves said they did. Perhaps for these reasons, these aggressive children had significantly more negative attitudes to school than the rest of the sample.

The Mortimore study clearly showed that age, gender, social economic status and ethnic group membership cannot be overlooked when considering pupils' behaviour at school and their attitudes towards it. Teachers cannot ignore these differences any more than they can assume that all children have the same ability. Strategies for tackling gender and racial inequalities in school now exist (see, for example, Weiner, 1990; Troyna and Hatcher, 1992), although in practice wide variations exist in how far and how successfully they are implemented. 'A school policy may be effective in reducing racist behaviour within the school but on its own it may do nothing to challenge the roots of racist behaviour' (Troyna and Hatcher, *ibid*, p. 199).

Not enough is known about the expectations children with emotional and behavioural difficulties have of school. Yet any attempt to change negative to positive behaviour is unlikely to succeed unless time and opportunity can be found to discuss these difficulties with the children concerned in a supportive and understanding way. Gersch (1990b) argues that pupils should be involved in the assessment of their behaviour for pragmatic, moral and legal reasons. From the pragmatic viewpoint, he says that 'it would seem sensible to ask pupils . . . what help they think they need (and) to negotiate . . . what counts as 'desirable behaviour' and 'what steps should be taken to bring about change' (p118). Morally, children have a right to be consulted if steps are to be taken to change their behaviour and legally it is also the case that any decisions taken regarding children should, as far as is practicable, take their feelings and wishes into account. At the primary stage anyway, it would seem that pupils are prepared to work along with school and to find their experiences of school satisfying on the whole. A 'whole school' policy towards behaviour, as discussed earlier in this chapter, can usefully be built on such attitudes.

Teachers' Expectations

(i) Of parents

Many efforts have been made over the past quarter of a century to bring teachers and parents together. Yet tensions still exist, making the relationship somewhat uneasy. Teachers are wary that parents may wish to question curricular content or pedagogical style and see parental membership of the school's governing body as open to abuse (as indeed it may be). Parents feel that teachers, while certainly more welcoming than previously, are only prepared to involve them on the periphery or as a financial resource.

In an investigation of children in the early years of primary education (Tizard *et al.*, 1988), almost twice as many teachers as parents believed that children's educational success was largely attributable to the family and the home background (58 per cent as compared with 30 per cent of the sample). As was said earlier in this chapter, there appear to be mismatches between the views of teachers and parents which will only be resolved, or indeed recognized, when schools make genuine attempts to become part of the community around them.

The introduction of the National Curriculum may lead to schools becoming more, rather than less, entrenched in their views for teachers will have little time to give to a consideration of parental interests. As is so often the case, the efforts of headteachers are of vital importance in making possible realistic and harmonious relationships (Cyster *et al.*, 1979). There have been so many changes in curricular content and structure that in-service training of teachers (INSET) has concentrated on offering help in these areas. Partnership with parents should remain an important INSET focus as schools are still some way from achieving the ideal interrelationship for their own individual situation.

(ii) Of pupils

After having carried out research at the primary and secondary stages, Nash (1973) states that 'teachers' perceptions of their pupils are closely correlated with the children's ability and behaviour' (p119). He accounts for this relationship by saying that teachers' expectations affect children's self-image so that children come to see themselves as their teachers see them and behave accordingly in school. Pidgeon (1970) suggests that this approximation of teacher expectation to pupil performance is the result of:

(a) lack of opportunity to perform differently as teachers alter the demands they make on pupils according to how they view these pupils; and

(b) changed motivation on the pupils' part in response to suggestions transmitted by teacher expectation.

Staines (1971) gives some good examples of how the interactions between teachers and pupils can, often unintentionally, affect children's views of their physical and cognitive attributes (for example, 'Jack, you're tall. Help me with this'; 'Wrong. You don't know your . . .') Children who are seen by their teachers as presenting emotional and behavioural difficulties in school are soon made aware that they are difficult and are liable to find circumstances conspiring to emphasize these difficulties, rather than alleviate them. David, it will be remembered, was innocent of theft but the incident did nothing for his expectations of teachers or their expectations of him.

Many teachers at the primary stage, although not all, do not report a high incidence of emotional and behaviour difficulties in their schools and, even when noted, the difficulties are often minor, though nonetheless stressful (Docking, 1990a). Whether or not this is an accurate picture of what goes on in primary classrooms is more difficult to determine. Teachers may be unaware of the significance of any troublesome or withdrawn behaviour displayed or prepared to tolerate it, believing that the children will grow out of it, or may not be willing to admit to researchers that they have difficulties with some children. It is probably true, however, that if teachers do not observe their pupils carefully and consider what they have observed, the expectations they have of their pupils' behaviour may be limited or even distorted and can produce in pupils feelings of being caught in a role they resent or dislike.

Expectations can present problems for the teachers themselves. Aggressive behaviour, for example, may not be expected of girls and so teachers may find overt aggression more difficult to cope with from girls than from boys (Mongon *et al.*, 1989). Withdrawn, very submissive boys may also be seen as having greater difficulties than would be the case if similar behaviour were shown by girls.

(iii) Of themselves

It is inappropriate to look in detail here at teachers' views of themselves as teachers and as persons (see, for example, Nias, 1984; Pollard and Tann, 1987). Woods (1981) suggests that teachers have to make a number of commitments to themselves and to their role in schools. These commitments may be vocational (feeling a 'call' for teaching) or professional (a desire to do a job well); they also involve the individual's identity (teaching allows people to be what they want to be) and 'career continuance' (there is a 'profit' in remaining in teaching and a 'deficit' in leaving the profession). Different teachers commit themselves more or less strongly in these four areas and may also find themselves under pressure in one or more of them either simultaneously or at varying points in their teaching career. Pressures in one area of commitment may cause a 'chain reaction' through the others, often with accompanying stress.

Children with emotional and behavioural difficulties present challenges to individual teachers, professionally and personally. These challenges — and the way in which they are dealt with — may threaten teachers' views of their competence in the classroom and their ability to achieve what they want from teaching for themselves and for the children. And these challenges must in most cases be stressful as, for any teacher, teaching is a major focus of their life. In a study of primary and secondary teachers (Travers, 1992), one of the main factors seen by them as sources of pressure was pupil-teacher interaction, this including verbal aggression, answering back, 'pupils trying to test you all the time' and maintaining discipline. Behaviour of this kind strikes at the core of teachers' self-identity. It is not surprising, therefore, that 'dealing with behaviour problems' should be seen by the teachers in Travers' study as having such high stress potential.

Overview

There are two main themes running through this chapter. One is that preventative measures are to be preferred to crisis control. Schools should be proactive rather than reactive; positive rather than negative. The other is that such a policy depends upon collaboration and consensus. Only when staff inside schools are pulling in the same direction will their efforts be productive. Staff must not overlook or dismiss the part that parents can play or fail to realize that what happens in schools is also shaped in no small degree by pupils.

There is, therefore, no question but that in-service training opportunities focussing on behavioural topics are essential. From these sessions can emerge a 'whole school' policy in which all interested parties within and outside the school have a part to play. The demand from teachers for help in implementing the curricular and assessment requirements of the National Curriculum cannot be allowed to squeeze out consideration of how all pupils can be encouraged to respond to such requirements and to find school satisfying.

Chapter 5

How Teachers can Help

In the previous chapter, it was suggested that a 'whole school' policy on how to cope with emotional and behavioural difficulties could provide a framework within which all concerned can work towards tackling these difficulties effectively. Such a policy has to be translated into classroom practice, with individual teachers taking their own decisions, within the agreed framework, as to what constitute difficulties. It is not possible to prescribe one particular way of helping children which will inevitably lead to correct decisions being made. It may be better to offer a variety of approaches so that teachers can select and adapt them to fit their own circumstances and preferred practice.

Before considering possible approaches, two points need to be made:

(i)   teachers' views as to what constitute behaviour difficulties may well differ (see chapter 2 and, for example, Furlong, 1985);
(ii) changing classroom practice is not easy for the individual teacher (Eraut, 1989).

To try to adopt an approach to helping pupils with EBDs which is at variance with teachers' long-standing beliefs about how children should be taught and the standards they should be expected to reach is unlikely to succeed. Rather, teachers have to experiment, to adapt the approaches they select to suit their own classrooms and to monitor results carefully with a view to further change. They must also be aware of how others view the members of their class and of those pupils who never disturb anyone but who may not be developing the educational and social strategies necessary for responding fully to the school programme.

How do Teachers View EBDs?

Mention has already been made in chapter 4 of the effect that teachers' expectations have on their pupils' progress. A closer look will now be taken at how expectations affect practice, as far as teachers are concerned.

(i)   To think of 'misbehaviour' in a global sense does not help teachers to understand what is happening in their classroom or to deal with it. Instead of thinking of their class as 'very naughty', 'a right lot' or 'lively to say the least', teachers might do better to list the behaviours they find worrying, identify times and places which seem to be major trouble spots and observe pupil interaction in the classroom. Shy, depressed, weepy children should not be disregarded.

(ii) Teachers' perceptions of what constitutes 'problem' behaviour are likely to be influenced by their cultural background. Langfeldt (1992) has shown that German junior high school teachers are not overly concerned about 'non-conformist' behaviour and appearance (for example, visiting discotheques; using make-up; dressing extravagantly), whereas Korean teachers, reflecting an Asian culture, find these 'problematic'. Teachers from both cultures were much more in agreement about 'dissocial-aggressive' behaviour being 'problematic' and 'withdrawal' behaviour (see chapter 11) being only 'somewhat problematic'. In this country, teachers' views of their pupils may be influenced by the expectations they have of how different ethnic groups behave and learn (see for example, Houlton, 1986 and chapter 2).

(iii) Teachers' perceptions of EBDs are also influenced by the age and sex of the pupils and by the length of the teachers' classroom experience (Borg and Falzon, 1990). Thus, teachers appear to view undesirable behaviours as being more serious in older than in younger children (with the exception of unhappy/depressed behaviour) and, in most cases, as more serious in boys than in girls. Borg and Falzon also found that the more experienced the teacher, the less seriously the various behaviours were viewed, except in the case of 'shyness' which the teachers with greater experience saw as a more serious problem than their colleagues.

(iv) When teachers perceive behaviour as presenting them with problems, especially if the behaviour is aggressive and/or disruptive, it is not surprising that many tend to resist having these pupils in their class (Kauffman *et al.*, 1989). D. Thomas (1985) has pointed out that teachers who feel reluctant about coping with pupils with special educational needs may, in some cases, manage very well when faced with such a child in their class. The quality of the teacher's skills is critical. Bennett and Cass (1989) would add that so is the quality of the support available to teachers, a point which will be looked at again later in this chapter.

How do Teachers Cope with EBDs?

Teachers would probably like to see in their classroom an orderly and uniform progression up a learning hierarchy, achieved by highly motivated pupils who are self-dependent without rejecting teacher direction, and creative without posing too many demands on teacher resources. The reality of the situation is much less tidy. Progression is followed by regression — two steps forward and then one back. Motivation varies from child to child and from topic to topic. Teachers, trying to approximate daily reality to their 'ideal' of learning, may well find it difficult to tolerate any behaviour which appears to them to be aberrant.

Croll and Moses (1985) found that 7.7 per cent of their sample of primary school pupils were considered by their teachers to have behavioural difficulties (see chapter 2). Of those with behaviour problems, about half (48.1 per cent) were felt to present discipline problems and over two-thirds to have learning difficulties. These are interesting results. They mean that, on average, there would be in a class of twenty-five, two children with emotional and/or behavioural difficulties, one of whom poses a discipline problem, and both of whom have some learning difficulties, one perhaps more so than the other. Two further considerations follow from the findings. One is that the number of pupils identified by their teachers as having EBDs is not, on average, large; the other is that to have even one child in a class who is challenging the teacher's management skills through indiscipline may be enough to upset the whole class.

It has already been suggested in the previous chapter that to adopt short-term, reactive strategies to cope with behaviour difficulties may not be as effective as taking long-term, proactive measures which will divert the difficult behaviour before it has even occurred. Short-term reactions include giving the pupil a 'good talking to', sending him/her to the headteacher, excluding the pupil from a lesson or keeping her/him in at playtime (or deprivation of other privileges). All of these may have an effect on behaviour the first time they are implemented. But this effect soon wears off and is rapidly disregarded by the child concerned, who often finds bad behaviour far more rewarding in terms of peer status or adult attention than conformity. What other approaches might be more effective?

Approaches to Helping Pupils with EBDs

Changing Teachers' Perceptions

Because perceptions are complex in nature, highly individual and seldom examined critically, they are resistant to change. If well-established preconceptions or approaches are to be modified, change must be carefully planned for and managed. Directives from above, whether from a headteacher or an educational psychologist, are unlikely to alter teachers' views on maladaptive behaviour unless they provoke teachers into observation of their interactions with their class. Such directives can seem remote from the practical problems facing the teacher or may require fairly far-reaching modifications to the class or school system. Innovation which is passed on from teacher to teacher may be much more readily accepted (Hanko, 1990), especially if the opportunity can be given for discussion and the formal transfer of information. Monitoring of the effects of any change is also essential so that teachers can have objective evidence of modification which might otherwise not be realized.

If teachers' perceptions are to be changed (and the attitudes and expectations reflected by these perceptions), a number of points must be borne in mind.

(i)   Changes in behaviour do not inevitably accompany changes in what people say. Teachers may quite genuinely express tolerance for some aspect of pupil behaviour when in the staffroom but react quite differently when faced with examples of it in their classroom or when the full implications of such tolerance for their time and patience are realized.

(ii) Perceptions which are linked to well-established attitudes are particularly resistant to change, especially if modification of one aspect conflicts with another.

(iii) If change is to be effected, it is likely to be because the individual can see gains for herself or himself in such a change.

It could be suggested, therefore, that the nature of the change (and all its ramifications) needs to be worked out in advance within the framework of the actual setting in which the change is to be attempted. Teachers have to take time to consider carefully the specific pupils who concern them, the implications of any change in approach for the class and school as a whole, and the extent to which the change can be sustained outside the classroom.

Help from others may prove extremely valuable. Callias and Rickett (1986), for example, describe how school staff worked with clinic staff in a neighbouring psychiatric hospital. Individual pupil problems were discussed as well as classroom management and the school's role in handling behaviour problems. In other instances, local authority support staff have worked in schools (see later in this chapter and chapter 7). Triandis (1971) warns, however, that crucial considerations in encouraging teachers to alter their preconceptions of their pupils include '*who* says *what*, *how* and *to whom*'.

The extent to which in-service courses (INSET) will produce change in teachers' behaviour in the classroom is, therefore, somewhat problematic. Some teachers may respond well to general discussion on maladaptive behaviour and realise how such information can be applied to their own circumstances; others may gain more from reading; while others may fail to see any relevance to their own teaching however proposed change is presented. Certainly if teachers try out a change in approach and find that it works, conversion is likely to be immediate and even long-lasting. It is perhaps prudent to suggest that, where teachers are concerned about any aspect of pupil behaviour, it would be constructive for them to clarify the focus of their concern, seek out help if it is required, introduce planned changes and monitor the effect of these on the pupil in question and on the remainder of the class.

Changing Normal Classroom Organization

A first priority for teachers is to ensure that the classroom environment is as conducive to learning as it can be (Hewett and Taylor, 1980). This not only involves taking care over displays and changing them in order to keep pupils' attention, but also means giving consideration to the arrangement of desks, tables, easels and chairs. It is not helpful to anyone if pupils are seated with their backs to the main teaching area or tucked away around corners or behind bookcases out of sight. Planning where pupils will sit in the classroom so that they can all see and be seen does not preclude seating them in groups. It merely entails a degree of rearrangement at times. It must also be possible for pupils and teachers to move around the classroom without disturbing those who are seated. Examples of classroom arrangements can be found in Mortimore *et al.* (1988), while Lawrence *et al.* (1985b) discuss the effects on pupil behaviour of the layout of the school buildings.

Criticisms have, with justification, been made of some 'informal' approaches to teaching which offer no structure or focus to children's learning. Where there is structure and focus, a well-planned, informal approach can be highly effective. Where these are lacking, whether the approach is formal or informal, little learning takes place and even less progression in the development of understanding. The teaching approach used is secondary to the quality of the learning experience. It was, after all, the doubts expressed as to how well children were learning when they were taught formally, seated in rows, that led to the move to informal classroom organization. A mixture of approaches will probably be most effective, with teachers changing from formal to informal strategies and seating arrangements depending on the objectives they have set for any particular classroom episode.

Wheldall and Merrett (1984) draw attention to what they call the teachers' ABC. What happens before a certain behaviour (B) occurs is the antecedent (A) of the situation. What follows the behaviour (B) is the consequence (C). Reorganizing seating in the classroom and trying to match teaching approaches to previously selected objectives are some of the antecedents which determine the pupil behaviour which follows. So also is modifying appropriately the curricular content, as will be discussed in the next section. Teachers often concentrate solely on the third part of the teaching interaction, the consequences, when difficulties in behaviour arise. Thus, they give all their attention to the pupil reactions they find unacceptable, instead of seeing them as the consequence of what has gone before. Tackling the antecedents to classroom behaviour in a flexible and sensitive way is an important factor in teachers becoming proactive rather than reactive in their interactions with their pupils.

Adapting the Normal Curriculum

The establishment of a National Curriculum to which all pupils must have access (unless specifically excluded) should have been beneficial to those with special educational needs. It was intended to safeguard their right to the same educational opportunities as any other pupil and to offer them equality of learning experiences at an appropriate level. The reality of the situation may be rather different, especially for those pupils with moderate learning difficulties whose slow progress makes it impossible for them to keep up with their peers. If their levels of attainment become quite incompatible with the rest of the class, teachers begin to question their position in the mainstream.

It has already been noted that the teachers in the Croll and Moses study (1985) felt that more than two-thirds of the pupils they saw as presenting behavioural difficulties also had learning difficulties. Yet at least some of these pupils have the intellectual ability to succeed at school. Were this to happen, their whole attitude to school and their motivation to learn might well change. Others, less gifted, have to be helped towards such a change. Can the National Curriculum help in this respect?

Learning difficulties can be seen as mismatches between pupils and task (Booth *et al.*, 1986). As Lewis (1991) points out, the National Curriculum could produce better learning 'matches' as it:

(i) provides common objectives for all pupils;
(ii) expresses these objectives in a curricular language accessible to all teachers;
(iii) ensures that all pupils are offered a broad, balanced curriculum;
(iv) emphasizes the importance of regular, purposeful assessment.

If these potential improvements are to be realized, then differentiation in the work provided for individual pupils may well be necessary. Differentiation, whether of language or content, is intended to achieve the desired 'match' between pupils' learning needs and their learning experiences. It requires careful monitoring and assessment of pupil progress, a sensitive understanding of pupil motivation and learning styles, and the ability to adapt educational objectives accordingly. In addition, as Barton and Smith (1989) note, teachers have to come to terms with 'new ways of relating to pupils as well as the contradictions which will inevitably arise when considering the individual versus the collective rights of pupils' (p. 87). Hard-pressed as they are, teachers may find it virtually impossible to achieve, single-handed, the differentiation of approaches and curricular content which individual pupils require without extra support.

Providing Additional Support for Teachers

Class teaching with some additional work for those who finish quickly and adjusted demands for those who are slow may not be adequate differentiation. The whole planning of lessons may need to be re-thought and additional resources be made available to ensure that differentiation is effectively achieved. It may also mean offering continuing additional help to pupils who, for a whole variety of reasons, have not reached the targets set for the majority of the class. A very good case can, therefore, be made for providing support for teachers in their classroom. Unfortunately, support teaching is expensive and so very much 'at risk' when school budgets are being considered. In many primary schools, the 'special' or 'opportunity' class, often the base for a teacher who could offer support to other members of staff, has disappeared. The expertise of the teacher may also have been lost through early retirement or redeployment, leaving the burden of differentiation on the class teacher alone. (An example of the work of a 'special' class can be found in chapter 7.)

Where a support system exists, class teachers find it successful provided that:

(i)   the teachers (or staff) in question can agree on class organization, lesson content and teaching approach;

(ii) careful records are kept so that both adults are fully aware of what has been tackled with all pupils and what level of understanding has been reached;

(iii) class teachers do not ignore the differentiation in core subjects required by some pupils when teaching other aspects of the curriculum;

(iv) the 'in class' support is linked to a 'whole school' policy on coping with special learning needs and to an ongoing staff development programme.

Evidence is available (Imich and Roberts, 1990) that it is effective to make additional expertise available to schools. By placing a specialist teacher (STB: Support Teacher Behaviour) in schools for up to three terms, Imich and Roberts showed that incidents of disruptive behaviour could be reduced, positive approaches to pupil management promoted and teacher confidence and skill in coping with behaviour difficulties increased. They argue that 'the service offered by a STB is one with many positive educational outcomes' (p. 209). Peripatetic support teams, usually consisting of a group of experienced, additionally trained teachers responsible to the School Psychological Service, have also been successful (Barnsley Education Team, 1981).

However, whether because of financial necessity or because of other more morally acceptable reasons, the move in primary schools today, as far as pupils with emotional and behavioural difficulties are concerned, is towards increasing the class teacher's coping skills from within the school itself. Hanko (1990) describes in detail how class teachers' expertise can be developed so that their confidence is restored and support made available from the rest of the school staff. She also discusses how parental help can be enlisted most effectively. School-based discussion groups of the kind she advocates may also meet the criticisms often levelled at out-of-school training as to its lack of relevance, for example. Kauffman *et al.* (1989) note that any help offered to school staffs must be highly individualized if it is to meet the teachers' perceived needs.

On occasion, adults other than professionally trained teachers may be present in classrooms — therapists, medical personnel or parents, for instance. Careful room management is then essential (G. Thomas, 1985). Also required is adequate prior discussion, easy communication at all times and 'follow up' by the teacher of any learning implications arising from the shared sessions. Only when all the adults concerned understand the purpose of the shared sessions and appreciate the role they are to play can pupils and teachers benefit from the help such support can give.

Specific Strategies for Coping with EBDs

Behaviour Management

Teachers faced with behaviour which causes them concern see the management of its change as their first priority. Often they attempt this change by concentrating on the unacceptable behaviour, inasmuch as they inevitably react to it and even anticipate it. Behaviour modification theorists would argue that such concentration merely serves to establish the unwanted behaviour even more firmly, as the pupils concerned quickly learn that certain actions ensure teacher attention as well as frequent class disruption (Fontana, 1985). If teacher and pupil attention were to be given to positive behaviour, with the negative behaviour being ignored as far as possible, the argument is that the ignored behaviour would decline and the positive behaviour become established (Leach and Raybould, 1977).

At the heart of this approach lie careful observation and consistency. The behaviour which is found unacceptable must be very carefully delineated so that its exact parameters are known. When teachers employ careful, methodical recording of individual behaviour, it is sometimes found that there are fairly straightforward explanations for it and obvious solutions which do not require formal modification programmes to be developed. For example, the difficult behaviour may only arise when the pupil in question happens to sit next to one other pupil in particular or when certain activities (for example, writing) are expected. Once such difficulties have been identified, extra supervision or support can be provided.

Careful observation does not, of course, always reveal simple explanations of undesirable behaviour. Further analysis is then required. Decisions have to be taken as to what behaviour would be considered acceptable, what in the pupil's present behaviour most nearly approximates to this desired behaviour, and what 'reward' can be offered to encourage the pupil to repeat that and, indeed, to shape it more and more closely to what is acceptable. Modification of behaviour may, therefore, take time. The detailed records essential to the approach show how far the programme is succeeding. It should be noted that it is positive behaviour which is encouraged. The punishment of negative behaviour has nothing to contribute to this strategy. Descriptions of how behaviour can be analyzed, modified and recorded can be found in Wheldall and Merrett (1984), Merrett and Wheldall (1990) and in the practical material they have developed, BATPACK (Wheldall and Merrett, 1988a).

Mention has already been made of the importance of consistency of re-action in establishing behaviour patterns. Teachers are well aware of this but, for a whole variety of reasons, may not always react to a particular behaviour in the same way. Behaviour theorists argue that, for any behaviour pattern to become habitual, it must be immediately and consistently 'rewarded' over a period of time. Everyone who interacts with the pupil in question should respond in the same way if a specific behaviour is to be established. A teach-er's programme will not be successful if other staff (or parents) do not coop-erate. The child's peers can also cause a plan to fail if they reward the undesired behaviour with their attention or support. Indeed, how to involve the rest of the class in a behaviour management programme and to use the reactions of fellow pupils to reinforce positive behaviour require considerable thought when planning any programme of behavioural change. Examples of pro-grammes and of 'rewards' selected by primary teachers in the modification of behaviour can be found in chapter 7.

Praise from a teacher is often believed to be effective in establishing desired behaviour in the case of young children, who are highly dependent on adult support. With older children, teachers have to be careful in their use of praise as, if it is used too frequently or directed only at certain pupils, it can be ineffective or have the opposite effect to that intended (Docking, 1990a).

Behaviour modification programmes, therefore, require considerable thought before implementation. They must also be carefully monitored. Teachers often use 'self-monitoring' activities which enable pupils to keep their own records of their progress towards the pre-determined behavioural objective. These activities include 'contracts' where pupil and teacher agree on the desired behaviour, the pupil endeavours to show that behaviour and the teacher indicates on a graph how often it has been successfully achieved. Rewards may be built into the programme, although frequently the graphical presentation of the success rate may be enough in itself to establish the behavi-our. Children can keep their own self-monitoring 'charts' showing progress. For example, the 'chart' may be in the form of a snakes-and-ladders game with a marker to indicate how near to the end of the game the individual is. Again, only positive behaviours may be counted. The chart could, for exam-ple, show a number of stages on a curve indicating the path of a spaceship landing on the moon. Self-monitoring techniques of this kind involve pupils in establishing control over their behaviour and avoid the criticism often levelled at behaviour modification strategies that they are purely manipulative.

Social Skills Training

Teachers who attempt to develop a behaviour modification programme in the classroom may be uneasy about the focus it brings to bear on one individual pupil and about the need for immediate and consistent reward for the appropriate behaviour. For younger children, activities intended to develop social skills in the context of the whole class may be more acceptable.

In the early years at school, children adopt behaviour patterns which seem to get them what they want and may not consider other ways of behaving which could be more effective or more acceptable than those they normally employ. Shy children, for example, find that by withdrawing from contact with others, by never taking hands in a group game or joining in 'pretend' play, they are left alone. Shy children do not want to be always in the centre of things but, equally, they may not want always to be left out or ignored. Being left alone means that they lack the opportunity to practise the social skills they badly need if they are to maintain the degree of social contact they wish. In the same way, aggressive children may know of no other approach to their peers than by grabbing, pushing or hitting.

Class activities, including discussion of alternative behaviour patterns, can prove helpful to most pupils at a time when normal development is leading to a considerable widening of children's social horizons and a proliferation of social contacts (see, for example, Spivack and Shure, 1974; or Curtis and Hill, 1978). For somewhat older pupils, the aim of social skills training remains the establishment of a range of behavioural responses so that the most appropriate (as the individual child sees it) can be selected as necessary. The aim is not to link only one response to any behavioural stimulus but to allow individual choice (after due consideration).

Cross and Goddard (1988) list the practical components of social skills training as:

discussion
modelling
role-play and simulation
feedback
transfer

They go on to stress certain essentials for the success of any training programme.

(i)   The activities must provoke genuine responses from the pupils. They are not means of teacher indoctrination but solutions to social problems which are relevant to the pupils.

(ii)   Group discussion skills (listening to others; contributing opinions; responding to suggestions; weighing up an argument) are prerequisites for any form of social skills training and, indeed, may themselves form the content of the early stages of any training programme.

(iii) In the early stages, teachers may need to cue the children in to important facets of social behaviour which they may not be fully aware of (for example, eye contact, body language, tone of voice).

(iv) Discussion of activities which have been modelled or simulated is vital and can usefully be followed up by re-enactments with attention directed to specific points. As children gain in confidence and in social awareness, feedback becomes more and more productive.

(v) The behavioural reactions considered in the training programme must be transferred into individual children's behavioural repertoire. Opportunities for practice outside the classroom must, therefore, be given and discussion of outside experiences (for example, television or video programmes) take place within the classroom.

Social skills training can be said to be successful if it increases children's insight into their own behaviour and their general feeling of well-being inside and outside school. The long-term effects of acquiring at least adequate social skills are immense both for present competence and for future child-rearing practices (see Trower *et al.*, 1978).

Details of specific programmes aimed at developing social skills can be found in a number of publications. Cartledge and Milburn (1980), for example, deal with role-playing and modelling (including the use of puppets, audio and visual tapes, books and live models) and offer suggestions for practising behavioural responses. Herbert (1986) stresses the importance of adult attention which provides immediate reinforcement if a new behaviour pattern is to be established. Leech and Wooster (1986) describe a series of activities suitable for older primary pupils, as does Spence (1980). Goddard and Cross (1987) show how classroom disruption can be successfully reduced, while Fontana (1990) suggests ways in which teachers themselves might manage their professional relationships more effectively by examining in a practical way their own exercise of social skills.

Children's personal and social education cannot be neglected or considered as something which happens outside school. For children with emotional and behavioural difficulties, it is particularly important that they should be helped to acquire appropriate skills in communicating and interacting with other children and adults. Successful participation in group activities is also important for the development of adequate social skills.

Group Work and Group Support

Children with EBDs may be awkward to place in working groups but can benefit enormously if arrangements are made to accommodate them. In the first instance, teachers must consider the general principles behind all successful group management (see Galton and Williamson, 1992), including the provision of clear objectives for each group and adequate resourcing. It is particularly important that groupings should be flexible, coming together for specific purposes and, therefore, changing in membership as appropriate. Secondly, groups may be constructed to encourage cooperative and independent learning experiences which would benefit all children.

When teachers specifically control the membership of groups, they are acknowledging the differential contribution made by individuals and providing opportunities for development through that individual contribution. A variety of strategies are open to teachers and Montgomery (1989) stresses the value to the teacher of thinking about the strategies as well as the content of group work. Strategies should also promote 'positive' interdependence, that is where all group members make a contribution to the activity rather than one child (or only a few) taking the lead and the others doing very little.

An example of 'positive' interdependence is the 'jig-saw classroom' (Aronson *et al.*, 1978). Here, pupils are grouped and then paired within each group. The groups are set the same task and each pair is responsible for a particular aspect of it, although all of the aspects are interrelated, decisions taken in one aspect affecting the outcome in other aspects. Thus, if each group were to be set the task of planning a class newspaper, decisions taken by the pair working on presentation would affect the decisions to be taken by the pair working on sporting activities. At certain times, the groups discuss overall procedures; at other times, the pairs work on their own; and at yet other times, all of the pairs tackling a specific aspect come together to compare progress. The group findings are then presented by one or more members of each group and the teacher chooses (or a vote is taken) which findings will be implemented.

Selection of the group, and especially the pair, in which a pupil with EBDs will work has to be carefully thought out. A degree of compatibility is essential; it is no use pairing two 'lame ducks' just because no-one else wants them. Ability to cope with the task must be considered although this may not be easy to estimate in pupils with behavioural difficulties. It may be that they can make a valuable contribution if their interest is caught and they are encouraged towards self-responsibility in their learning.

Barnes and Todd (1977) have shown how group discussion can enlarge pupils' understanding of the topic being examined. Their work points to the importance in individual personal and social development of having the language appropriate to the task and Tann (1981) charts the ways in which discussion develops in groups. She suggests that pupils should have acquired the skills of questioning, listening and managing disputes if group work is to be successful. There is, therefore, clearly an overlap between group approaches and the development of social skills discussed in the previous section of this chapter.

Pairing pupils has also been used effectively in paired learning or peer tutoring schemes (Topping, 1988). As far as pupils with EBDs are concerned, there are two potential benefits to be gained when this strategy is used successfully. First, pairing a competent reader with one who has reading difficulties (some pupils with EBDs lag behind in reading development) can give the poorer reader the benefit of one-to-one attention. Secondly, pairing an older with a younger child in the pre-reading stage can enhance the self-esteem of the older pupil.

Teacher involvement is essential in all of these grouping strategies if learning is to take place. Involvement does not mean interference and the ultimate aim could be seen as the group taking over the teacher's functions of directing, reviewing and supporting (Biott, 1987). There will always be a place for teacher membership of a group, providing that this membership is genuine and not covert leadership.

Mention should also be made of group therapy, originally devised in clinic settings by Slavson (1947). His work was the basis for the therapeutic strategies devised by Foulkes and Anthony (1965) for 5-to-9-year olds. Therapeutic groups are intended to help children with fairly severe emotional problems and allow them to release their fears and tensions in a non-authoritarian setting outside of school where other group members may offer help as problems are worked through.

The use of therapeutic groups within the school setting is described by Kolvin *et al.* (1981). In their research, they investigated various strategies which could be used to help pupils with EBDs at 7 and 11 years of age. Group therapy was one of the strategies examined. With the younger children, it took the form of small playgroups in which the children were given time to work out their problems through play under controlled conditions. For the older children, discussion groups were set up with the pupils themselves controlling the discussion (Rogers, 1952). Although school-based, the groups were led by specially trained 'therapists' who were in close contact with the research team.

On measures of fairly immediate benefit and of 'good outcome' in the longer term, group strategies came out well in comparison to the others (for example, parent counselling; behaviour modification) in Kolvin *et al.*'s study. It must be remembered, however, that the help offered, although within the school, was outside the classroom and required additional, well-supported staff. The use of groups specifically for therapeutic purposes would seem, therefore, to require help from clinical personnel, even if the groups meet in school. Working groups within the classroom, on the other hand, can be very valuable especially when, as Tann (1988) points out, teachers are fully aware of the potential benefits arising from well-structured groups which are part of a 'whole school' policy.

Cognitive Approaches

It has already been said that teachers may be more effective in dealing with EBDs if they can prevent their manifestation rather than simply reacting to their display. It could equally be argued that changing children's ways of thinking about themselves and their behaviour might enable them to inhibit unacceptable behaviour and to find acceptable behaviour self-enhancing. Cognitive approaches aim to provide children with the opportunities to become reflective and prescient, able to use verbal reasoning and be open to what others think.

Instrumental Enrichment programmes, as devised by Feuerstein (see Sharron, 1987), are intended to enable children to think coherently. This is achieved through a variety of exercises ('instruments') which mediate (intervene) in children's experiences enabling them to develop meaning from them, as well as purpose and the ability to generalize. The 'instruments' are also intended to promote self-control, sharing and a sense of personal worth. An exploratory study using Feuerstein's materials in the UK with pupils aged 10 years and over (Weller and Craft, 1983) found many positive features in the reaction of special school children and their teachers to the 'instruments' and they have been used since in ordinary and special schools. Teachers have to be trained to use the materials as the approach has a strong theoretical basis which must be fully appreciated if it is to succeed in developing intellectual capacity.

Other programmes for cognitive development make use of somewhat different approaches. For example, Lipman *et al.* (1980), in their programme on 'Philosophy for Children', propose a dialogue-centred approach based on the discussion of specially written, short novels. They stress that pupils require some ability in expressing opinions and listening to others prior to entering the main programme and provide suggestions as to how these skills can be acquired (see, for example, Lake, 1989). Others who also stress that thinking is a learnable skill include the advocates of 'process learning' (Robb, 1989), and of 'mastery learning' in which pupils are helped to develop the study skills necessary for successful educational progress (Bloom, 1971). Pupils with EBDs are often prone to careless thinking or over-rapid foreclosure in arguments, and programmes such as these, devised to develop study skills or strengthen existing ones, can be of use. As with group strategies, they can be implemented in the classroom for the benefit of the whole class.

Deliberate linking of social skills training (see earlier in this chapter) and cognitive problem-solving approaches (Spivack *et al.*, 1976) can also be considered. The latter advocate training in the process of problem-solving, that is identifying the problem, working out alternative solutions to it, considering the consequences of these and selecting what seems to be the most suitable solution. This emphasis on the need to develop forward-planning skills can be applied to social behaviour (Frederickson and Simms, 1990) so that pupils are encouraged to think about how they interact with others and how social relationships could become more productive. The programme outlined by the writers was carried out in a clinical setting and also involved meetings with parents before and after it was implemented with the children (boys aged 8–11 years). It used an approach based on psychodrama (Moreno, 1955), namely scene setting and role-play, alternative solutions to problems being enacted by group members. The various episodes were discussed fully by the group and homework intended to make each individual think about his personal situation was given. The writers claim that the results of this intervention strategy show promise but that it might be even more effective if it could be used in the classroom with the involvement of the normal peer group. Not only do

cognitive and social skills need to be integrated but also 'therapeutic and preventative work with children (in) the social environment in which they are
functioning and relating' (Frederickson and Simms, 1990, p. 15).

The importance of involving children in working towards the solution of
their problems is, therefore, clear and it would appear that such involvement
is possible at quite an early age, certainly at the ages of 7–11 years. At this
stage, pupils should also be encouraged to develop metacognitive skills (Nisbet
and Shucksmith, 1986). It is claimed by these educationists that metacognitive
skills are essential to the development of study skills. They argue that 'the
factor which differentiates good from bad or inadequate learning is the ability
to monitor situations, tasks and problems and respond accordingly' (p. 25). It
has to be admitted that pupils with EBDs are often poor at just such monitoring. Nisbet and Shucksmith suggest that learners need to know both what
they know and what they do not know about learning and to have effective
strategies which will enable them to see where they are and where they are
going in their learning. These strategies must be learned in context (i.e.,
pupils must actively participate in the learning episode); they must never be
purely specific to one task but always related to an overarching understanding
of learning or thinking in general; the stress should be on the process rather
than the product; and 'discussion, whether formal or informal, will probably
remain the teacher's foremost tool' (p. 72).

The content of such discussion is elaborated by Brown and DeLoache
(1983). Metacognitive skills, they suggest, include predicting the consequences
of any action; checking on the results of one's own actions; monitoring one's
own progress; and reality testing (i.e., does what I am doing make sense in
these circumstances?). In all of these, especially with pupils at the primary
stage, teachers can offer valuable guidance. Pupils can be helped to extract the
main idea or theme, scan a visual presentation to pick out the essential details
and retrieve information which they have previously stored. Indeed, the ability to store information in a manageable format and with appropriate cues for
easy retrieval is in itself an important cognitive strategy.

Overview

It is impossible in a book of this size to do more than offer fairly brief discussions of the variety of ways in which teachers can help pupils with EBDs
to display behaviour patterns which are not only more acceptable to others
but also more productive of satisfaction to themselves. Lewis (1991) points
out that 'children benefit from having opportunities to work in a variety of
individual, paired, small group and whole class contexts' (p. 90). They also
benefit from experiencing within these various contexts opportunities to increase their self-knowledge and their personal skills of interacting with others
and with the educational programme. All children can benefit from acquiring
enhanced social and learning skills but they are particularly important for

those with emotional and behavioural difficulties. Teachers have to approach pupils with EBDs with compassion and objectivity (Laslett, 1977) but also with an understanding of how classroom activities can best be selected and implemented in order that behavioural difficulties may be pre-empted or helped.

Chapter 6

How Parents and Others can Help

Children are not only part of the school system, they are also (and primarily) members of a family. For professionals (teachers and others) to act in isolation from the children's carers at home cannot be as productive as for them to cooperate. To say that all concerned should work towards a common objective is not to see their functions as duplicating one another. The Warnock Report on Special Educational Needs (DES, 1978) argued the case for 'parents as partners', ideally equal partners, engaged in a productive, two-way dialogue with the professionals involved with their child. The Report goes on to say that parents need information, advice and practical help from professionals in all aspects of special needs which must include emotional and behavioural difficulties. But, in their turn, parents have access to information which it would be difficult for professionals to obtain. With regard to behaviour at home, sleep patterns, eating habits and sibling rivalries, they alone have first-hand knowledge. They can also advise on how their child might react to any suggested behavioural intervention (or prevention) programme and they can contribute to the practical implementation of that programme. As Lennox (1991) emphasizes, the development of normal and maladaptive behaviour is a product of all the aspects of the child's environment — home and family, culture and sub-culture, community and school.

Schools have realized for a fairly long time now that the curriculum which they offer should have relevance for their pupils, that is, it ought to be embedded in the children's experience and environment. They also hope that what the school is trying to do will be supported by the home. Schools may, however, be somewhat unrealistic in both of these aspirations. Social, emotional and cognitive dimensions within homes vary enormously and teachers' assumptions about these dimensions are not always correct. The relevance that they hope for may not exist. Families may be indifferent to what is going on in schools or absorbed in other activities or even actively hostile to the whole educational system. The reactions in the home, however, will nevertheless have considerable impact on children and their behaviour in school.

Because the contribution made by their families is so important to children's behaviour, adjustment and emotional well-being in school, this chapter will look at the influences which parents have on the emotional development and behaviour of their children and how links between home and school can be effectively established. It will then go on to consider the contributions made in these areas by those professionals who are usually not school-based but who work directly with the home.

How Parents Affect Children's Emotional Development

Education goes on all the time in families but it is organized and transmitted differently from what goes on in school. It is casual, informal, largely unassessed, more or less supervised and carried out with varying degrees of skill and intention. The crucial element may well be the patterns of social communication which exist in the family (Melnick, 1991), that is, the ways in which information, values, organization and so on are transmitted as patterns which children observe and absorb as they grow and develop. From these stem the ways in which children view themselves as members of society, including their view of themselves as members of a class and a school.

An illustration of this point is the case of two sisters, *Leonie* and *Magda*, then aged about 7 and 9 years respectively. Teachers had been concerned about both children over the years because of their withdrawn, silent response to any activities. They looked pale and underfed but there were no signs of abuse and the girls seemed to prefer being at home to being in school. Matters came to a head when the pilfering of small amounts of money and sweets was found, almost by accident, to be the work of Leonie. Simultaneously, Magda was discovered weeping in the playground and a fairly prolonged history of bullying by the other girls in her class was extracted. Home visits confirmed that their mother was having to cope on her own, the children's father having moved out. The house was bare and cold, with few signs of comfort — or food. Clearly the mother was finding it impossible to cope; she looked as thin and neglected as her children. Social Services were alerted and things began to improve materially. What messages the girls were absorbing with regard to parental responsibility, school achievement and self-esteem (to mention only a few aspects affected by the social communications they were receiving) can only be hypothesized. Further aspects of how parents and schools interact will be discussed below.

Parents and Their Children's Mental Health

Child-rearing practices

As Richman (1988) points out, the influences of the family are paramount in children's early years. These influences are not one-way; the children growing up are part of the family and influence it in their turn. Nor are difficulties in the early years irreversible if good quality experiences can be offered later (a good start may be adversely affected by later poor experiences). If the family, therefore, is suffering severe stress of any kind (for example, marital breakdown, maternal depression, bereavement), the children are not unaffected both in the pre-school years and later. Indeed, children in the 7 to 11-year-old range may have particular pressures put upon them as parents turn to them to fill the gaps in their own lives or expect them to take over roles which are not appropriate for the level of emotional development the children have reached. Woodhead (1991) quite rightly warns of the dangers inherent in making generalizations such as those above. The inferences drawn may well be simplistic, bearing in mind how complex family relationships are and also how context-specific are the effects of stress on the children concerned. Nevertheless, stress within the family cannot be ignored when trying to help children with emotional and behavioural difficulties.

Children in the 7–11-year-old age range are vulnerable to other pressures within the family, not perhaps quite so potentially traumatic as severe stress. Take, for example, sibling rivalry. Leonie and Magda clung to each other, excluding other children. In other families, the demands of other siblings may be the cause of unhappiness or even hostility. There are plenty of examples: the arrival of a new, much wanted baby (or a new, unplanned baby) where the existing relationships and responsibilities are changed; a bullying older sibling (or an 'omnipotent toddler', Besag, 1989); uneven academic ability, where more (or less) is expected of some children because of the achievements of their siblings; the birth of a child with special needs. As children develop socially, they become more and more aware of the attitudes and expectations of those around them and of differences between their family and that of others.

Comparisons by children of one way of being brought up with another way can be the source of much friction. Different rules with regard to expected behaviour, different sets of values, different reactions to everyday happenings are observed and considered. Where there is a degree of flexibility, such differences can promote development. But where the family does not adapt to changing circumstances or where no discussion of differences is possible, children's behaviour at home and in school may reflect their confusion or resentment.

Social and emotional deprivation
Behaviour problems in the early pre-school years are often related to deprivations of various kinds in the home background (for example, restrictive housing conditions; domestic crises; unsatisfactory parental attitudes and practices). Many of these problems are short-lived, but in some cases where the adverse circumstances are particularly marked or where they are numerous (Macfarlane *et al.*, 1954), children bring these problems with them to school where they may well affect their early educational progress and adjustment (Chazan *et al.*, 1977). Age inevitably broadens the experience of young children, whether for good or ill, but what happens to children at home in the years from 7 to 11 remains crucial for their social and emotional development. The making of at least one good relationship (such as with a teacher) can be very beneficial (Rutter, 1972). Children who come to school unduly restless

(many of them boys) may persist in presenting problems, or be expected to present problems. Teachers find these children difficult to handle and so may inadvertently deprive them of opportunities to establish good relationships.

Andrew, who has already been mentioned in chapter 4, is a good example of how tiresome behaviour can disrupt the learning atmosphere of a whole class. In his early school years, Andrew was considered 'a right nuisance' by his teachers who individually devised their own way of trying to cope with him. There was no father figure at home and Andrew's mother had never really been able to control him. As he grew older, so his restless activity in the classroom was exacerbated by his increasing inability to cope with the learning demands made on him. Because he seldom attended to what was being said or done, he had largely failed to acquire the skills which might be expected of him, as he was not lacking in intellectual ability. He constructed a position for himself in school which derived from his challenges to the teacher's authority and his following of younger pupils who provided the incentive for further displays of bad behaviour.

As far as Andrew is concerned, parental guidance was either inadequate (in the case of his mother) or non-existent (in the case of his father). It could almost be said of him that he came to school pre-programmed for failure. He had never had the opportunity to learn self-control and, because of this, the relationships he made with adults were poor and those with other children somewhat ambivalent. To sum up Andrew in this way may well be over-simplistic but he does serve to illustrate how family privations can have long-lasting effects.

It is always dangerous to have preconceptions about children, their behaviour and their progress. To accept a label for any child may well change how he/she is viewed. Labelling can lead to extra efforts being made to help but it can also lead to an acceptance, or even exaggeration, of patterns of interaction which may be definitely unhelpful. Material poverty does not inevitably lead to a lack of care, concern and love in the homes so affected any more than material wealth guarantees emotional well-being in all the family members. What can be said with a degree of assurance is that emotional well-being will be at risk if children feel that their home is not providing the support, concern, interest and acceptance they need, as well as the guidance and control which will enable them to develop socially and emotionally within a secure framework.

Traumatic incidents in the home
In the years from 7 to 11, children may have to cope, often for the first time, with highly stressful incidents (traumas) in the home. In the early years, care may be taken to protect them from stress but, as they grow older, their developing understanding of family circumstances and greater sensitivity to the interactions within the family structure make them vulnerable to anything which threatens the system which they know. The arrival of a new baby, the death of a grandparent, parent or sibling, the break-up of the relationship

between the parents or the departure of one of the parents from the family home are traumatic happenings which children in this age group feel intensely but may still not be old enough to understand fully. They may also be put under pressure to act in a way which demands greater maturity than they possess.

Children are often aware of death early. They may lose a loved member of the family circle; their dog may be killed; the cat they have known all their life may die of old age. Death is depicted many times on television, whether real or contrived. As Kitzinger and Kitzinger (1989) say, 'Anguish, pain and grief cannot be avoided. They *can* be borne, understood and used for growth' (p. 186). To achieve such growth, however, puts considerable demands on the adults who have to cope at a time when their own grief has to be dealt with effectively. Failure to realize the confusion or hurt which children may be experiencing is understandable but if such feelings in children are not recognized and if no opportunity is given for their expression, children may show these feelings in changed behaviour. They may become withdrawn or aggressive, may develop sleeping or eating problems, may take to bed-wetting or stealing or be unable to go to school. Not all children are similarly affected. Some, whether because of their temperament or their experiences, are more resilient than others, just as some adults are. But for adults to pretend that death has not occurred is seldom helpful. The quality of the care which the child receives before and after the bereavement is crucial if psychological disorder is not to develop (Black, 1992).

The concept of dissonance (Thomas and Chess, 1977) remains a useful one. By this is meant that the circumstances which are upsetting to children are those which they find are not at all in keeping with their ability to cope or those where there is a marked lack of consistency. Thus, if parents disagree over the handling of their children, for example if one parent is easy-going and the other expects strict and immediate obedience to rules or demands, some children may find the consequent tensions impossible to deal with. More adaptable children may have no great difficulty in such a situation. Again, some parents may realize their inconsistencies and try to achieve congruity while others may find the disagreements becoming a major source of friction. Parental discord, whatever its source, creates dissonance and so may be stressful to children, especially if they become pawns in the parents' struggle for power. Separation or divorce may further complicate matters. Rutter (1972) states that 'distorted relationships are most important in the genesis of antisocial behaviour' although, as he goes on to add, 'the presence of a deviant model may well be a contributory factor' (p. 14).

Not all children are fortunate enough to find love, affection and concern in their home. Children can be neglected or even rejected by those who should be providing care. Parents, particularly if under financial or emotional stress themselves, may feel they have neither the time nor the energy to nurture their children effectively. They may even reject some of their children, perhaps because of a disability, difficult behaviour (especially confrontations over eating, sleeping or general control) or family circumstances, such as a second marriage or a death in the family. Adults can take their own negative feelings out on their children, constantly criticizing them whatever they do. The unhappiness and insecurity this engenders in children and young people may well be released in emotional disturbance and problematic behaviour. Parental rejection must be the greatest 'dissonance' of all. A major complication is the interactive nature of relationships and reactions. Difficult children provoke adverse and negative behaviour from others (Hetherington, 1991), causing any breakdown in emotional bonds to escalate, forcing those concerned further and further apart.

In dealing with marital breakdown, as with other traumas in the family, opportunities for discussion, with no attempt to apportion criticism or blame, are invaluable. Clarke (1990) warns, however, that children are not like tapes which can be wiped blank. Immediate measures, which she terms 'first aid', must become longer term measures aimed at improving the self-control and self-esteem of all those concerned. Social workers may also be involved, a point which will be discussed later in this chapter. Marital counselling or family therapy may be helpful in resolving disagreements and laying the basis for a rather more favourable environment in which to bring up children. Schools as such may not be places where family discords can be resolved but they can serve two useful functions: to listen to parents and to suggest where help is available; and to be alert to displays of behaviour or changes in behaviour which may indicate that children are under stress at home. Only when parents and teachers trust each other can the conditions exist in which teachers may be able to carry out these functions to the benefit of those at risk. Consideration will be given to linking home and school later in this chapter.

Parents and Their Children's Adjustment to School

It has been suggested that one of the dimensions along which homes can be placed is that which runs from 'democratic' to 'controlled' (Mussen *et al.*, 1992). In the former, children can express their views, be listened to and be talked to; in the latter, parents are much more authoritarian and rules are set and adhered to. Clearly there may be distortions at both ends of this scale with either too much choice being offered so that children do what they want, or too little room being available for the child to develop cooperation and self-control. The idea of such a continuum may have some use, however, in indicating possible discontinuities between home and school routines.

In school, a degree of control has to be exercised if programmes are to run smoothly, although the extent of that control may vary from school to school (or even from teacher to teacher within the same school). For children from 'democratically'-oriented homes, compliance may come hard. They are accustomed to expressing their views and being largely self-activating. By the time they are 7 years of age, they may have learned that such self-dependent modes of behaviour are not always acceptable and may have made various adjustments to the school's demands, but this does not always happen. *Lester*, for example, was a lively, intelligent boy, an only child of parents who expected him to join in family decision-making. His language development was excellent, he could read and count before he went to school, and his general knowledge was extensive. In the infant school, he posed problems for his teachers as he knew most of what they were trying to teach and had no hesitation in saying so. Relationships with the other children were not particularly good as Lester really preferred the company of adults. The infant school regime was, however, sufficiently flexible to be able to cope with him but when he entered Y3 (at 7-plus years) his teacher was much more formal in outlook. The result was that Lester lost interest in school, finding the lessons boring and restrictive, and both his performance and his attendance deteriorated.

Ruth shows another aspect of how home and school can fail to work together. At 11 years of age, her school attendance (like that of her elder sister) was poor. Her parents were older than average, the father never coming to school and the mother appearing only to complain about some injustice which she felt had been done to Ruth. Ruth had no friends in school, largely the result of her withdrawn behaviour and her sporadic attendance. The parents, especially her mother, condoned these absences, always providing excuses for them. Attempts to involve Ruth more in school merely led to further complaints from her mother that the teachers were 'picking on Ruth'. Indeed, the girl had missed so much because of her absences that it was difficult to keep her within the main programme.

One final example of the effect of parental attitudes on children's school adjustment can be given. Many, many other examples are possible. *Ben* had an accident in the fairground when he was in the reception class. He missed a term's schooling and his parents, who had been with him at the time of the accident, entered into prolonged litigation with the fairground owners. They claimed Ben's behaviour had changed very much for the worse since the accident. The school, however, had seen some displays of poor behaviour before the accident took place but these had not been recorded. As Ben grew, his behaviour caused ever more concern as he was a big boy for his age. His Y5 teacher, however, seemed to be able to cope with Ben. He now said to her that he was going outside as he needed to be on his own. He then absented himself, did not respond to conversation but returned to the classroom when he felt ready. The parents' concern for their child seemed to have encouraged difficulties in self-control which may have been present before the fairground incident. Their attitude led Ben to see himself as beyond control, a view which at nine years of age he was only just beginning to think about for himself.

In the primary school years, home-school relationships are usually much more productive than the above examples might indicate. Johnson (1991) points out that these are the years when parents are familiar with much of what the school is doing; schools are relatively small and non-threatening; teachers are known to the parents and know them and other members of the family; and parents are encouraged to come to school for various purposes and activities. It is to practical links between home and school that attention will now be given.

Linking Home and School

The current stress on parental choice with regard to their children's schooling has encouraged in many parents an increased awareness of what schools have to offer and of their own educational responsibilities. Some confusion remains, especially over the ever-growing number of acronyms in use and the frequent changes which occur with regard to programmes, content and method. Where greater involvement than previously of parents in school activities has resulted, most would regard this as beneficial. Some, however, see parental involvement as potential interference or query the 'benchmarks' which parents are offered as the bases of their choice. Whatever the views taken by individual schools and parents of their relationship, the wide chasm which formerly existed between many schools and their parents has in most cases been bridged. Would any school today dare to put a notice on the playground gate saying, 'No parents beyond this point'? To increase parental choice of school may be viewed by many somewhat ambivalently but to increase parental involvement in school is in most cases seen as welcome.

Parental participation in the work of the school
There are many pressures on teachers in primary schools, not least those concerned with teaching and testing nationally prescribed programmes of study. There may be little time over for relaxed discussion with children, other members of staff, visiting professionals, governors or parents. Parental participation in school can, therefore, be a mixed blessing, especially as the parents concerned may have a whole variety of reasons for offering to participate ranging from a genuine wish to help the pursuit of vested interests which may do little to help at all.

Genuine involvement, which may still require teachers to find time to plan and organize parental contributions, has been used in primary schools in many different schemes, for example, to service school libraries, to supervise trips and journeys, to provide transport and to support children's reading (Cyster *et al.*, 1979). The latter is usually carried out at home, although monitored by schools or other professionals, and has been shown to be successful in most cases (Topping and Wolfendale, 1985). Other subjects may also be part of a home-based programme (Griffiths and Hamilton, 1987). Children with emotional and behavioural difficulties may complicate parental involvement, whether in school or in home-based programmes, by making it difficult for parents to establish a cooperative, working relationship or by withdrawing from such a relationship altogether. Indeed, the problems they may pose to those who are trying to help constitute one of the reasons why schools are sometimes unsure of the benefits of parental involvement.

Noreen at 8 years of age quickly realized that the parents who ran the school library were not able to control her restless behaviour as well as her teachers could. She disturbed the books, pushed the other children out of the way, defied the volunteers and created upheaval every time she came, although never quite going beyond the tolerance limits of the adults. Her reputation had spread among the parents long before the teachers realized what was going on. Again, confrontations may take place at home. Parents, already perhaps feeling inadequate in controlling their child's behaviour, may find a clash of wills more likely over their attempts at reading support, for example, than enjoyment in a cooperative exercise.

Parental interviews in school
Parents whose children show emotional or behavioural difficulties in school are not without experience of being called to school to discuss them. These interviews should be seen as 'enabling', that is giving parents and teachers access to information which might help to resolve the situation. As has already been said, the concept of 'parents as partners' was set out in the Warnock Report (DES, 1978) but the achievement of this ideal is far from easy. Wolfendale (1989) points out that, to achieve partnership, parents and teachers when talking together must agree on three fundamental issues:

(i)   they must share common basic principles (for example, if the school is striving not only to contain the child in question but also to promote maximum educational development, partnership is unlikely if parents are not concerned about educational progress);

(ii) they must recognize that teacher/parent time and availability are not unlimited and adjust demands accordingly;

(iii) they must show 'mutual respect for each other's roles and responsibilities' (p. 116).

In the absence of agreement on these principles, discussion with children's parents is likely to prove unproductive to all parties. Teachers blame parents for not trying to carry out their suggestions for change; parents blame teachers for not listening to them or not making the suggested changes clear or relevant or practicable. 'The essence of good communication is that it is a two-way process in which each participant can seek and give information and each attends to what the other is saying' (Atkin *et al.*, 1988, p. 123).

Parents of children with emotional and behavioural difficulties are at a disadvantage in school interviews. Their position is made worse if the school's policy is one of only calling parents in when there is a crisis. Successful (and productive) interviews are more likely when the school has found the time to think out the purposes of interviews and their format. Staff making themselves available at specific times on an informal basis, interspersed with more formal interviews at least once a year (with follow-ups of parents who do not attend either formal or informal sessions), can provide a framework around which real contacts can be made. Children's difficulties cannot be fully discussed in a corner at a Parents' Association disco but the beginnings of a working relationship can be made there. At all costs, what must be avoided is articulate teachers or headteachers telling bemused or resentful parents how their inadequacies at home are at the root of their children's difficulties in school.

Parents and teachers working together
So far, emphasis has been given largely to the differences between home and school and to the effects on school progress of home circumstances. To promote partnerships often requires no more than a change of attitude from both parties but it should be remembered that attitudes are not easy to change (see chapter 5). While many schools are genuinely trying to become more 'user friendly', some parents still retain views of education which are based on their own (not always happy) experiences. Teachers may be critical of some parents' methods of coping with behavioural difficulties in the home or astonished that some parents are prepared to tolerate ways of interacting that most people would reject. Yet whatever is done at home, as indeed whatever is done at school, is what seems to the participants to be the only possible action at that time.

Schools may find themselves reacting to emotional and behavioural difficulties in ways which they do not really find satisfactory, just as families may. Carpenter and Treacher (1989) warn of the dangers of getting stuck in patterns of interaction so that the same responses are repeated again and again, because change would lead into the unknown which might be much worse. Many factors are involved in creating 'stuckness', including frustration, anger and hopelessness on the part of all concerned. But adults involved in trying to help children with emotional and behavioural difficulties would be wise to remember two points: that it is ineffective to go on repeating a programme which has failed repeatedly; and that if the adults involved are not part of the solution of the difficulty, they have become part of the problem. And to complicate matters further, it should also be remembered that the 'problem' itself is seen differently by the child, the class teacher, the headteacher, the meals supervisors, the parents, the grandparents, the neighbours and so on. Finally, 'stuckness' must be distinguished from consistency. The latter is all-important in establishing patterns of behaviour.

What constructive suggestions can be made with regard to bringing parents and teachers closer together in coping with emotional and behavioural difficulties?

(i)   Rigidity of response should be avoided. This is not to advocate inconsistency in approach but to recognize that different individuals, whether children or adults, have different needs. In some cases, for example, parents are not uninterested in their child's school progress, they simply cannot attend for discussion during the school day. Arrangements have to be made to accommodate their life style. There needs to be a bit of 'give and take' on both sides. Parents, too, may have to shift their point of view.

(ii)   It is almost always better to deal with a difficulty early on rather than to wait for it to escalate. Parents can alert schools to the possibility of difficulties in behaviour (for example, by warning class teachers that worries about moving into another class are upsetting an already withdrawn child) or inform them of family upheavals or losses. Schools should have created the relationships with parents which enable them to raise concerns about their child's behaviour before it becomes established.

(iii)   There are many barriers in the way of good communication between schools and parents. Notes for parents and advance arrangements for school events get lost between school and home; parents find they cannot (or do not choose to) attend parent group meetings; family circumstances intervene in intentions to attend meetings with staff and vital information is not full understood when conveyed at second hand; using English as the only medium for communication may lead to confusion and misunderstanding. Access to school staff and school governors is now easier than it used to be for parents who know, and can cope with, the system. But, for some parents, access may be just as difficult to achieve as it ever was. If schools and parent associations could reach these parents, involvement might lead to considerable change in pupil behaviour.

(iv)   The greatest enemy to developing effective home-school relationships is time. Many misunderstandings arise because neither parents nor school staff have the time to think through how matters could be better organized. The only comment that can be made is that it is usually infinitely more time-consuming to cope with a behavioural crisis than it is to arrange home-school relationships in such a way that all involved are trying to work together to avoid any crisis.

It may seem in the discussion so far that more has been said about the help that parents need than about the help that they can give in the matter of emotional and behavioural difficulties. But only when parents feel that they are coping adequately, and believe that the school also feels this, can emotional and behavioural difficulties in their children be avoided or managed with some degree of success. Helping parents, therefore, to help their children may be the most effective approach available. It is not only schools that can offer this help. Other agencies, as may be seen below, can also make their contribution.

Help from Other Professionals

As well as the additional educational support which can be offered to schools (see chapters 5 and 7), there are many other sources of help in coping with emotional and behaviour difficulties which are available to teachers, parents and children (Davies and Davies, 1989).

Educational Psychologists

Their contribution has already been referred to briefly in chapter 5. What educational psychologists (and the staff who work with them in the School Psychological Service) offer is a professionally trained viewpoint on the difficulties in question which is grounded on educational understanding and psychological expertise (for example, a knowledge of how children learn; how skills can be assessed; individual differences; and a variety of therapies which might help). Educational psychologists should also have the time to discuss the situation with those involved (including the child) and to see the child functioning in school and at home. They can advise teachers and parents, devise special programmes, and arrange for additional support from a number of other services if this is required.

Educational psychologists are usually linked to specific schools and should, therefore, be known to staff and pupils. It is a pity if their expertise is only called upon when the difficulties involved have become crises. A preventative approach to EBDs — providing in-service training, informal discussion with staff and so on — may be the most productive way to use their time.

Child Psychiatrists

Educational psychologists have a particular interest in children's progress and behaviour at school, although they are also involved with EBDs which appear to affect children outside but not inside school (for example, bed-wetting; being out of parental control). Child psychiatrists are medically trained and have additionally specialized in dealing with a wide range of mental health problems in children. They function mainly from a base in the health service, which provides out-patient child psychiatric clinics in many districts, but they may also work in local authority child guidance centres and within schools. In cooperation with educational and clinical (health service based) psychologists, social workers and sometimes psychotherapists, they contribute to the assessment and treatment of children and adolescents referred by a variety of agencies. These include parents, schools, family doctors, other medical specialists such as paediatricians, magistrates and the social services.

Child psychiatrists tend to be involved in the more serious cases of emotional and behavioural disturbance, and to use a variety of therapeutic approaches depending on their own orientations and the nature of the problem being tackled. They are well placed to decide when further medical investigation is required, for example, by neurologists, and to provide access to appropriate hospital services, including in-patient provision. They may offer family and group therapy as well as help for individual children (for example, psychotherapy or behaviour modification; medication; advice to parents).

Family Doctors

In some instances, parents may feel it appropriate to contact their own doctor. This is particularly the case when the behaviour which is causing concern shows physical symptoms (for example, sleep problems; anorexia). Parents may wonder if a depressed, withdrawn child has some physical disorder, as may also be the case if the child complains of persistent headaches, sickness or phobias. These symptoms may, of course, be psychosomatic in origin (i.e., more to do with emotional disturbance than physical disorder) but to approach the family doctor, especially if he/she has been associated with the family over a number of years, may be easier for those concerned than going to school with their worries. Pressures on GPs, however, are considerable and they may not have the time available to examine fully the nature of the behavioural difficulty. They can, however, refer the difficulty to an educational psychologist or a child psychiatrist. Thus, family doctors have an important role to play in children's mental, as well as physical, health and should be alert, just as teachers should be, to changes in children's behaviour or development which could show that all is not well.

Special diets and drug treatment can prove helpful in alleviating the emotional difficulties which may be associated with the child's medical condition (see chapter 3, pp. 39–40). Hyperactivity in some children may be reduced by avoiding certain foods or food additives; in others, special diets (or vitamin supplements) appear to have no positive effect. Children who are obese may find it easier to make friends and join in peer group activities when they lose weight but, again, improved social relationships do not inevitably accompany changes in physical shape. Coping with the physical symptoms may have to be supported by giving attention to the emotional concomitants.

Therapists

The contribution made by speech therapists to children's development is well known to teachers and parents and invaluable in promoting emotional well-being in their clients. To be able to communicate freely with peer groups and adults prevents misunderstandings, criticisms or jeers. Other therapists can also help. The work of play therapists and family therapists has already been outlined. It is a pity that the invaluable service which they can give to parents and children is limited by their very scarcity. The intentions of the various therapies are always to 'provide support, skills, energies and hope' and to forge a 'therapeutic alliance' within which those in difficulties 'can retain responsibility for solving their problems' (Carpenter and Treacher, 1989, p. 235).

According to Carpenter and Treacher (*ibid*), the work of therapists (especially those involved in family or marital counselling) should follow certain guidelines if it is to be successful. These guidelines can usefully be considered in any situation in which help is offered to adults or children.

(i)   The responsibility for change rests with the client. Help, however well-intentioned, cannot be forced on the recipient.

(ii)   Goals set as the objectives of the therapy need to be realistic and obtainable in the view of the client, not the therapist.

(iii)   The client must be an active participant in the helping situation, not the passive recipient of advice from an 'all-knowing expert'.

They also point out that, as the interaction between therapists and clients is flexible and ongoing, therapists may find the relationship with their clients changing and must adapt accordingly, even to the extent of asking for help themselves if they find that what they are doing seems to be getting nowhere.

Social Workers

The nineteenth and twentieth centuries have seen great changes in every aspect of the family, including child-rearing practices and expectations of children's place within the family. Thus, children are no longer seen, in Western society, as economic assets who will become the main supporters of the family in their turn. Children are now expensive to rear and see their future in much wider terms than previously (Levine and White, 1991). As a corollary of the changing role of the family in society, others have stepped in to say what should happen to children and how they should be educated. Children's experiences within their own home have become the concern of national, and even international, agencies. Statements of children's rights have been drawn up and internationally agreed (if not always fully implemented); Social Services Departments see their role as including the support of a family and the protection of the children in that family, whether or not the family agrees.

The Children Act 1989 (see, for example, Feldman and Mitchels, 1990) aims to place the welfare of the child at the centre of any decisions taken and sees parents as having responsibilities towards their child rather than rights over him or her. The legislation, therefore, widens the basis on which decisions are taken by stressing the importance of the wishes of the child (or young person), the contribution of the whole family network and the need for advice from a variety of professionals. Children 'in need' ought to have greater protection and increased attention to their well-being under the 1989 Act, whether or not they are the subject of a court order. The Act is 'user friendly', provides guidelines which should be adaptable to individual cases and stresses flexibility in responding to crises or potential crises (Bennett, 1992).

Nowhere are societal changes to be seen more clearly than in the current concern over child abuse. The extent of physical and sexual abuse within industrialized, developed countries is still not fully known. Nor is the extent of neglect among children. The recent growth in public awareness of these problems, and concern over them, may have led to a reduction in the incidence of child abuse (Frude, 1991) but it remains an area which is difficult to define and even more difficult to deal with effectively. Social Services Departments do not, therefore, always get it right. Their work is likely to be enhanced in value when social workers and teachers cooperate (not collude). As has been said before, teachers are well placed to spot changes in children's normal behaviour which may indicate that something is going wrong.

Family breakdown, poverty and deprivation, sometimes in combination as in the case of Leonie and Magda (see earlier in this chapter), bear down particularly heavily on children in middle childhood. Easy communication between teachers and social workers is again vital so that the contribution of Social Services to the alleviation of the difficulties in the home can be supported by the school if appropriate. Financial and housing problems, for example, have no small effect on children's behaviour in school and yet are not normally within a teacher's competence to deal with. More than that, societal problems are usually extremely complex. Recognition by the school of the help which social workers can give and the passing on of information from the Education and Social Services to each other must enable a wider (and more supportive) perspective to be taken.

Educational Welfare Officers

The work of EWOs is to link home and school when a gap has appeared between them. Absence from school may be the reason why EWOs are alerted in the first place but home visits may reveal much useful information for schools and, of course, may lead to further involvement from Social Services Departments. Of particular concern to EWOs are 'condoned' absences (when the parent/s accept or even encourage non-attendance), truancy and school refusal (see chapter 11). These are all problems which schools cannot fail to be aware of and which parents should be aware of. If families are to help in overcoming these problems, they need opportunities to come to terms with them in their own way, information, support, encouragement and the feeling that they are collaborating in some way in a joint effort. Schools, too, have similar needs and the role of the EWO can be crucial in attempting to meet these needs and in bringing together all concerned.

Overview

Dowling and Osborne (1985) have described three scenarios, all of which are unhelpful to children with emotional and behavioual difficulties.

(i) The home blames the school for what is happening. Parent(s) claim that there is no problem at home and shrug off any responsibility for the behaviour which is causing concern.

(ii) The school blames the home for what is happening. Teachers are only too aware of the behaviour in question but see it as an inevitable reaction to home circumstances and so beyond their control and not their responsibility.

(iii) Both home and school blame the child for what is happening. This may be the most unfortunate scenario of all as there is no respite for the child. Whether at home or in school, he/she is the focus of negative pressures which push the entire responsibility for the unacceptable actions away from the adults involved.

In order to help children with emotional and behavioural difficulties, there must be consultation and cooperation between all concerned. Clark (1988), discussing young children, lists four Cs which are important preconditions for development — coordination, cooperation, communication and continuity — all set in the framework of a relevant and stimulating curriculum. These preconditions still hold for somewhat older children, especially in the context of home-school relationships and support from other agencies. Discontinuities, lack of communication, failure to work together towards agreed objectives, reluctance to accept responsibility leading to the neglect of the difficulty, all mean that help is not forthcoming for the children concerned.

It is almost impossible to overemphasize the importance of parental attitudes in any discussion of emotional and behavioural difficulties. When home and school are at least compatible, children know where they are. They may not accept the guidelines for acceptable behaviour which are indicated but at least these guidelines are fairly consistent. Lack of such consistency creates uncertainties and these may be compounded if agencies other than the school are also involved. Teachers who are not sure of what additional support is being offered, or who may not even know that others have been called in to try to help, cannot work effectively with the children in question. Therapeutic and supportive help may be similarly ineffective. Parents, particularly those who are facing stresses of whatever kind in their own life, need to feel a sense of agreed purpose if they are to become part of the process of helping their children. If they are no part of this process, the outcome is unlikely to be positive. 'What appears to matter most is parents' sense of confidence and competence and their expectations in relation to a realistic appraisal of the possibilities' (Fontana, 1985, p. 297).

In many localities, there are schemes to link schools and the communities they serve and some offer 'parent education' programmes. Alexander (1992) lists forty-seven strategies used by thirty primary schools in Leeds to develop and build on such links and many other writers over the years have outlined possible schemes with similar aims (for example, Edwards and Redfern, 1988; Wolfendale, 1989). That establishing good relationships is not always easy can be seen in discussions by Pugh and De'Ath (1984), Partington and Wragg (1989) and Wolfendale (1992). All of these writers remain convinced that problems can be overcome, even in times of increased public scrutiny and growing awareness on the part of parents of their rights with regard to their child's education. Indeed, it may be that the current changes in educational outlook will enable the various lines of communication and support to come together to the benefit of all children, but especially those with emotional and behavioural difficulties.

Part III

Educating Children with EBDs

Chapter 7

Integration

During even a brief visit to a school catering for pupils in the 7–11+ year-old range, teachers' ways of coping with emotional and behavioural difficulties can be identified. The visitor will overhear instructions designed to modify unwanted behaviour: 'Walk, don't run in the corridor'; 'Turn around and listen to what I'm saying'. He or she may see pupils set apart from their peers, for example, sitting alone at the teacher's desk or waiting outside the headteacher's office. He or she may also see other pupils misbehaving and teachers electing not to reprimand them or not having observed the behaviour in the first place. Most of the examples of unwanted behaviour will be mild in character and will appear to have little effect on the smooth running of the establishment.

Most teachers expect to have to cope with mild behaviour problems as part of their normal duties, and they do so by adjusting their classroom organization and managerial style or by giving attention to the demands of the curriculum. Some teachers will be proactive and will set ground rules, plan strategies and evaluate the effectiveness of any changes made, while others will be reactive and will respond in an *ad hoc* fashion to a situation once it has occurred. When unwanted pupil behaviour is mild and confined to a small minority of pupils, it is unlikely to motivate teachers to collaborate and plan 'whole school' responses to emotional and behavioural difficulties. The demands placed upon teachers' time in recent years, including the implementation of the National Curriculum, statutory assessment and recording, mean that teachers already feel under considerable pressure. However, failure to set aside time to consider emotional and behavioural difficulties and to plan the school's response to pupils who experience them may, in fact, be a central factor in placing individual teachers under considerable stress which might otherwise be avoidable. Neglecting to deal with the problem may also lead to a move towards segregating such pupils in special units or schools outside mainstream education.

Galloway *et al.* (1982) define disruptive behaviour as that which disturbs teachers and is viewed by them as being problematic and inappropriate. This emphasis on the teacher's viewpoint underlines the variations which occur in what is perceived as being disruptive. It follows naturally that, if teachers define problem behaviour differently, they are likely to attempt to deal with that behaviour differently. At the level of mild behaviour problems, therefore, it is unlikely that continuity of practice will ever be achieved but, despite wide variations in teacher response, integration of pupils exhibiting mild behaviour problems remains the norm. For such pupils, schools are generally flexible enough to provide an environment in which their behaviour is tolerated, moderated or even eliminated.

Not all disruptive behaviour falls into the category of being 'mild' or even 'moderate'. There are other more serious types of behavioural problems which may on occasion call the mainstream placement into question. Robertson (1989) categorizes these under three main headings:

(i) those behaviours violating the pupil's own interests, for example, endangering his or her health or safety;
(ii) those behaviours violating the school's interests, for example, challenging adult authority; and
(iii) those behaviours violating the interests of other pupils, for example, bullying or distracting pupils from their work.

However, while more serious forms of behavioural difficulties present schools with greater challenges, they do not always result in a call for segregation (i.e., moving children out of mainstream integration). It is evident that some schools feel able to cope with problems while others look to the removal of the child as the solution. What then are the barriers to integration which result in some schools feeling unable to own and deal with problem behaviour?

Barriers to Integration

It might be expected that the main barrier to integration would be the degree of severity of the emotional or behavioural difficulty. While the seriousness of the behaviour is undoubtedly a factor in whether or not a child can be integrated in the mainstream, the overall picture is far more complex than this. Take, for example, the case of 8-year-old twins, *James* and *Jason*. The twins broke into their school during a weekend in the company of a third boy from a different school. Once inside, they daubed graffiti on walls, carried out various acts of vandalism and were caught in the process of leaving the building with some stolen goods of limited value. Staffroom conversation on the following Monday centred on the break-in and, while there was much discussion about what punishment would fit the crime, no mention was made of removing the twins from the school.

If the seriousness of the twin's actions did not constitute sufficiently disruptive behaviour to warrant their removal, one might well ask what factors supported their continuing presence in the mainstream. These might be summed up as follows:

(i)   the break-in was not confrontational with regard to teachers. At the time of the break-in, the twins were in their parents' care and so were breaking their rules and the law rather than teachers' rules;

(ii)   the twins were not perceived as troublesome in class. James and Jason were within the acceptable range in terms of their in-school behaviour;

(iii)   they posed no threat to teacher authority.

Although their actions damaged the school building, they were not directed against any individual and so there was no loss of any teacher self-esteem as a result of the misbehaviour. Even the boys' classteacher did not feel in any way challenged as the twins were contrite in her presence on the Monday following the break-in.

If pupils can be integrated even when they have broken the law through unacceptable behaviour, then what factors will cause integration to be questioned and segregation to be seen as an appropriate alternative? Tattum (1982) emphasizes the damage done to interpersonal relationships when children display disruptive behaviour. Teachers in a school or unit for pupils with emotional and behavioural difficulties may well feel that they personally are not contributing to those difficulties because the children will have come to them already labelled. In the mainstream, however, teachers may feel that they are somehow to blame or have failed to cope with a particular child. Thus there may be a loss of teacher self-esteem and a desire to return to the status quo by the removal of what is perceived as the root of the problem — the child. It may be that, if teachers were shown how to manage problem behaviour within their own schools and helped to see that the cause of unwanted behaviour is seldom the result of a single factor, the barriers to integration would be, at least in part, removed.

It is necessary, therefore, to consider what schools and the teachers within them lack if they fail to provide the support necessary to sustain pupils in the mainstream. Gow (1988) lists a substantial number of points some of which are given below.

Lack of Appropriate Planning and Resourcing

Resources for offering additional support to mainstream teachers are inevitably finite. In view of this, the need for planning takes on even greater significance. Indeed, lack of coherent planning may create integration 'by default' where pupils are mainstreamed, not because their needs are being met by such a placement, but because the school has not sought (or cannot obtain) appropriate help. Where integration is sustained in an unsatisfactory manner, classteachers bear the responsibility of knowing that they are not meeting children's needs, with a resulting detrimental effect on the education of other children.

Duality of Provision

The Warnock Report (DES, 1978) emphasizes the need for a continuum of provision to meet the special educational needs of a wide variety of pupils. Where no planned response has been made to the needs of pupils with emotional and behavioural difficulties, it is possible that scarce funds will be tied up in providing segregated special schools at the expense of innovative interventions in mainstream settings. Conversely, it may be the case that so much money has been put into supporting integration that insufficient funds are left to provide appropriately for a minority of pupils whose needs cannot be met in the mainstream.

The Lack of a Relevant Curriculum

Individual teachers may not have fully recognized the links between providing a relevant curriculum and the reduction in unwanted behaviour. Bird *et al.* (1980) identified four main ways in which pupils might be disaffected by the school curriculum: if they could not meet its demands; if it left them feeling a failure; if they felt it was irrelevant; and if they could not relate to its academic slant. Pupils who exhibit unwanted behaviour may be helped if the curriculum is differentiated (see chapter 5) so that they can access it and achieve success within it. Some teachers may be reluctant to take on board the work involved in differentiating the curriculum to meet individual pupil needs; some may be unaware that adaptations to teaching style, classroom organization, task setting, materials etc. can reduce disaffection and improve behavioural standards.

The Lack of Appropriate Training Opportunities

Few teachers leave their initial training with well-established strategies for dealing with a whole range of unwanted behaviours. Even those who have such strategies will have to adapt them so that they fit the demands of the children with whom they work. Teachers, therefore, have to build up through trial and error a selection of effective strategies and may feel, from time to time, that they are not coping adequately with certain situations. The need is for in-service training from individuals who have specialist expertise and may be able to suggest additional or alternative approaches which teachers can utilize in their own classrooms. Because of financial restrictions or lack of suitably qualified staff, this need is not always met.

Making Integration Work

Just as it is important to examine barriers to effective integration, so it is also important to consider how schools which do manage to sustain integration succeed in doing so. Chapter 5 looked at how teachers can be helped to provide more effectively for pupils with EBDs and also at some specific approaches which they might adopt. The section which follows examines how individual teachers have responded to particular pupils and how they have availed themselves of others' expertise. How schools may undertake a 'whole school' response will also be described and how one LEA has organized its provision in order to support the full integration of 7–11+ year-old pupils with EBDs. In some instances, a single approach to changing unwanted behaviour has been adopted but frequently individuals and institutions have made use of more than one technique in order to reach the desired outcome. An overview of the various approaches which individuals and institutions adopted is given at the end of the section.

Teachers and Pupils

Michael, Y3

Mrs. W., who teaches a class of 7–8-year-olds, found that she was having problems with the behaviour of one particular boy, Michael. He presented few unwanted behaviours when occupied with classwork but was a very disruptive element in the class during the inevitable introductory and clearing-away sessions which preceded and succeeded lessons. Mrs. W. had reprimanded Michael many times but this seemed to be having no effect on his behaviour. Over time, she found that Michael's failure to conform was interfering with the smooth start to her lessons and that she was dismissing the pupils at breaktimes in a very stressed manner. Partington and Hinchcliffe (1979) stress the importance of events at the beginning and end of lessons and see control by the teacher at these times as being part of establishing his or her status in the class.

Mrs. W. sought the help of an advisory teacher who was visiting the school in respect of another child with learning difficulties. Without knowing Michael, but having had his actions described to her, she suggested that Mrs. W. initiate a star chart to draw attention to, and reward, those occasions when Michael behaved well. As a result, Mrs. W. divided Michael's day into quarters and rewarded good behaviour in any one quarter by a star. At the end of each day, the chart was reviewed with Michael and, if three or more stars had been earned, Michael was allowed to select and take home a reading book. This may not seem like a particularly motivating reward but Michael was, in fact, a very keen reader and, at the time, the school had no take-home book arrangement.

Michael quickly realized that he held the responsibility for whether or not he had earned a book and his behaviour improved considerably. Mrs. W. was able to do away with the chart and provide only oral feedback on each quarter day. Michael now accepts that Mrs. W.'s evaluation of his whole day determines whether or not he will take home a book. Mrs. W. has not yet decided what her future action in respect of Michael will be but, at some point, she will have to consider whether or not the improvement in Michael's behaviour is sufficiently well established that she can reduce the frequency of the oral feedback.

Tina Y3

Another Y3 teacher, Miss M., in a different school, adopted a similar approach with far less effective results. Miss M. was concerned about Tina who was working well below her ability level and disrupting the work patterns of her fellow pupils. Miss M. had tried seating Tina apart from the others but Tina's facial expressions and gestures proved as disruptive as her physical proximity had done.

Miss M. adopted a star chart on the suggestion of another teacher but, unlike Mrs. W., she opted for a once-a-day evaluation. Tina would get a star if she worked well during the day and allowed others to work also. Four or more stars over a period of five days would earn Tina a certificate on a Friday afternoon which she could then take home. There was no noticeable change in Tina's behaviour and the system was discontinued after three weeks with no certificate having been earned.

Clive, Y3–Y6 Special Class

Mrs. B., the teacher of a class for a range of pupils with learning difficulties, found an effective system for changing the behaviour of one boy, Clive, who was then 9 years of age. Clive was sullen, difficult to motivate and would often respond rudely to the teacher's requests to do anything he had not selected for himself. Mrs. B. felt that Clive's academic abilities were such that he would be able to cope with the mainstream curriculum if only he could improve his attitude in class. She, therefore, felt that one of her teaching priorities in respect of Clive was to establish a system which would motivate Clive to work.

Left to his own devices, Clive would paint or draw all day and would produce very attractive work which gained the admiration of staff and pupils alike. Mrs. B. placed a paint pot containing four paintbrushes behind her desk and removed a brush each time Clive was uncooperative. If two or more brushes remained at 2.45 p.m. then Clive could spend the remainder of the school day painting. Mrs. B. drew Clive's attention periodically to the number of brushes remaining.

Alan, Y4

Mr. K. knew that sweets were a motivating force in the life of one of his pupils, Alan, who showed aggressive behaviour toward younger pupils in the school. Alan's behaviour in class was not a problem but Mr. K. was regularly told by other adults that Alan had caused problems in the corridor, or on the yard, or at lunch-times. Mr. K. enlisted the help of Alan's parents and adopted a system whereby Alan's day was divided in two. If Alan's behaviour was not remarked upon by another adult in the morning, Alan was given a sticker and the process was repeated in the afternoon. On Friday afternoons Alan took his stickers home and, if they amounted to eight or more, his parents rewarded him on Friday evenings by allowing him to select the sweets of his choice to a pre-agreed value. Mr. K. was well aware that using sweets as a reward in the mainstream might motivate individual pupils to improve their performance but might also actually encourage pupils with currently acceptable behaviour to misbehave! He nevertheless felt that it was worth taking such a risk in Alan's case.

Leanne, Y4

Mrs. T. grew increasingly concerned about the behaviour of one of her pupils, Leanne, following the death of the child's grandmother. Leanne and her unmarried mother had shared the grandmother's home and she had cared for Leanne so that Leanne's mother could go to work. When her grandmother died unexpectedly, Leanne appeared unmoved and was back at school the next day. However, in the weeks that followed Leanne became increasingly unkempt in her appearance and considerably less communicative. When Mrs. T. attempted to talk to Leanne, she was accused of 'picking on' her and Leanne would often become tearful. Other teachers commented upon the fact that she had become a loner in the yard at playtimes. Mrs. T. spoke to Leanne's mother but she herself was under considerable pressure following her mother's death and Mrs. T. felt uncomfortable about adding to this pressure.

In an attempt to reopen the channels of communication, Mrs. T. used worksheets from the 'Picture my Feelings' pack (LDA). Initially she gave a group of children, which included Leanne, those worksheets which were concerned with positive feelings for example, 'I feel proud when . . .', 'I feel excited when . . .' and, when these were established as part of a normal routine, she introduced sheets which invited the pupils to record more sensitive emotions, for example, 'I feel embarrassed when . . .', 'I feel sad when . . .'. Leanne found it possible to respond to this less direct approach. Although the process was a long one, Leanne regained her pleasant disposition and came to terms with her grandmother's death.

Carl, Tom, Adrian and Jeremy, Y5

Initially Y5's classteacher, Mr. J., referred Carl for additional help because of his apparent learning difficulties. Carl was failing to progress in reading and his written work, although well produced, was weak in content. He appeared to have a very short concentration span. When a peripatetic teacher was deployed in respect of Carl, Mr. J. mentioned the disruptive behaviour and learning difficulties of a further three boys in the class. The peripatetic teacher began working with Carl as part of this group and took note of the boys' poor learning strategies, the lack of differentiated work and the increasing disaffection from school being shown by the boys.

In view of the limited time he was able to offer the school, the peripatetic teacher advised Mr. J. on differentiating the tasks to make them more accessible. He also undertook aspects of the Instrumental Enrichment Programme (see chapter 5) with the boys in order to improve their learning skills. These content-free activities were something the boys were unfamiliar with and they were highly motivated during the sessions. This intervention is still ongoing and so it is not yet possible to evaluate fully its effectiveness, but the behaviour of the four boys is noticeably better.

In the above case studies, the attempts to change behaviour have been confined to individual classrooms and have been orchestrated by particular teachers who, in some instances, had consulted with others. In the following case-study, a whole school examined its approach to unwanted behaviour and attempted to create a cohesive policy on behaviour.

A School Approach

Fernlea School
This school, catering for pupils in the 4–11 year age-range, was without a permanent headteacher for a considerable period and, by the time a new appointment was made, standards of behaviour had deteriorated. Two children had been suspended and a number of others were felt to be 'beyond control'. The noise level in the open-plan school was such that it was a stressful working environment for all concerned. These factors provided the new headteacher with a dramatic contrast between this and her previous school and she made it known that the creation of a policy for 'discipline' was one of her priorities.

Staff were asked to make notes on those things which were causing concern and to bring these along to a staff meeting. Where there was consensus over matters such as behaviour during assembly, movement around the school or acceptable noise levels, rules were framed so that definitions of minimum requirements could be stipulated. These rules were framed positively (i.e., in this school we expect pupils to . . .). Children were told of these rules by the headteacher during assembly; they were displayed in each classroom; and copies were sent home with an invitation for parental comments to be sent to school. The rules concerned six areas of school life: staff/pupil behaviour; pupil/pupil behaviour; respect for property; concern for others' well-being; dress codes for pupils; and movement around the school. The rules and the consequences for breaking them were made explicit in the school's prospectus.

Techniques Used by the Schools

Behavioural approaches
In these case studies, reference has been made to a number of techniques examined in chapter 5. The first four case studies all employed a form of

behaviour management although each teacher adopted a slightly different approach and experienced varying degrees of success. Modifying behaviour by means of a reward system can only be successful if the rewards offered are meaningful and motivating to the child concerned. Miss M., for example, might have experienced more success with Tina if she had negotiated with her a reward which was appropriate. Clearly a certificate was not motivating in Tina's case. Jones (1983) stresses the need for teachers who adopt a behaviour modification type of approach to check the preferences of their pupils before selecting a reward. However, care must be taken that the reward is also appropriate within the ethos of the mainstream classroom. Mr. K. ensured that the sweets which motivated Alan's improved behaviour were earned in school but purchased and eaten at home. Failure to ensure that rewards are in keeping with existing school norms may result in management problems with respect to other pupils in the class.

In addition to ensuring that rewards are motivating and appropriate, teachers must take care to monitor the frequency of feedback and the form this feedback takes. Miss. M. failed to recognize that Tina needed to receive feedback more often than she was given it. Mrs. B., on the other hand, not only provided periodic feedback for Clive but also recognized the importance of a tangible reminder (the paintbrushes) with direct links to the reward in the case of a child with moderate learning difficulties.

Teachers attempting to undertake behaviour management can also be helped by the existence of a framework within which to work when confronted by pupils who cause concern (Bird *et al.*, 1980). Such a framework could be provided by a 'whole-school' policy such as that which was created at Fernlea School. A common rule system makes explicit to staff and pupils what is acceptable behaviour as defined by that school. Consequently, pupils know when they have broken a rule and what the outcome is likely to be. More importantly, they are given clear patterns of desirable behaviour.

Social skills training and group support

A teacher acting alone can effect change in a child but that child does not exist in a vacuum. Rather he or she is part of a complex social network of peers. Utilizing these other children in effecting the change is a very powerful tool for the teacher. When Leanne appeared pressurized by her teacher's attempts to get her to put her feelings into words, this pressure was reduced in two ways:

(i)   by allowing Leanne to write down her feelings rather than expressing them orally; and

(ii) by involving her in a group engaged in the same activity from which she could draw support and retain a degree of anonymity.

The other group members had not been made aware of the teacher's aims or their support explicitly sought but their involvement through a shared task was, in this case, successful. In other cases, teachers might need to structure group support in order to bring about behaviour change but for Leanne the very fact of being asked to communicate as part of a group, rather than as an individual, was sufficient.

Cognitive approaches

Teachers may not be fully aware of the Instrumental Enrichment approach (see chapter 5) and so it is hardly surprising that it is not often employed. The case of Carl and his group highlights not only the contribution of innovative strategies in changing behaviour but also the role of professional help. Teachers are never going to be competent in every aspect of intervention with those who exhibit emotional and behavioural difficulties. What is important is that teachers should have access to those who are appropriately trained and equipped with special skills, such as the peripatetic teachers.

If pupils with EBDs are to be retained in mainstream schools, then some support system must exist to provide resources for teachers in terms of advice, manpower and training. Some LEAs have organized themselves to this end and the following section examines one LEA which is committed to the integration in mainstream schools of primary-aged pupils with emotional and behavioural difficulties.

An LEA Approach

Northfield LEA

Northfield LEA serves a mixed rural and urban area. For a number of years this LEA has maintained no special schools or off-site units for EBD pupils in the primary age range. This commitment to integration has meant the setting up of a specialist team of appropriately-trained and experienced teachers, led by an educational psychologist. These specialist teachers work alongside their mainstream colleagues, with the stated aim of making schools more effective in dealing with pupils who are perceived as having behaviour problems.

When a child is referred by a school through the appropriate educational psychologist, details have to be provided of what has already been tried in school with that child. This has the effect of making the school examine its own responses to unwanted behaviour and acts as a filtering system if the referral is premature. The psychologist may suggest alternative strategies if he/she feels that the school has not fully carried out its responsibility. If, however, he/she feels that the school has done all it can from within its existing resources, then the referral will be passed to the head of the specialist team.

One of the strategies the school will be expected to have undertaken is the involvement of the child's family. The team sees its role very much as one of working with all the individuals who are influencing the child and, not least, the child him/herself. Consequently, the specialist teacher may be involved with the child, the teacher, the headteacher, the parents, the siblings and the grandparents or any combination of these. Problem behaviour is dealt with within the context in which it occurs, i.e., the educational setting of the school, rather than by removal to a clinic.

Challenging perceptions which exist and may have become fixed is central to the LEA's approach to enabling children with EBDs to be supported in the mainstream. However, the specialist team goes to great lengths to avoid being seen to be critical of the school or to support any one aspect of a situation in preference to another. The school that feels it is being judged as wanting by the team's support for the parents is unlikely to be responsive to suggestions for change. Parents would react similarly if they were to feel that the team has joined forces with the school in being critical of discipline at home. Specialist teachers do not aim to be viewed as experts, but rather to be seen as additional resources which can help all concerned to make a difference.

While there are common problems which, on the surface at least, appear to affect a number of schools, the actual variables which exist in terms of pupils, staff, resources available, family situations and previous experience mean that no one format for involvement will suit all cases equally well. The LEA retains a guiding philosophy for all interventions but the precise nature of each intervention will be determined by the individual situation within any school.

In general, the involvement of a specialist teacher in a school will be intensive (i.e., one hour per day, four days per week) and highly focused so that his/her withdrawal can be achieved after a period of six to eight weeks. One involvement with the service does not preclude a school from referring the same child again if the problem persists. However, only by negotiating a sensible withdrawal time, can the LEA ensure that the school does not become dependent upon the service and that the resource is available to many schools rather than being indefinitely tied up with a few.

Following the involvement of the specialist team, schools report a greater understanding of, and confidence in, using behaviour modification techniques, counselling and group support work. They are shown the relationship between curriculum and behaviour and how differentiation can lead to success which may motivate more acceptable behaviour patterns in certain children. The modelling of particular techniques in the setting of the mainstream classroom does not de-skill the teacher, and the specialist teacher will offer in-service training to the whole school so that other members of staff can benefit also. However, in spite of the clearly thought-out, relatively well-resourced intervention of the specialist team, the needs of the children continue to cause concern. A number of these children have had two or more inputs from the team and yet they still present behavioural difficulties in school. With respect to this small minority, the LEA is considering the setting-up of an 'off-site' unit for pupils in the 7–11+ age range.

Overview

Just as the term 'learning difficulties' encompasses a variety of problems, so emotional and behavioural difficulties are similarly multi-faceted. This chapter has looked at children with EBDs in mainstream schools and at some of the factors which may inhibit their integration or even serve to prevent it. Such factors can be influenced by appropriate planning and resourcing, if integration is felt to be the correct method of meeting the needs of the pupils concerned. Even where an LEA is not committed to integration, integration may occur 'by default', but this is often unfair on both pupil and teacher and may adversely affect the education of the child's classmates.

Within mainstream schools, teachers have shown themselves to be resourceful in attempting to reduce unwanted behaviours. Some act individually, utilizing knowledge they already have; others involve professionals who have greater expertise; yet others band together as a staff to create a 'whole-school' response. If, in turn, an LEA has adopted a structured policy for responding to the needs of pupils with EBDs, then schools can look to additional support. This may assist with continuing integration and reduce the need for the segregation of pupils' with EBDs. A separate special system is the focus of the next chapter.

Chapter 8

In Special Provision

Regardless of the prevailing educational thinking on integration or segregation, most pupils exhibiting emotional or behavioural difficulties will be educated in their local school at the primary stage of schooling. However, at different times, varying influences on education have produced trends towards particular types of provision in preference to others. The Underwood Report (Ministry of Education, 1955), for example, recorded and described the increase in provision for difficult children, and this provision was almost entirely in the form of separate special schools.

According to Rennie (1993), provision for pupils with EBDs has, to some extent, mirrored that for pupils who have learning difficulties. First there were special schools and then there were units (both on- and off-site). Elliot and Carter (1992) maintain that by 1980 the vast majority of ascertained pupils with EBDs were being educated in such units. Since then, there has been a growth in the provision of peripatetic support within the mainstream. This peripatetic support has been provided by teams of behaviour support teachers often under the management of an educational psychologist.

Such changes in the nature of education for pupils with EBDs have not taken place in a vacuum. They have been symptomatic of the growing awareness that problems (whether of learning or of behaviour) do not lie solely with an individual but are the result of that individual's interaction with the learning environment of the school, including those individuals whom he/she encounters within it. This awareness has resulted in changes to the terminology used in respect of such pupils and in a move away from segregation towards greater integration. When the focus changes from the individual child to the child as part of the education system, then it rapidly becomes evident that a response which seeks to change the child without changing the system cannot be wholly effective. Galloway (1985b) points out that there is '. . . a false premise, namely that disturbing behaviour which occurs in one context can be successfully treated in another' (p. 112).

However, we have not yet seen the demise of segregated provision for pupils with EBDs and its replacement with in-class behavioural support. Indeed, there are indications that schools are becoming increasingly reluctant to tolerate behaviour deemed unacceptable and that, in the increasingly competitive world of education, more pupils may find that they have to receive their education outside the mainstream. The National Exclusions Reporting System

(NERS), introduced in 1990, provides data on schools' exclusion practices (see DFE, 1992b). Such data is notoriously unreliable but in the returns it made to the DFE in its first year it indicated that:

(i) approximately 3000 permanent exclusions had been reported over a one-year period;

(ii) 13 per cent of the total were pupils in the primary school phase; and

(iii) of the total, 44 per cent were receiving home tuition, 22 per cent were in special units, 5 per cent had been admitted to a special school, and 29 per cent had secured an alternative mainstream placement.

In view of the numbers of pupils receiving their education outside the mainstream, whether in special schools, in units or even in their own homes, the nature of such provision needs to be closely examined.

Special School Provision

Maladjusted children were first officially recognised as a category of handicapped children in the School Health and Handicapped Pupils Regulations of 1945. Segregated special schools, both day and residential, for such pupils were established and the numbers of these schools increased rapidly between 1950 and 1974.

Much of the research during the period centred on residential, independent schools (Wills, 1960; Lennhoff, 1960; Burn, 1964; Shaw, 1965). Such schools were able to exercise considerable autonomy in relation to their treatment of pupils. They were not answerable in the same way as their state-maintained counterparts and, by removing pupils from the influence of their parents and home environments, the staff could control many more factors than would be possible in a day school. Despite these advantages, the schools' results were mixed (Galloway and Goodwin, 1987), but the approaches adopted within them had a substantial impact on the training of teachers for, and the thinking within, state-maintained day schools. Given the mixed results of such approaches and the difficulties involved in replicating them in an entirely different environment, it is hardly surprising that these special schools were not totally successful.

Independent schools were able to offer smaller classes, teachers with experience of working with pupils with EBDs and specialized techniques, such as behaviour modification. They were, however, left with the problem of reintegrating their pupils into the society of the home and the ordinary school. Cooling (1974) and Dawson (1980) found that only between 20 and 24 per cent of pupils from residential special schools returned to their neighbourhood schools.

Day schools have some advantages over their residential counterparts in terms of making reintegration more likely. However, they inevitably cater for pupils from a number of neighbourhoods and introduce an enforced artificiality at the primary phase in terms of peer group, transportation to and from school, and links with the respective mainstream schools. This artificiality and the cost of maintaining segregated provision may be a small price to pay if such schools can significantly reduce or eliminate emotional and behavioural difficulties in pupils. If, however, as Galloway and Goodwin (1987) suggest, their success does not '. . . exceed the improvements we should expect on the basis of spontaneous remission' (p. 57), then the question of what advantages they have over mainstream schools must be raised.

Laslett (1977) writing in the period directly preceding the publication of the Warnock Report (DES, 1978), sounded two notes of caution in relation to special school provision. First, he questioned the ability of specialized teacher training programmes to keep pace with the demands for appropriately qualified teachers to staff the increasing number of special schools. He suggested that such a shortage might create a situation in which pupils were being taught by teachers who lacked the necessary specialist skills and relevant experience. Secondly, he commented on the dearth of research into the effectiveness of such schools and called in particular for outcome research into many aspects of the education being provided.

Since then, research has been undertaken, including that carried out by the Schools Council Project on the Education of Disturbed Pupils and reported by Wilson and Evans (1980) and Dawson (1980). They confirmed that in 1974 there were 188 schools for maladjusted pupils listed by the then DES, but the project confined its survey to the 114 schools with whom they were able to make contact via a returned questionnaire. While Laslett (1977) provides factual data on a greater number of schools, his data do not go into as much detail as the findings of the Schools Council Team. The survey found that only 15 per cent of the schools surveyed catered solely for younger pupils, i.e., those below 12 years of age. A further 36 per cent were 'all age' schools and contained within them some pupils in the 7–11 years age range. This lack of similarity to the age divisions common in mainstream education immediately calls into question the organizational structure of special schools and their subsequent ability to provide appropriately for the educational needs of their pupils in the 1990s.

Special schools tend to cater predominantly for boys with anti-social problems. They tend to be small, catering for between thirty and fifty-five pupils on average, in classes of approximately seven pupils (Dawson, 1980; HMI, 1989b). The atypical gender distribution in schools catering for pupils with EBDs further distances the educational experiences of pupils of both sexes from the mainstream educational experience common in the 1990s, which is largely coeducational with a relatively even distribution of both sexes.

Segregated special schools began as an attempt to make '. . . some positive discrimination in favour of pupils seen as handicapped' (Bowers, 1984, p. 1). However, accountability, as encouraged in recent legislation, as well as economic forces and the need to update and justify practices, means that laudable aims cannot of themselves be enough. There needs to be evidence that segregated special schools can provide pupils with the advantages of mainstream schooling while offering the necessary expertise and facilities required to produce change in the pupils' behaviour.

These requirements would prove challenging at any time but especially so in an educational era dominated by attention to:

(i)   the importance of, wherever possible, educating pupils with their peer group;

(ii) the need for breadth, balance and accountability within the curriculum; and

(iii) the encouragement of parental choice.

Education with the Peer Group

Fish (1984) suggests that the reasons for the existence of special schools have significantly changed. Instead of the assumption that special schools are the right place for pupils with special needs to be educated, a proactive role, they are increasingly viewed as institutions which cater for pupils whose needs cannot be met in the ordinary school, a reactive role. Special schools have, therefore, been forced into extending their links with mainstream schools and there are examples of this association bringing benefits to both (Hegarty *et al.*, 1982; Hackney, 1985; Doyle, 1988; Jowett, 1989). However, this contact, while necessary, does not always result in the anticipated collaboration or cooperation.

The changing role of separate provision can be illustrated by the contrasting experiences of two children, Nicholas and Gavin, both currently being educated in special schools but whose experiences en route have been very different.

Nicholas became known to a variety of agencies during his pre-school years. His family had periodically required help from Social Services, his older siblings had both been in receipt of special education, one in a special school for pupils with moderate learning difficulties and one in the special class at his local primary school, and a specialist health visitor was involved. Nicholas' mother had difficulty in establishing a routine with her youngest son and complained of his being 'hyperactive'. She also maintained that he 'never slept' and 'never listened'. When he was 2-years-old, Nicholas was enrolled in a Social Services playgroup but continued to present problems in the form of tantrums, aggressive behaviour and destructive attitudes towards toys and equipment. Despite advice and support, Nicholas' mother found it very difficult to control his behaviour and seemed almost afraid of him when she was asked to describe her son. When he reached 4 years of age, Nicholas was admitted to the assessment class of a school for pupils with EBDs and has since progressed to a regular class for younger pupils within that school.

Gavin, on the other hand, entered the nursery class of his local school at 4 years of age. During his first year in the education system, his mother, a single parent, was frequently called to school to be told of her son's misbehaviour and asked to cooperate with the school in matters of discipline. Gavin used bad language and showed aggression towards staff and a lack of respect for other people's property.

He moved into the ordinary reception class and on into Y1 with his peers but had established a reputation as a 'problem' within the school and was felt to be beyond the control of his mother. His behaviour had an increasingly detrimental effect on his learning and by Y2 he was experiencing difficulties with the whole curriculum, most noticeably reading, writing and listening skills. He was referred for assessment with a view to statementing. Despite the additional help that statementing secured, Gavin's school situation in Y3 continued to worsen in respect of both behaviour and learning difficulties. Gavin's LEA had no special schools catering specifically for pupils with EBDs and so his learning difficulties, which staff in the mainstream attribute largely to behaviour problems, were used as a reason for transferring him to a school for pupils with moderate learning difficulties.

Nicholas and Gavin are now both in segregated special schools and may well remain there for the rest of their school careers. Nicholas has never known what it is to socialize with a mainstream peer group or experienced the academic expectations of a mainstream curriculum. Gavin, on the other hand, has had a largely negative experience of both. The staff of his special school believe that many of their recently admitted pupils are, in fact, children of average intelligence who have failed to acquire knowledge and skills because of their EBDs. The staff have developed a somewhat cynical attitude towards their mainstream colleagues and see themselves as having to pick up the pieces after the mainstream schools' failure. The special school now admits far fewer pupils in the early years than once it did but receives larger numbers of referrals at 7+ and an even greater number at 11+. Staff believe that their job would be easier and more successful if referrals and placements were made earlier but can offer no hard evidence to support this view.

The cases of Nicholas and Gavin appear to indicate that, while early segregation is open to criticism based on the known difficulties of special schools in avoiding an artificial and restrictive educational environment, prolonged integration, unless it is carefully supported and monitored to ensure its effectiveness, can produce a climate of repeated failure for both pupil and teacher. This adversely affects the child's educational experience and the view of mainstream education held by staff in special schools.

Clearly the educational history of the two boys raises a number of issues including the need for closer liaison and greater understanding between mainstream and special schools. It also highlights the need for clear criteria to be adopted with respect to placement in special schools. Despite the 1981 Education Act and its emphasis on a needs-led system, local variations in attitudes to integration and segregation, along with the provision of places in appropriate establishments, contrive to exert a major influence over the type of education a child will receive. Malek and Kerslake (1989), in a study of English and Welsh LEA practices in placing children in residential special schools for pupils with EBDs, found clear placement policies to be lacking and social reasons taking precedence over meeting the children's special educational needs as defined in the 1981 Education Act.

Breadth, Balance and Accountability Within the Curriculum

Recent changes in education have placed enormous strains upon the resources of every school. The 1988 Education Reform Act requires all schools to provide a broad and balanced curriculum for pupils, whether in the form of the National Curriculum or a specified alternative curriculum. This requirement has not been met in the mainstream without great difficulty. The number of subjects children in the primary phase must be taught, coupled with the extent of the content within each subject, means that no minute of the school day can be wasted. There is little, if any, room for aspects of the curriculum which are non-statutory, despite advice that the National Curriculum should form only part of the school's actual curriculum.

Special schools experience all of the challenges facing mainstream schools and many more besides in their attempts to teach the breadth and balance of the National Curriculum as well as to assess pupil progress within it (Humphreys and Sturt, 1993). These challenges include school organization, teaching aims and objectives and training opportunities, amongst others, and can be illustrated by the case studies of three teachers.

Mrs. Graham teaches, along with the other two teachers, in an all-age day school for pupils with EBDs. She has responsibility for six pupils aged between 8 and 11 years. The children in her class are brought to and from school by taxi, with journeys varying from five miles to twenty miles. On average, lessons begin at 9.25 a.m. despite an official starting time of 9.00 a.m. The taxis begin collecting pupils from as early as 3.10 p.m. although school officially ends at 3.30 p.m. The reasons given by the taxi firms include contractual difficulties and the excessively early time some pupils would have to be collected in order to meet the specified registration time. Whatever the reasons and however justified they may be, the result for pupils and staff is a daily loss of teaching time amounting to approximately forty-five minutes daily, a little under four hours in the course of a week.

In view of the complaints made by mainstream staff that their teaching day is not long enough to cover all the ground they are required to cover, Mrs. Graham in her special school cannot hope to fit in as much teaching, and hence stimulate as much learning, as her mainstream colleagues. Additionally, she includes in the curriculum a number of lessons which are less overtly taught in the mainstream, a point which will be enlarged upon in the next section.

Mr. Markham teaches 10 and 11-year-olds in a day special school. The children in his class are taught through individual education programmes based on a series of short- and medium-term goals designed to meet their individual needs. These programmes show evidence of an emphasis on social skills (for example, cooperation, turn taking), communication (expressing thoughts and feelings in non-aggressive ways, improving the use of body language) and self-help skills (basic hygiene and health care). The opportunities for teaching these skills vary but there is a marked contrast between the academic nature of a mainstream school and the developmental curriculum on offer in Mr. Markham's class.

The relevance or otherwise of these two approaches is not at issue here but rather the fact that the educational experience offered in both placements is essentially different. This needs to be borne in mind when decisions regarding the placement of any child are taken.

The Warnock Report (DES, 1978) stated that the aims of education are the same for all children and that the scope of the special school curriculum should be as broad as that of ordinary schools. Wilson (1981) called for a close association between the curricula of special and mainstream schools and the 1988 Education Act made a broad and balanced curriculum the entitlement of all children. None of this, however, solves Mr. Markham's practical problem of attending to the learning and social/emotional priorities of his pupils as expressed in their individual programmes while attempting to fit in the range of subjects and quantity of subject matter these pupils should experience as part of their schooling.

Miss Giles, a recently qualified teacher, had only one year's teaching experience before being appointed in a temporary capacity to her present residential special school for pupils with EBDs. She is enthusiastic about the job with a class of six 9–11-year-olds and would like a long-term career in special education but cites three sets of circumstances which serve to prevent this. Her initial training made little reference to children with EBDs although some work was done on how to differentiate the curriculum to meet individual need. Secondly, the only courses available designed specifically for teachers working in the field are outside the LEA and have a financial implication which Miss Giles feels is too great for her present circumstances. Thirdly, the school-based INSET provided seems inadequate to Miss Giles in comparison with what she experienced during her first year of teaching. She attributes this to the school's difficulties in appointing subject coordinators which have led to weak curriculum development in some areas. Miss Giles feels that, while she is growing in experience, she is not getting the broad overview, theoretical expertise and professional guidance which appropriate training opportunities could provide.

Increased accountability through teacher appraisal and statutory testing of pupils is intended to lead to improved standards in our schools. Care must be taken that modifying all of these aspects of the education system in special schools (for example, disapplying pupils in large numbers from SATs) does not become a mechanism for placing special schools outside the mainstream of education in such a way that movement of staff and pupils between the two can no longer be achieved.

Parental Choice

Recent changes in legislation and the 1993 Education Act have recognized and encouraged increased parental decision-making in education. However, not all parents are finding that the 1990s are promoting a more positive partnership between themselves and the education system. For example, the issue of children's exclusion from school on the basis of unacceptable behaviour is being given increasing emphasis in educational publications.

Exclusion may be permanent, indefinite or fixed-term, and the Advisory Centre for Education (ACE, 1992a) records an increase in the incidence of all three categories. In view of the fact that a percentage of those excluded pupils find themselves in a segregated special school, the ways in which these exclusions are handled is of particular interest during a period of supposedly increased parental choice.

Garner (1993) notes that there is an over-representation of boys, especially those from minority ethnic backgrounds, being excluded. He also adds that 15 years was the peak age for exclusions to take place. ACE (1992b), however, carries an article written by a governor of a 5–9 county primary school in which the increasing pressure on governing bodies to exclude young children is examined. Of those parents contacting ACE in 1991, 70 per cent felt that they had not been sufficiently consulted before matters reached the stage of requiring their child's exclusion. Some, but not all, of the dissatisfaction may result from feelings of anger but there is evidence that up to a third of parents were denied their legal rights. Thus there was evidence of failure to follow legal procedures such as requiring parents to find alternative placements for their children, parents not being given written notification of the exclusion and the reasons for it, refusal on the part of the school to reinstate a pupil despite being so instructed by governors and the use of 'blacklists'.

Provision in Units

Many of the issues affecting special schools catering for pupils with EBDs apply to unit provision for such pupils. However, provision in units is characterized by certain factors which apply less forcibly or not at all to segregated special schools.

Unit provision for pupils with EBDs takes a variety of forms. Mortimore *et al.* (1983) list provision which is:

    (i)   on-site and functioning as part of an ordinary school;
    (ii)   off-site and serving clusters of schools;

(iii)   local authority run through social services; and
(iv)   run by the voluntary sector.

Mortimore *et al.* describe this type of provision as presenting a 'bewildering array' especially when contrasted with the relative uniformity of the mainstream educational system.

Generally speaking, unit provision was intended to offer a more short-term solution for the problems of pupils with EBDs than segregated special schools. According to Galloway and Goodwin (1987), the majority of units were established with reintegration as an expressed aim but 'in the overwhelming majority of units this aim was rapidly, if tacitly, abandoned' (p. 58).

The best examples of unit provision exploit their position outside the normative ethos of the mainstream classroom with its inevitable pressures on some pupils, while acknowledging that their pupils must contrive to share many educational experiences with their mainstream peers if they are to stand any chance of subsequent reintegration. Less successful units tend to fail in this latter requirement while inevitably falling short of the facilities which can be provided at a special school.

Elliot and Carter (1992) list the advantages and disadvantages of unit provision in comparison with mainstream placement. The advantages include:

(i)   an improved teacher-pupil ratio in the units;
(ii)   more teacher time for mainstream pupils in the absence of certain pupils;
(iii) a reduction in stress for mainstream teachers.

The disadvantages include:

(i)   the loss of good peer models;
(ii)   the risk of labelling and negative expectations especially from mainstream teachers;
(iii) de-skilling of mainstream teachers in respect of their handling of pupils with EBDs; and
(iv)   potential difficulties in achieving reintegration.

The picture is further complicated by the fact that placement is often determined not only by what provision would best meet an individual child's needs, but by the range and type of provision available within an LEA. The occasional conflict between pupil need and placement availability is illustrated by the case of Lee described below.

Lee, aged 9 years, is currently being educated in an off-site unit for pupils in the primary age-range. This placement has only recently been made despite an acceptance of the extent of Lee's needs which goes back some two years. Lee was perceived as a 'discipline problem' throughout his years in the infant department of his primary school but his case was not referred to any outside agencies although his parents were frequently involved. His Y3 teacher, however, insisted that the educational psychologist be informed and consequently a referral was made.

Lee's behaviour included overt defiance of teacher instructions, aggression towards pupils and staff, walking out of lessons and leaving the school premises without permission. Sanctions such as the loss of privileges and action such as increased parent/school cooperation had failed to produce change and the psychologist elected to involve the LEA's behavioural support team. The psychologist's range of options was severely limited. The LEA had no special schools for pupils with EBDs and no unit provision for children under the age of 11. Some pupils who had learning difficulties in addition to behaviour problems had been placed in schools for pupils with moderate learning difficulties (see the case of Gavin earlier in this chapter), but Lee's academic performance was well within the normal range for his age.

Lee received two periods of intervention by the specialist team with some short-lived gains but, a month after the second intervention, Lee physically attacked the headteacher and was indefinitely excluded from school. Lee then began an extended period of home tuition, a solution which was recognized as unsatisfactory by all concerned. Almost a year later, Lee and three other primary-aged boys became the first pupils in a specially formed, off-site unit opened as an emergency measure in response to the needs and demands of the four excluded boys.

If the LEA had had at its disposal a continuum of provision for pupils with EBDs it is unlikely that Lee's experience would have been so unsatisfactory. During the year that Lee did not attend school, the number of teaching hours he received was greatly reduced and the stress on his family was considerable. However, the mere existence of unit provision is insufficient to meet pupils' educational needs; the latter can only be met by attention to a number of factors, including curriculum content. Lee's educational experience continues to give cause for concern as indicated by a further examination of his case.

Technically, Lee's primary school retains ownership of the 'problem'. As part of the conditions for acceptance by the off-site unit, Lee's school must agree to have him on the register and to undertake a programme of phased reintegration beginning with a one day a week attendance at the school in the company of a member of staff from the unit. Potentially this arrangement should:

(i)   maintain links between the unit and mainstream school;
(ii)   facilitate continuity of curriculum across the two placements;
(iii)   avoid the de-skilling effect on mainstream staff of engendering behavioural change in a totally segregated setting;
(iv)   remove the stress on staff in the mainstream and enable the pupils in the mainstream to experience more teacher time; and
(v)   aid full reintegration in the future.

Lee certainly presents no problems in terms of behaviour on these occasions. However, the school operates a thematic approach to the curriculum and this raises the question of what the learning experience of these isolated days means to Lee. Some effort is made by unit staff to undertake follow-up work on the other days but they are left with the problems of:

(i) balancing Lee's curricular needs with those of the other unit pupils who are engaged in different topics on their days in school;

(ii) differentiating the curriculum so that it meets Lee's needs, which have increased since missing almost a year of schooling; and

(iii) fitting in the aspects of social learning and behavioural approaches which the unit staff feel must be addressed if Lee and the other unit pupils are to reintegrate successfully.

Lee currently has a temporary disapplication from the National Curriculum. Even if this were not the case, the unit staff of two full-time teachers would find it difficult to provide the necessary expertise to coordinate, differentiate and teach the full range of National Curriculum subjects which includes Welsh as a second language.

White (1990), a teacher in an all-age, off-site unit for pupils with behaviour problems, maintains that staff in such units must carry out most of the duties of a mainstream teacher but also find opportunities to include:

(i) a flexible teaching style to cater for mixed-age and mixed-ability groups;

(ii) the development of programmes to enhance both academic and social development;

(iii) liaison with parents where appropriate;

(iv) the encouragement and extension of cooperation between the unit and mainstream schools including the support of reintegration; and

(v) the undertaking of multidisciplinary work.

In view of the workload currently being experienced by the average mainstream classteacher, these additional duties seem to add an almost intolerable burden to those teaching in unit provision.

As yet, it is too early to judge how successful unit placement will turn out to be in Lee's case. The current arrangement is certainly preferable to the situation prior to his admission to the unit, but it provides many challenges to Lee, the unit staff and the mainstream school. Some of these challenges will be met and overcome but others appear almost insurmountable.

Future Trends

Exclusion

Already there are indications that the growing trend in exclusions and the pressure that this places on support teams, home tuition, special schools and unit provision are being recognized by the DFE. Currently, the educational climate with its emphasis on competition, parental choice, financial autonomy and reduced LEA support, does little to encourage schools to view children with EBDs positively. Exclusions can, for some schools, bring double benefits in terms of removing troublesome pupils while at the same time allowing the financial input accruing to such pupils to remain.

In response to the trend to exclude, the DFE Discussion Paper (DFE, 1992b) outlines several ways in which schools might be encouraged to retain and adopt positive strategies towards their pupils with EBDs. Two points, amongst many others, can be considered with regard to exclusion (see also chapter 9, pp. 151–2).

The publication of statistics concerning exclusions
In a competitive school ethos, the factors by which a successful school may be judged might well include a low exclusion rate. This could be taken to indicate a successful 'whole school' approach to the emotional and behaviour development of pupils including matters of discipline, just as a low absence rate is considered to enhance a school's reputation. There is, however, another side to this argument. It might be said that schools which publicize a relatively high number of exclusions are presenting themselves as having strict codes of conduct which they are not afraid to enforce. Such schools might actively employ high exclusion rates to promote their image.

Financial disincentives to exclusion
Schools which lose pupils because parents exercise choice incur financial penalties and so may be prompted to seek ways by which they can make themselves more attractive. Schools which exclude, on the other hand, may retain money in respect of a pupil who is no longer being educated there. Allowing funding to follow the pupil might discourage schools from excluding any pupils other than those for whom all possible in-house approaches have proved unsuccessful.

Recognizing successful schools

Schools have traditionally had curriculum innovation recognized and rewarded at local and national level. Similarly, schools which provide effectively for pupils' social and personal development should have their efforts publicly celebrated. Over time this might encourage more schools to improve their functioning in terms of catering for pupils with EBDs.

It seems unlikely that any or all of these strategies, good though they are, will prove totally effective in eliminating requests for segregation although they may prove successful in reducing the numbers of exclusions. There will continue to be demand for separate placement in the form of special schools or unit provision. Such establishments came into being during an educational era which shares some aspects in common with the 1990s but also differs in some important ways. A growing emphasis on meeting academic goals, teacher accountability, inter-school competition and parental involvement in decision-making permeates our schools. These factors are accompanied by the notion of 'entitlement' which brings the education offered by segregated establishments under the same umbrella as mainstream education. This 'entitlement' was intended to protect pupils and, as such, is laudable, but it also reduces autonomy and it is this autonomy which has characterized segregated provision in the past. If special provision is expected to conform to the content of mainstream education and additionally provide all those educational experiences which are deemed necessary to provide specialist help for pupils with EBDs, then the challenge facing special schools and units is great indeed and may prove too great.

Peagam (1993) calls for clarification and intervention before the pressures of expectation and ability to meet these expectations split apart the service for pupils with EBDs. He argues for LEA guidelines in respect of which pupils need and will benefit from placement in segregated, specialist provision; nationally validated professional qualifications for the teachers working in such provision so that there can be continuity in terms of the theoretical underpinning of the educational approaches adopted; clarification of the ways in which staff can properly contain some pupils while still attending to such issues as the protection of LEA property and the avoidance of nuisance to people living near the establishment; and coherent LEA monitoring policies. The future of segregated specialist provision seems to rest on an acceptance that it will continue to be required for some pupils (Elton Report, DES/WO, 1989). It also now deserves and demands a review which will enable clear codes of practice to result for the benefit of both staff and pupils.

Overview

Pupils with EBDs receive their education in a variety of settings and there is considerable variation, both locally and nationally, in the nature and location of that education. While segregated provision caters mainly for older pupils, there are a significant number of pupils in the primary age range receiving their education in such schools and units. Once a decision is made to segregate a young pupil, he/she will inevitably experience an education which differs significantly from that of mainstream schooling, despite the continuing entitlement to a broad and balanced curriculum, including the National Curriculum, enshrined in the 1988 Education Act. As a result of these significant differences, care needs to be taken to ensure that the decision to segregate is in the best interests of all concerned.

The likelihood of reintegration has been shown to be low but relatively recent legislation may have helped in terms of providing a National Curriculum to which all pupils are entitled. This same legislation and other recent changes in education have, however, provided many challenges to segregated provision for pupils with EBDs. If, despite the DFE's efforts to stem the flow of exclusions, segregated provision continues to be needed, and there seems little doubt that it will be, the problems faced by specialist staff and the educational experiences and needs of the pupils concerned seem ripe for re-examination.

It may be that the autonomy which allowed segregated provision to select and direct the approaches adopted has, in fact, become the greatest challenge of all. Increased LEA involvement and a national consensus on the criteria for segregation may enable separate special schools and units to re-evaluate the education they provide and equip their staff with the necessary confidence to provide meaningfully for pupils in the future.

Part IV

Specific Behavioural Difficulties

Chapter 9

Disruptive Pupils

Low-level disruptive behaviour in school is likely to cause teachers a great deal of stress. For example, as previously mentioned (see chapter 2, p. 21) Wheldall and Merrett (1988b) report that teachers found 'talking out of turn' and 'hindering other children' to be their most frequent problems. The Elton Report (DES/WO, 1989), on discipline in schools, also drew attention to the adverse cumulative effects on teachers of having to deal with prolonged incidents of non-cooperation, even if minor, that called for disciplinary action of some kind. Frude (1990) points out that, while some degree of aggression is a natural part of school life, common forms of misbehaviour such as 'messing about' and 'clowning' may well develop into more severe forms of disruption.

It is not surprising, therefore, if teachers regard as particularly unacceptable and stressful seriously challenging behaviour such as disobedience, impertinence, verbal abuse and physical aggression directed towards themselves or other pupils (Kauffman *et al.*, 1989). Nor is it surprising that teachers tend to regard acting-out, externalized behaviour more negatively than withdrawn, internalized behaviour. Indeed, they are justified in their concern about disruptive behaviour. Quite apart from the damaging effects that such conduct has on the morale and self-esteem of teachers, and their ability to carry out their everyday functions, clinicians and researchers have shown that anti-social behaviour in childhood tends to have long-term implications. Robins (1991) points out that children prone to conduct disorder can typically be identified between 8 and 10 years of age (if not earlier). It is important, therefore, that attention should be given to these children as soon as possible in their school careers, in the hope that the escalation of their anti-social tendencies may be prevented (see chapter 2, pp. 25–7, and later in this chapter for a further discussion of the long-term consequences of anti-social behaviour in childhood).

Teachers differ in their reactions to disruptive pupils. Some will maintain a degree of control of the situation, and persevere for a lengthy period in seeking ways of encouraging such children to modify their behaviour while retaining them in their usual class. However, many teachers, for their own self-protection as well as in the interests of the class as a whole, will wish the offending pupils to be removed from their responsibility. Teachers are likely to feel a sense of failure if they cannot control a child, particularly one of primary-school age. Such failure usually results in lowered self-esteem as well as anger and frustration in response to disobedience or disruption of the normal class routine. The most patient and tolerant of teachers may not be able to cope when faced with a persistent, deliberate flouting of his/her authority by an individual or group.

Much has already been said in previous chapters which is of relevance to the identification, assessment and management of disruptive pupils. This chapter will focus particularly on cases of serious disruption in middle childhood. It will discuss the nature and prevalence of such behaviour; explanations and consequences; prevention and intervention. Cases of total disruption of the life of primary schools are rare, though some have been reported in the 1980s (Frude and Gault, 1984); and while relatively few pupils are suspended from primary schools following disruption, some are transferred to special provision outside the mainstream for this reason (Galloway *et al.*, 1982; DES/WO, 1989).

Nature of Disruptive Behaviour in School

In recent years, the term 'disruptive' has become increasingly used in connection with a wide range of forms of misbehaviour in schools, and is often used in a vague way. However, to call a pupil 'disruptive' is meaningful to an extent to most teachers, implying that the child is interfering with either his/her own efficient learning or that of other pupils (Topping, 1990). As Galloway *et al.* (1982) state, different teachers have different ideas about what constitutes disruptive behaviour, and have different levels of tolerance. Pupils, too, behave in different ways in different contexts, and they may challenge the authority of one teacher but not another. For the purposes of their own discussion of the subject, Galloway *et al.* define disruptive behaviour as any behaviour which appears problematic, inappropriate and disturbing to teachers. Badger (1985) defines disruption as behaviour which significantly interferes with the teaching process and/or the routine operations of the school.

Gray and Richer (1988) emphasize that disruptive pupils tend to work less than others; to misbehave for a high proportion of their time; to have a short attention span and to switch activities frequently; to ignore the teacher to a great extent; and to be comparatively uninfluenced by what the teacher does or his/her attempts to relate to them. Gray and Richer point out that the many forms of behaviour which disrupt lessons include rudeness; abusive language; physical attacks on teachers; shouting out; distractibility; fidgeting with materials; making unusual noises; and fighting or squabbling between pupils. Groups within the class may plan disruption, for example, engaging in practical jokes at the teacher's expense. Disruptive behaviour may occur outside as well as inside the classroom, for example, in corridors and assembly hall.

Some case studies of disruptive pupils have been given in chapter 7. A further illustrative case is that of *Rodney*, aged 8+ years, in year 4. Rodney is an example of a child whose disruptive pattern of behaviour begins at an early stage in his schooling. He was perceived as a behaviour problem at the nursery and infant school stage, but even more so when he entered the junior department. Here he was soon known to every member of staff.

Rodney was a handsome child, dark, sturdy and with a most attractive smile. However, he had no respect for authority and the school's attempts to get him to conform had no effect whatsoever. In year 3, the class had three supply teachers to replace the usual class teacher who was away ill. Several children showed ill-effects as a result, but Rodney reacted worst of all. His concentration span was short and he quickly became bored with any task. Any attempt to prolong an activity was met by acts of deliberate destruction. He would hurl crayons, tear books, and scribble over his own and others' work. In year 3, the supply teachers regularly sent him to the headteacher. Verbal warnings proved of no avail and his mother was asked to come to the school.

Rodney's mother was a single parent with an older child in the same school. This child, a girl, presented no problems whatsoever as a pupil but was embarrassed by her brother's behaviour. Rodney's mother claimed that he was 'out of control' at home. He was obsessed with car badges and stole these. He stayed out late and wandered far from home, often taking another child's bicycle to travel even farther than he could on foot. The mother blamed the lack of a male role model for Rodney, and her own poor health. The school suggested behaviour management strategies, with appropriate rewards and sanctions, but these were inconsistently applied at home.

When the year 3 class teacher returned to her duties, she found Rodney impossible to control. He and a small group of boys appeared to delight in disrupting lessons and they took up a disproportionate amount of the teacher's time. Playtime and lunch-time provided no respite. Rodney carried out acts of vandalism on or near the yard — scraping car paintwork, kicking down fences, and pulling branches off newly-planted saplings. At lunch-time, he had to be held by the hand by the assistants, who consequently had less time to give to the other pupils.

At the beginning of year 4, the educational psychologist was consulted, and Rodney was referred to the behavioural support team. During the period of intervention (one hour per week special attention for eight weeks), Rodney threw a chair across the classroom, hurting another child, and he was suspended for three days as a 'cooling-off period'. As Rodney's mother had difficulty in coping with him at home, and as the boy seemed oblivious to the effects of his actions, this period served only as a respite for the school staff. However, the suspension galvanized staff action in school, and the headteacher came under intense pressure to exclude Rodney.

Nothing tried by the school had had even short-term success in altering Rodney's behaviour, and it was likely that the school would ask for the boy to be removed to an off-site special unit before he moved into his third year at the junior school.

This case illustrates how much havoc a young child can cause, and the difficulties which a school can have in modifying behaviour sufficiently to keep a disruptive pupil in his usual class, despite considerable efforts to achieve this objective.

Extent of Disruptive Behaviour in Middle Childhood

It is not possible to arrive at a reliable estimate of the prevalence of disruptive behaviour in school during middle childhood. Different schools experience such behaviour to differing extents and deal with it in different ways (Galloway, 1987). Even among schools in catchment areas providing them with an entry of potentially difficult pupils, the proportion of children perceived as disruptive varies greatly — between 0.5 per cent and 40 per cent in a survey of primary schools undertaken by Lawrence and Steed (1986). An analysis of referrals from schools to the support services does not help in obtaining a true picture of the numbers of serious cases of disruption as compared with those of other kinds of EBDs for which outside help is sought. For example, Todman *et al.* (1991) point out that primary teachers are reluctant to refer children with special educational needs to the School Psychological Service unless they are a disruptive influence in class. When they do refer difficult pupils, there is often the expectation that they will be removed to some form of special provision.

It is difficult to uncover even the extent of exclusions from school, as some children are 'unofficially' excluded rather than reported to the LEA and school governors, as required by the 1986 Education Act in the case of fixed term, indefinite and permanent exclusions adding up to more than five days in any one term (Stirling, 1992). These 'informal' exclusions may be disguised as medical problems, or else parents may be persuaded to keep a child at home while special provision is being arranged. Further, not all schools are forthcoming in their response to surveys. These considerations affect the interpretation of surveys undertaken by the government, such as that carried out by the Department for Education (1992b), mentioned in chapter 8 (p. 122). This survey found that exclusions were more common in secondary than in primary schools, but the latter accounted for 13 per cent of the total number of about 3000 permanent exclusions reported over a one-year period.

As Docking (1989) states, even carefully executed independent studies of disruptive behaviour cannot eliminate subjective opinion, since the concept of 'disruption' is necessarily based on personal perceptions of the problem. This has to be borne in mind in considering the findings of research into the extent of troublesome behaviour in schools, though there is general agreement that serious disruption is relatively rare at the primary school stage.

Croll and Moses (1985) found that teachers in junior schools made a distinction between pupils with EBDs and those who presented discipline problems in the classroom, although in practice these types of behaviour overlapped considerably (see also chapter 2, pp. 19–22). Of their sample 4.1 per cent were nominated as presenting problems of discipline in class, of whom about 84 per cent were seen by their teachers as also being behaviourally or emotionally disturbed. Difficulties arising from a combination of emotional disturbance and problems of discipline were attributed to over two children per class on average in junior schools. Pupils said to present problems of discipline mainly had low levels of work involvement and were prone to distractibility and fidgeting. Mortimore *et al.* (1988), on the basis of class teachers' ratings in fifty London junior schools, report that 10 per cent of pupils were considered to be 'disobedient'.

Dawson (1982) asked teachers to nominate pupils causing them 'an unusually high degree of concern for behavioural reasons'. He found that 1.5 per cent of pupils in one English LEA met this criterion as far as 'conduct problems' were concerned. In many cases, other problems (such as learning difficulties and absenteeism) accompanied 'conduct problems', which included 'aggressive', 'disruptive' and 'uncooperative' behaviour. A somewhat lower percentage of pupils in primary schools were nominated than in secondary schools as having conduct problems.

Wheldall and Merrett (1988b) found that, on average, 4.3 children per primary school class (of whom three were boys) were identified by their teachers as troublesome, but mostly not to a serious extent. Only 1 per cent of teachers overall ranked 'physical aggression' as the most frequent misbehaviour, with 2 per cent ranking 'disobedience' as first of a list of misbehaviours in terms of frequency. As mentioned earlier in the chapter (p. 137), most of the teachers rated 'talking out of turn' or 'hindering other children' as the misbehaviour most often encountered.

The Elton Report (DES/WO, 1989) confirmed that the prevalence of seriously disruptive behaviour in primary schools is generally low. In a survey carried out for the Elton Committee, about one in twenty primary teachers reported that they had verbal abuse directed at them, and about one in fifty had to deal with some form of physical aggression directed against them, though not necessarily intentionally. About one in ten primary teachers thought that the discipline problems in their schools were 'serious'. This was especially the case in socially disadvantaged areas or in schools with high proportions of pupils with 'below average' attainments.

Recent surveys have suggested a substantial increase in disruptive behaviour leading to exclusion from school, but, as pointed out above, it is difficult to know the true extent of any rise in behaviour disorder which may have taken place (Pyke, 1993).

Explanations of Disruptive Behaviour

Background

Children who are disruptive in school during middle childhood may have a history of aggressive behaviour dating back to their pre-school years. Many young children exhibit aggressive tendencies, and indeed much aggressive behaviour is entirely natural in the early years of life, particularly in the face of frustration (Manning and Sluckin, 1984; Laing and Chazan, 1986). However, most children gain more control over displays of anger after the age of 5 or 6 years, and these who remain highly aggressive and hostile at the stage when other children's aggression is lessening are likely to be immature or disturbed (Maccoby, 1980). Persistently aggressive children may have shown hyperactivity, excessive irritability and uncooperativeness, as well as developmental delays (Robins, 1991).

Associated factors

The discussion in chapter 3 (see pp. 36–47) of the wide range of factors associated with behaviour problems in middle childhood is relevant to the consideration of explanations of disruptive behaviour. Here, only brief mention will be made of those factors particularly related to disruption in school.

Frude and Gault (1984) suggest that the concern about the growth of disruptive behaviour may be due to panic induced by the media; the general stress experienced by teachers as a result of increasing pressures on them; the rise of violence in society; less acceptance of authority; and/or social problems such as mass unemployment.

The social milieu in which schools function has certainly to be taken into account in seeking to explain disruption in schools, even if teachers can do relatively little to counteract the general conditions in which their pupils are growing up.

Factors related to the individual and his/her immediate environment include:

(i) temperamental and personality problems, for example, being of an aggressive disposition;

(ii) the family background, especially where there is faulty discipline, parental conflict, a cold and rejecting atmosphere, or models of resistance to authority. Children of criminal or alcoholic parents are vulnerable to conduct disorder, particularly if the mother is affected; and a strong correlate of behaviour disorder is a pattern of poor parental control (Robins, 1991);

(iii) the neighbourhood, especially where there is low morale associated with material deprivation;

(iv) peer pressures: the sub-culture of a class may be antagonistic to learning, though this is less likely to be the case in the primary school than towards the end of the secondary stage. Disruptive pupils, too, may be disliked and rejected by their classmates;

(v) the general ethos and organization of the school; and the level of control achieved (see chapter 5);

(vi)   the situational context in the class, especially when there is poor class control, unstimulating teaching, or an unsatisfactory teacher–pupil relationship (see chapter 4). Disruptive pupils may well be those who are under-achieving or failing in class. The following account of an unsatisfactory classroom situation, while not necessarily a typical or common one, will serve to illustrate factors related to the classroom context, particularly in regard to teachers' attitudes.

Mrs. Taylor was in her late fifties. She had repeatedly applied for, and been refused, early retirement. She was clearly disenchanted with teaching and was frequently absent from school for occasional days or longer periods.

Mrs. Taylor had effectively opted out of staff development programmes within the school. She paid lip-service to changes agreed at staff meetings but appeared to put them into practice to a very small extent in the classroom. Consequently the curriculum provided in her Y5 class (age range 9–10+ years) was less well-planned, structured and managed than in other classes in the school.

Mrs. Taylor's comments in the classroom made it clear that she saw problems in behaving and learning as entirely emanating from the child. Pupils who failed to make progress were, to her, 'lazy', 'dull' or 'no-hopers', and those who misbehaved were 'difficult', 'delinquent' or 'wasters'. Even when another member of staff indicated that the child was not a problem in his/her class, Mrs. Taylor did not realize that her attitudes might be a contributory factor.

Mrs. Taylor's lessons tended to be formal and teacher-centred, but she was not a harsh disciplinarian. Her classroom was quiet and the standards in the basic subjects were, on the whole, quite high. She believed that a child had to conform rather than that the education system should be flexible enough to adapt to a range of needs.

One year Mrs. Taylor had a particularly stressful time with three boys in her class causing trouble. Several teachers had found these boys demanding in terms of a tendency to talk all the time and to be easily distracted from the task in hand, but they were not considered to present serious behavioural difficulties. Within the first month of their move to Mrs. Taylor's class, she was saying that the boys 'should be in a special school'. She frequently sent them to the headteacher, demanding that he should 'do something'. Attempts by him to consider strategies for dealing with the boys in class were not greeted by Mrs. Taylor with enthusiasm. She felt that she was 'doing all anyone could do' and should not be expected to put up with such behaviour.

The boys' parents were asked to come to the school in advance of the normal parents' evening. They were quite taken aback to hear their sons being described in such strong terms. Over time the boys' behaviour appeared to deteriorate in the eyes of other staff. They became troublesome at playtime and lunch-time, and began to be seen as a gang of three for the first time: until year 5, they had not been close associates.

Their end of year reports were far from good, and all three boys took longer than usual to settle down in their year 6 class. However, they did adjust reasonably well after a time. Mrs. Taylor did not appear to find it strange that the three boys were no longer the subject of staffroom concern or discussion.

The Pupils' Point of View

However serious the disruption caused by a pupil may be, there is always the need for an appreciation of the child's perspective of the situation (Cooper, 1989). The views of disruptive pupils may at times be exaggerated or distorted, but they may well throw some light on the possible reasons for their misbehaviour. The very act of calmly asking a child for his/her own view of an incident may help to lessen tension on all sides (see also chapter 4, p. 69).

Pupils' reasons for disruptive behaviour include blaming teachers for being boring; lacking control of their class; failing to respect pupils; and not being fair in applying rules. Some criticize the school for badly arranged timetables and for a lack of institutional authority. Others say that they only intended to 'have a laugh'. Unmalicious and inoffensive laughing and joking may be differentiated from clowning directed at undermining the teacher's authority (Tattum, 1982).

Pupils' complaints about class management or school atmosphere should be taken seriously and, where they have some basis, appropriate action should be taken.

Consequences of Disruptive Behaviour

The consequences of disruptive behaviour in school are usually serious, both in the short-term and the long-term. Physical injury to pupils or staff may result, and the reputation of the teachers involved may suffer. Work, learning and teaching all become difficult if not impossible in disrupted classrooms, which are characterized by noise, anger, abuse and violence and where much damage is caused to the relationship between teacher and class (Gray and Richer, 1988). Disruptive pupils are likely to fail to keep up with the demands of the curriculum and to become educationally retarded if this is not the case already.

If disruption persists in spite of internal action by the school, it may lead to suspension or exclusion from school. Even if home tuition is provided while pupils are not allowed to attend school, this is usually only for a limited time each day. Excluded pupils, therefore, are likely to roam around streets in an aimless way and possibly to become involved in delinquent acts.

Many children with mild conduct disorder do not grow up to be permanently anti-social, but seriously aggressive and disruptive behaviour in childhood has a poor prognosis for adult life (Robins, 1991). Conduct disorder predicts not only mental ill-health in adulthood, but high rates of marital break-up and poor job history, as well as involvement in criminal activity (West, 1982; Farrington *et al.*, 1988). Appropriate action by schools and support agencies may help to prevent these effects.

Prevention

As the causes of a pupil's troublesome behaviour may, at least partly, lie outside the school, disruptive incidents may arise in the best regulated schools and classes. A child may, for example, be difficult in class because he/she is in a disturbed state as a result of crises at home, and a blameless teacher may become the target of aggression as a displacement for a parent. Nevertheless, the ethos of the school and the general atmosphere in the classroom are likely to have a bearing on the occurrence or absence of disruptive behaviour (see chapters 4 and 5).

Gray and Richer (1988) emphasize that disruption may be prevented by effective teaching and class control; harmonious pupil-teacher relationships; clear and reasonable rules, commands and expectations; avoiding threats; ensuring fairness; and providing appropriate models of behaviour. Cooper (1989) stresses that teachers should ensure that their dislike of particular behaviour does not extend to individuals and that pupils are given a chance to express their own perceptions of a situation in a non-threatening way. Scarlett (1989) points out that the fewer rules there are, the more chance there is of pupils accepting and identifying with them, especially if they are involved in formulating the rules; also, that pupils differentiate between personal and institutional authority and acceptance of one does not necessarily mean the acceptance of the other.

Galloway (1987) asserts that more can be learnt by analyzing the characteristics of successful schools than by providing short-term solutions from a classroom-based analysis of problem behaviour. Much can be learnt, too, from a consideration of how successful teachers operate in the classroom. *Mrs. Cotton* is an example of an effective teacher who helps to prevent disruptive behaviour.

Mrs. Cotton teaches a year 4 class (age range 8–9+ years). She is in her late 30s and has been teaching for twelve years. Mrs. Cotton organizes her class mainly in groups, tolerates quite a lot of conversation and promotes active learning. She is a PE specialist and organizes a variety of games throughout the school. She is popular with colleagues and pupils.

Two years ago a child named *Evelyn* was transferred to her class from another school. This child had been sexually abused by her stepfather, and her mother subsequently left the man and moved, with Evelyn and her brother, to a new school catchment area. Mrs. Cotton was given brief details of the child's background and told to expect behaviour problems such as temper tantrums, vandalism and petty theft. It was arranged that a support teacher would visit weekly in order to advise and guide the school in dealing with Evelyn.

Mrs. Cotton quickly established rapport with Evelyn, mainly through encouraging the girl's prowess in gymnastics. Praise and success in this area counter-balanced Evelyn's relatively poor achievements in the basic subjects.

Mrs. Cotton had class rules which everyone was expected to keep. These were linked to the school's social development policy which was designed to emphasize a smooth-running school ethos for all. Mrs. Cotton's rules were particularly related to classroom management and discipline. They were framed in a personal way — 'We will . . .' — discussed and illustrated by pupils, and made known to parents. On a rota basis, the pupils were given specific class-room responsibilities which they took very seriously. Evelyn found this structure motivating. On a few occasions, she defaced other children's books in response to perceived insults and she appeared to find the last half-hour of the day stressful. If temper tantrums did occur, it was during this period.

Mrs. Cotton's relationship with Evelyn was so good that it was decided that the specialist support teacher should have the whole class for a time, to allow Mrs. Cotton to give attention to Evelyn on a one-to-one basis. During these sessions, it emerged that the girl was afraid that her stepfather would come to school for her, and this was causing the difficulties at the end of the school day. Mrs. Cotton was able to reassure Evelyn and the tantrums effectively disappeared.

Mrs. Cotton's success appears to be based on her skill in balancing the needs of a whole class against the needs of individuals within the class. Conformity is respected for the contribution which it makes to the smooth running of the class, but it is not allowed to outweigh the problems faced by some children in conforming to standards set. It is also worth noting that the availability of a support teacher, even for a short time, allows a successful class teacher (who might appear not to need support) to devote some attention to pupils with special needs.

Evelyn has since moved on to other teachers. She is not considered an 'easy' child but neither is she in regular or frequent trouble. She still finds opportunities to speak to, and help out, Mrs. Cotton, who clearly played a considerable part in preventing this pupil from becoming disruptive.

Action

As an immediate response in the case of seriously disruptive behaviour in the classroom, Gray and Richer (1988) advise that the teacher should attempt to defuse anger and aggression and calmly separate pupils who may be fighting: if physical restraint is needed, the teacher should get help. It is wise to avoid touching a pupil if this is possible, especially if another adult is not present. Abuse directed at the teacher should not be answered in kind.

In the longer-term, the school has to consider what action is most appropriate to halt the disruption and to help the pupils involved in a constructive way. As the Elton Report (DES/WO, 1989) pointed out, schools use a variety of strategies and sanctions. With the exception of 'reasoning with pupils outside the classroom setting', which was generally seen as effective, no strategies or sanctions were uniformly endorsed as being highly successful or unsuccessful. Schools may choose to use punitive sanctions or positive strategies (or a combination of these approaches), or, as a final resort, to remove the child from school in their response to disruptive behaviour.

Punishment

Gillham (1984) warns that the labelling of pupils as disruptive is encouraged rather than avoided by the typical authority response in schools, which is a series of reactive non-sequiturs, such as punishment or warnings. Docking (1987) states that, although punishment in school may be intended to deter children from behaving unacceptably, whether it actually does so is a different matter. Punishment may produce undesirable side-effects. Adults who engage in a punitive style of child management may unwittingly be instrumental in producing undesirable behaviour, feelings and dispositions in children. Punishment may fuel dissatisfaction with school, and exposes children to an inappropriate model of adult behaviour. Wheldall and Glynn (1989), too, assert that punishment may lead to the teacher being regarded as someone to fear or avoid, and is unhelpful in maintaining an educational context based on shared control between teachers and learners.

In spite of the undesirable effects of punishment, it is generally accepted that fair and reasonable punishment does have its place in school. Children have to learn that society imposes penalties for anti-social behaviour, and punishment acts as a deterrent in the case of most children. Scherer (1990b) favours the use of rewards and positive reinforcement to encourage appropriate behaviour, but recognizes that changing to the use of positive methods in a predominantly punitive school may lead to increased difficulties over discipline, as traditional controls are relaxed. Scherer advises that it is sensible for teachers to assess the needs of, and best consequences for, each pupil and regularly review such assessment.

Whatever punishment is used, and schools have only a limited range of sanctions at their disposal, it should play only a minimal role in the school's approach to difficult pupils. The child should always be told the precise purpose of any sanctions which are applied, such as 'time-out' (for example removing the child from the class, or making the child sit in the classroom away from others), loss of privileges, or being put 'on report'. Cooper (1989) advocates the use of a daily report form with difficult pupils, through which positive as well as negative behaviour is recorded, and which can be used to forge links between pupils, teachers and parents. This can be combined with negotiating a more constructive use of the 'leisure time' of a disruptive pupil, and targeting the pupil for praise by teachers and supervisory staff.

Following the 1993 Education Act, the government issued draft guidelines on pupil behaviour and discipline (DFE, 1993b; Pyke, 1994). These guidelines advocate 'whole school' approaches to discipline, and stress that schools should help to promote moral standards in behaviour. A draft circular on the education of pupils with EBDs, issued at the same time (DFE, 1993c), also recommends the avoidance of degrading or humiliating punishments.

Positive Measures

Meeting individual needs

The removal of punishment options from teachers without training in alternative positive methods can have a demoralizing effect on teachers and it is, therefore, essential for schools to provide their staff with such training. The Elton Committee (DES/WO, 1989) found that schools had developed a variety of approaches in their systems of incentives and support, in improving teacher-pupil relationships, and in talking things through with pupils; but much more remains to be done in this area in both initial and in-service training. Positive measures aimed at improving the behaviour of disruptive pupils include behaviour modification strategies, counselling, and social skills training. Schools may institute such strategies internally, or invite the help of the School Psychological Services; outside agencies may provide psychotherapy.

Galloway (1987) considers that counselling and psychotherapy are not very successful with disruptive pupils, and that behaviour modification programmes are difficult to implement properly in schools. He stresses that responses should be institutional rather than individual in nature. However, this seems a rather sweeping statement. Attention has to be given to individual needs, and some pupils have been helped by counselling, therapy, social skills programmes or behaviour modification (see chapters 4 and 5). Yule *et al.* (1984), for example, consider that with appropriate help, teachers in ordinary schools can integrate behavioural techniques to produce significant changes in a child's behaviour: often this means considerable modifications in the teacher's own behaviour. Yule and colleagues cite a case of a 10-year-old boy in whose case ignoring inappropriate off-task behaviour while praising and rewarding appropriate actions was successful in reducing disruptive incidents caused by the boy and in improving the teacher-child relationships.

Resources for INSET

There are now available several resource packages for individual study or for use in staff development and INSET courses related to behaviour problems, especially disruptiveness. For example, the set of materials designed by Galvin *et al.* (1990) aims to help schools in the formation of behavioural policies as well as to develop the skills of individual members of staff in managing behaviour problems. The nine study units include 'Curriculum Organization' and 'Behaviour Management', 'Preventive Classroom Management' and 'Working with Individual Children'. In this scheme, both theoretical and practical considerations are stressed.

Luton *et al.* (1991) have devised a comprehensive resource and training package for primary schools, which covers such topics as rules and reinforcement; support for teachers; and producing a school policy on behaviour management. The package developed by Smith (1993) relating to managing pupil behaviour in school and classroom includes suggested forms for recording incidents of disruption by the teacher and pupil; a behaviour monitoring form to be used by a pupil to give an account of his/her own behaviour over a period and as a basis for discussion between teacher and pupil; and a pupil/ teacher/parent form of contract. Teachers will also find useful the publications by Fontana (1985), Montgomery (1989), Jones (1989), Maines (1991), McGuiness (1993) and Wragg (1993).

Support systems
Since the early 1980s, many local education authorities have established peripatetic behaviour support teams of specialist teachers to help schools to meet the needs of children with EBDs within the context of the mainstream system (see chapter 5, pp. 78–80, and chapter 7, pp. 118–9). These teams usually work closely with the School Psychological Service, and to a considerable extent have replaced off-site units, which were proliferating up to the late 1970s. They operate in a variety of ways, but in general they aim to provide help in schools to pupils and teachers by supporting the class teacher, individual children or small groups and/or offering a withdrawal service through which pupils can be given intensive help (Drew, 1990; Elliott and Carter, 1992; Rennie, 1993). Very recently, the tendency has been for support personnel to focus on acting as consultants to teachers rather than directly working with pupils.

Hanko (1990), whose own approach to supporting schools is based on work with groups of teachers to widen their perception of a problem, points out that support teachers may be faced with tensions between parents and teachers, and between members of staff within and across departments. They may also meet with conflicting advice from different school services, and have to contend with pressures arising from increasingly limited LEA budgets (Mittler, 1992; Copeland *et al.*, 1993). However, support teams tend to find their work rewarding, and the service they offer is generally appreciated by schools (Ashley, 1987; West, 1989; Imich and Roberts, 1990).

The role of a specialist support teacher is illustrated by the following account of an episode in the working life of Miss Quinton.

Miss Quinton works as part of a specialist behaviour support team. This team's services are avaiiable through the School Psychological Service, but before a referral is accepted, the school must undertake some positive intervention including parental involvement.

Cynthia was referred to the support team at the age of 9, when she was in year 5 of the primary school. During her time in the first year, she had been described as 'selfish' and 'spiteful'. In the second year, her behaviour became more of a problem. She was functioning considerably below the norms for her age in English and mathematics, and was behaving aggressively towards fellow pupils as well as showing a lack of respect for authority. The educational psychologist considered that the school had acted responsibly. They had already involved Cynthia's mother, who found the girl a 'handful' at home too.

With two younger children and a broken marriage, Cynthia's mother found difficulty in being consistent with her elder daughter. She praised Cynthia's practical skills around the house, but said that this seemed to lead the child to 'take advantage' in actions and attitude.

The school did not have a policy on behaviour or social development but they had attempted, via the headteacher, to provide guidelines for Cynthia. The psychologist felt that the school and the girl would benefit from specialist help and Miss Quinton began her twice weekly sessions at the school.

She began by speaking to the whole staff at a suitable opportunity. This enabled her to explain her role and the school's responsibilities. As a result, the deputy headteacher began to co-ordinate a policy on behaviour for future implementation in the school.

Miss Quinton observed Cynthia at various times during the school day and asked the class teacher to maintain an 'ABC diary' of any incidents involving the girls. She explained that knowledge of antecedents, behaviours and consequences would provide a very useful monitoring tool at this stage of the intervention. She also spent short periods along with Cynthia, getting to know her and gaining her confidence. Two of these sessions were conducted in Cynthia's home and were followed by discussions which included her mother.

In school, documentary evidence was beginning to show that Cynthia's outbursts were often reactive responses to other pupils' comments. Sometimes these comments were lighthearted and perfectly normal school behaviour, but, at other times, they were directed at Cynthia's poor clothing, her lack of material possessions and her family. The girl's coping strategy was to 'lash out', both physically and verbally. As her behaviour was much more overt than the others, she was often caught and considered to be the sole culprit.

Miss Quinton talked to the staff about this and also to Cynthia. The staff were surprised but anxious to reduce the insidious 'bullying' of Cynthia. They agreed to be more careful in their responses to playtime incidents, looking at all aspects before reacting. Cynthia was helped to see the difference between innocent name-calling and insults which she should not have to endure. She was told that there were adults who could help her to deal with the latter, thereby removing the risk of her getting into trouble.

Miss Quinton discussed with Cynthia's mother the possibility of the girl spending more time with children of her own age and less with her two younger siblings. The mother said that she did use Cynthia a great deal to help out and had often felt that this was unfair. She agreed to let Cynthia attend the summer play-scheme which was restricted to pupils of 9+ years.

Progress with Cynthia has been slow. She is not a popular child but has two loyal friends with whom she seems content. The three play together and this has lessened the need for interaction resulting in aggression. Her attitude to staff has certainly improved and now more energy can be devoted to being proactive in relation to her learning difficulties rather than reacting to her behaviour difficulties.

Peer support groups
Mosley (1991) discusses the establishment of peer support groups for disruptive pupils who wish to gain more control over their behaviour. As a consultant, she developed a four-day model which involved:

(i)   an introductory course for headteachers to raise awareness of 'whole school' policy formation and ways of raising pupils' self-esteem;
(ii) on being invited to work in a particular school, holding a preliminary meeting with all staff;
(iii) the use of what is called the 'Circle Approach', which brings in the whole class and also the teacher, having them seated in a circle and engaging them in a wide range of cooperative activities, tailored to meet different ages, abilities and needs. A disruptive child might, for example, work jointly with others on an action plan with certain behavioural targets to be reached by the child, with social rewards for achieving these targets;
(iv) meetings with welfare assistants, lunch-time supervisors and clerical assistants with the focus on the theme of children's self-esteem; and
(v)   arranging a staff meeting to discuss issues raised, and to review the school's system of rewards and punishment.

This seems a useful model for the involvement of a whole class in responding to disruptive behaviour (see also Mosley, 1993).

Removing a Disruptive Pupil from his/her Usual School

If other measures fail, schools will seek to have a disruptive child transferred elsewhere, mostly to a special unit or school but sometimes to another mainstream school. While the pupil is awaiting transfer, he/she may be suspended or excluded from school. Such action may reduce pressure on the school and on the teachers suffering from disruption, and allow normal routines to be re-established. However, removal tends to have serious consequences for the pupil. It is likely to cause him/her to have difficulty in keeping up with curricular demands, though perhaps less so in the case of primary school pupils than at the secondary stage. Further, once a child is removed from his/her original school to provision outside the mainstream, considerable difficulty is often experienced in achieving a successful return to the school, even if the pupil settles down well in a special unit or special school.

The functions of special schools and various kinds of special unit, as well as the use of exclusion, have been discussed in chapter 8. Following concern about the alleged growing number of exclusions from school and the lengthy delays in completing the necessary procedures and in securing alternative provision, the 1993 Education Act has modified existing legislation with regard to pupils excluded from school: the new legislation will come into force in September 1994 (Morris *et al.*, 1993). Headteachers will no longer be able to exclude pupils for indefinite periods, or to exclude pupils for more than fifteen school days in any one term. Procedural stages in the exclusion process will have to be completed within specified periods, and funding will follow any pupil permanently excluded from an LEA-maintained or grant-maintained school. The Act places LEAs under a specific duty to provide education otherwise than at school where it is necessary to meet the needs of an individual child: this duty covers excluded pupils who otherwise might not receive suitable education unless such arrangements are made for them. The Act also gives LEAs the power to make provision otherwise than at school for pupils of compulsory school age in free-standing units, to be known as 'pupil referral units'. These units are intended to be small, catering on a full-time or part-time basis (but for as short a stay as possible) for between fifteen to thirty pupils, across a wide age range.

They are not meant to be a long-term alternative to mainstream schooling, but Morris *et al.* warn that the very existence of pupil referral units may well encourage exclusions because if they are successful, headteachers and governing bodies may continue to exclude, secure in the knowledge that provision will be made, perhaps for many children to a standard better than that currently available.

The following account of Bernard illustrates a case where it was generally considered that a placement in special provision would be beneficial to the pupil.

Bernard (aged 9+ years) is now in a special class for pupils in the 7–11 age range with learning difficulties. Of the six children in the class, three have pronounced behaviour problems. Bernard is very small in stature but his impact is totally disproportionate to his size. In his local school he was known as a 'runner': if he was chastised, put under pressure or teased, his reaction was to 'take off'. Bernard would yell verbal abuse at the teacher, fellow pupil or school assistant and run out of the school.

During Y1 and Y2, Bernard's behaviour was predictable: left to his own devices, he would be pleasant and cooperative but if he was asked to improve his work, stop talking, or try harder, he would change completely and storm out of the room.

Bernard's mother had been through the special education system and was considered to be of limited ability. She loved her son, but had few parenting skills. His father lived in the family home occasionally but was often away. Bernard appeared to admire his father and devised complex excuses for his absences from home.

In Y3 and Y4 Bernard began using his behaviour as a threat, for example, 'If you make me do that again, I'll run out'. This created a sense of tension in the classroom that was transmitted to other pupils. The school had by now established a routine for dealing with Bernard's actions. Rather than chasing him, they would notify the police and the family, and wait for Bernard to return or to be brought back to school. His behaviour and its effect on his learning led to his falling behind his peers. He was considered to be in need of a high teacher/pupil ratio and a learning environment where there was an emphasis on personal/social development. This was available in a nearby transitional slow-learning class and Bernard was referred for placement there shortly after his eighth birthday. So far this move appears to have provided an answer. Bernard sulks when once he would have run off and all those involved with him are optimistic about his future emotional, social and scholastic progress.

Overview

Much stress is caused to school staffs and parents by pupils who disrupt school life in some way. Even young children can interfere with normal school and class routines, and serious anti-social behaviour in middle childhood may well have long-term consequences if not adequately dealt with. It is difficult to discover the true extent of disruptive behaviour in schools, or whether the problem has grown as much as is commonly alleged. However, surveys suggest that most primary schools experience between 4 and 10 per cent of their pupils as causing disciplinary problems to a relatively minor extent, and about 1 or 2 per cent as seriously disruptive.

Disruptive behaviour may be caused by a variety of factors, including personality make-up, family background, peer pressures and the ethos of the school and class, as well as current social trends encouraging violence and attitudes challenging authority. Disruption may be prevented, at least to some degree, by well-considered school policies related to discipline allied to effective teaching and class control. A wide range of positive strategies may be applied by schools or the support agencies to deal with disruptive pupils, including behaviour modification, social skills training, counselling and psychotherapy. LEAs have in recent years developed behaviour support teams, in which specialist teachers help schools to keep disruptive pupils in their usual classes. However, in some circumstances a disruptive pupil may be transferred to a special unit or school, sometimes after being formally or informally excluded.

Chapter 10

Bullies and Victims

It is only in recent years that bullying in schools has become a matter of widespread concern among teachers and parents. The Elton Report (DES/ WO, 1989), on discipline in schools, gave voice to this concern by drawing attention to the damage caused by bullying both to individual pupils and to the emotional and social climate of schools. The paucity of the literature on bullying until recently is surprising, since much has been written on other aspects of aggressive behaviour and since bullying causes great distress to many schoolchildren, as will be shown later in this chapter. Perhaps this lack of attention to bullying is at least partly because in a mild form it is so common among children and adults that it is not necessarily seen as a problem, and is largely accepted as a normal part of social interaction. However, in the last few years, publications have appeared which not only report on research related to bullies and their victims but which also offer practical advice to teachers and parents on dealing with the problems arising from incidents of bullying (see section on intervention strategies later in this chapter).

This chapter discusses definitions of bullying; the extent and nature of bullying in middle childhood; factors associated with bullying; characteristics of victims; identification, assessment and possible strategies for helping both bullies and their victims.

Definitions

Various definitions have been suggested to highlight what distinguishes acts of bullying from other forms of aggressive behaviour. Most of these (see, for example, Crabtree, 1981; Manning and Sluckin, 1984) stress that bullying involves deliberate intent to: (i) cause physical injury; and/or (ii) cause distress by psychological means (teasing, taunting, mocking, sarcasm); and/or (iii) extort something from another; also that a particular individual or group is selected as the target for attacks of these kinds, by individuals, groups or gangs. Olweus (1978) defined bullying by boys as the systematic use of physical and/or mental violence and oppression by one or several boys against another boy.

Stephenson and Smith (1989) view bullying as a form of social interaction in which a more dominant individual (the bully) exhibits aggressive behaviour intended to cause distress to a weaker individual (the victim): the aggressive behaviour may take the form of a direct physical and/or verbal attack, or it may be indirect, for example, hiding a victims's possessions or spreading false information about the victim. This definition assumes that the victim experiences the intended distress and does not successfully defend him/herself from the attack.

The use of the term 'bullying' usually implies that the hostile acts referred to are unprovoked and repeated over a period (Besag, 1989; Smith and Thompson, 1991). However, some victims of bullying seem to go out of their way to provoke aggression against them (see below, pp. 160–1). It may help to prevent the escalation of aggressive behaviour if early signs are acted upon, rather than waiting for further incidents to develop.

Nature and Extent of Bullying in Middle Childhood

Early Beginnings

In the past, bullying has tended to be considered more as a feature of secondary school life than as occurring frequently at earlier stages. However, a number of studies have found evidence of bullying in various forms in nursery and infant schools (see Chazan, 1989). Manning *et al.* (1978), for example, found cases of physical or verbal harassment (unprovoked aggression directed at another child, often the same one repeatedly) in a sample of 3–5-year-old nursery school children. In a study of infant school children in the Isle of Wight conducted by Yule (1970), teachers rated 1.4 per cent of 209 boys and 1 per cent of girls as 'certainly' bullying other children.

As children move into the post-infant school stage, bullying may become more highly organized and involve calculated strategies on the part of the aggressors (Gregory, 1992). Tattum and Herbert (1990) stress that bullying can be experienced in the form of racial and sexual harassment and intimidation. Bullies may use blackmail or physical force to secure financial or other benefits, including the bolstering of dominance status within the group. They may make victims steal money or other things, or they may deliberately damage another's school work or equipment. As small gangs begin to form in class around the age of 8 years or so, the likelihood of group bullying becomes greater.

Difficulties in Ascertaining Extent of Problem

The precise extent of bullying in middle childhood is not easy to ascertain, since, as with behaviour problems generally, a variety of factors affect any estimates of prevalence. In particular, children are often reluctant to inform adults, particularly their teachers, even when they suffer greatly at the hands of bullies (Whitney and Smith, 1993), perhaps out of fear of the consequences or because they feel that it is unacceptable in the peer group to 'tell tales' on other children. The make-up of any school population in terms of gender and home background will also have a bearing on the prevalence of bullying. As will be seen from the studies discussed later in this section, boys tend to be more prone to bullying than girls, and any racial tension which exists in a school and its catchment area may result in some victimization of ethnic minority groups. Further, whether or not a school has an explicit anti-bullying policy will have a bearing on the extent to which bullying is experienced in school.

If systematic attempts are made to discover the extent to which bullying is occurring in a school, the methods used will be an important factor in determining the estimates arrived at. Questionnaires answered in writing, anonymously and in confidence, are probably the best means of obtaining as true a picture as possible of the prevalence of bullying in a class or school (Ahmad and Smith, 1990), but some children of 7 and 8 may have problems in responding to questionnaires in writing, such as children with learning difficulties, who may well be particularly susceptible to bullying in a main-stream class. Ahmad and Smith found that interviews can yield much qualitative information of value, and also that peer nominations tend to be accurate but are time-consuming.

Surveys of Prevalence

A number of recent research surveys have thrown light on the nature and extent of bullying in middle childhood, although the context and methodology of each study have to be kept in mind in the interpretation of the results. The work of Olweus (1978, 1987) in Scandinavia has influenced the methodology of surveys carried out in other countries, including the United Kingdom (see also Roland and Munthe, 1989). In an extensive study using an anonymous questionnaire, Olweus (1987) found about 12 per cent of 8–12-year-olds in Norway being bullied 'now and then or more often' considerably more than among 13–16-year-olds, of whom only about 5 per cent were victims of bullying. No such age trend, however, was apparent in terms of the reported incidence of bullying others, which was about 7 per cent in both age groups. O'Moore and Hillery (1989), using the Olweus self-report questionnaire, estimated that 10 per cent of 783 children aged 7–13 years in four schools in Dublin were involved in serious bullying, either as bullies or victims.

Three surveys carried out in England have reported an even higher prevalence of bullying than those indicated above.

(i)   *Stephenson and Smith (1989)* asked forty-nine teachers to rate 1078 final year primary school pupils (aged 10–11+) attending twenty-six schools in a North-east England local education authority. The teachers reported 10 per cent of the sample as bullying other children at the time of the study, though mostly not seriously; 7 per cent as being victims; and 6 per cent as having the dual role of bully and victim. In all, 23 per cent of the sample were involved either as bullies or victims. There were individual differences in prevalence among classes and schools: the larger the class or school, the greater the problem of bullying tended to be.

Stephenson and Smith suggest that there are two main types of bullies in middle childhood. Most are confident, assertive and physically strong. These bullies are unpopular with teachers, but usually of average popularity in the peer group. However, some bullies are anxious, lacking in self-confidence and in general not popular. In their studies, Stephenson and Smith found that bullying tended to be persistent. In most cases, the bullying had been going on for at least a year, although it did occur in phases too. Gregory (1992) reports a case of bullying lasting for nearly five years. Stephenson and Smith suggest that the nature of bullying may differ for boys and girls. The girls were more often involved, as bullies or victims, in verbal attacks, whereas the boys were more often prone to physical bullying, perhaps combined with verbal taunts.

(ii) *Boulton and Underwood (1992)* used a modified version of the Olweus self-report questionnaire in their study of 296 children (142 girls and 154 boys) attending three urban middle schools in England with an intake of pupils with predominantly Asian and white English working-class family backgrounds. The questionnaire invited answers to twenty-five questions: (i) about friends; (ii) about being bullied; and (iii) about bullying other children, in terms of never/once or twice/sometimes/two or three times a week. Overall, about 20 per cent of the sample reported being bullied 'sometimes' or 'more often'. In this sample, significantly more younger children (mean age 8.5–9.5 years) than expected admitted to being bullied several times a week and significantly fewer of these younger children reported never being bullied, whereas the opposite was the case with the older children (mean age 11.5 years). Significantly more boys than girls said that they were being bullied, but there were no significant between-school differences in regard to being bullied. With regard to bullying others, 17.1 per cent of the sample acknowledged that they participated in bullying others 'sometimes' or more often. Significant differences were found for age (more younger pupils committing acts of bullying); between the sexes (more boys involved); and between schools.

Boulton and Underwood report that about 58 per cent of the victims in the sample of 8–12-year-olds which they studied stated that the bullying took the form of teasing; around a third complained that they had been hit or kicked; and about 10 per cent said that they had been subjected to other kinds of physical or mental assault, such as hair-pulling or being sworn at. The researchers found no significant age, sex or school differences as far as forms of bullying were concerned.

(iii) *Whitney and Smith (1993)* gave anonymous questionnaires on bullying to over 6000 pupils in seventeen junior/middle and seven secondary schools in the Sheffield LEA. The sample of junior/middle school pupils totalled 2623 (1271 boys, 1352 girls), aged between 8 and 11 years. The results were averaged over class and schools. Of these children 27 per cent stated that they had been bullied at least 'sometimes' in the current term; 10 per cent of the sample alleged that they had been bullied at least once a week; 16 per cent of the junior/middle school pupils admitted to bullying others 'sometimes', with 6 per cent of the sample stating that they did this once a week or more. Considerable differences were found between schools, the reported range in junior/middle schools being from 6 per cent to 21 per cent with regard to being frequently bullied and from 2 per cent to 8 per cent with regard to bullying frequently. These figures were about twice as high as those reported by the secondary school pupils. There was only a slight difference between boys and girls in their reports of being bullied, but at least twice as many boys as girls admitted to bullying others. Name-calling was the most prevalent form of bullying, but intimidation took a variety of forms, physical and psychological. In the junior/middle schools, bullying was carried out mainly by individual boys, both bullies and victims being mostly within the same class or year group.

Bullying Line

The child's point of view in regard to bullying is discussed by La Fontaine (1991) in an analysis of calls to the Bullying Line, set up by Childline in 1990 and funded by the Gulbenkian Foundation. Over three months, 2000 calls were received, about two-thirds being from girls. 19 per cent of the calls were from 7–10+ year-olds, and 50 per cent from 11–13+ year-olds. In the 7–10+ age group, 44 per cent complained about being picked on, 17 per cent about troubles with peer relationships, 28 per cent about physical assault, and 11 per cent about extortion or theft of property. Over half of the bullies in the various age-groups were of the same age and likely to be classmates; 44 per cent were older than the victims. In interpreting these figures, it must be borne in mind that children who make use of a telephone service such as the Bullying Line are not necessarily a representative sample of those who are bullied. However, it emerged strongly from the analysis that the victims felt rejected, isolated and lonely, and that they wished the bullying to be stopped without them being implicated as the cause of any intervention.

Why do Children Become Bullies?

There is no simple explanation of the reasons why children become bullies, and some disagreement exists about the main causes of bullying. Much that has already been said in this book (see, in particular, chapter 3) about the sources of EBDs in general applies to a consideration of factors associated with bullying: temperament, physique and the child's situation (in the school, home, playground and street) all may play a part. It is easy to understand how children with an aggressive temperament combined with low-esteem arising from a physical disability, unattractive appearance or learning difficulties may seek to compensate by bullying weaker contemporaries. There are clear links between aggression and rejection, and these links are especially strong round about 9–10 years of age (Malik and Furman, 1993). Some pupils, too, may wish to establish themselves as leaders in the class or smaller group and attempt to achieve power through the use of force when necessary.

Olweus (1978 and 1984) stresses temperamental factors rather than aspects of the environment as possible causes of bullying, but others assert that bullies often have problems at home and that bullying is more common in some schools than in others. Stephenson and Smith (1989), for example, report that far more children who are bullies have problems within the family than other children. These difficulties include a lack of firm, consistent discipline; marital disharmony, financial and social strains, and poor relationships between the children and their parents. Parents themselves may provide models of bullying and use excessive physical punishment. Some children who are subjected to parental pressure and undue chastisement at home may react not against their parents, but against weaker children at school.

Olweus does not regard school factors as of great importance in the causation of bullying, finding no relationship between bullying and the size of class or school, or teachers' job satisfaction in his Scandinavian studies. In a different school context, Stephenson and Smith (1989) reported that bullying occurred much more frequently in some schools than in others, on the basis of a study carried out in a sample of schools in England. Bullying tended to be more prevalent in schools located in socially disadvantaged areas, and in larger schools. Those schools where the incidence of bullying is very low tend to be the ones which have a well-planned, specific policy directed at the prevention of bullying as far as possible and dealing with it effectively when it does occur.

Boulton and Underwood (1992) found that many out of a small sample of bullies aged between 8 and 10 years tend to excuse themselves on the grounds that they had been provoked by the victim. Other reasons given by the bullies included that they disliked the victim, that the victim got on their nerves, or that they (the bullies) were hard, tough or strong. Some could not give any reason for their behaviour.

Whitney and Smith (1993) found that rates of bullying reported by pupils varied with year, gender and school location, partly as a result of opportunities for bullying. In their study, school size, class size and ethnic mix were not linked with bullying; social disadvantage was correlated with bullying to a small extent.

Victims

In the past, even less attention has been given by researchers to the victims of bullying than to the bullies themselves, but it is now increasingly recognized that children who become victims may well be maladapted to school life and be failing to fit into the peer group. Studies of victims of bullying in middle childhood suggest that these children tend to be generally anxious and insecure; possessing low self-esteem; non-aggressive, weak, passive and socially ineffective; and reluctant to retaliate in the face of provocation (Olweus, 1978 and 1984; Stephenson and Smith, 1989). A small number of victims, however, may be assertive and provocative, appearing to invite aggressive acts against them (Besag, 1989). Most victims are lonely, unhappy, socially isolated and unpopular in the group, and have below average school attainments (La Fontaine, 1991; Boulton and Underwood, 1992; Nabuzoka and Smith, 1993). Children from ethnic minorities are particularly vulnerable to racist taunts. Moran *et al.* (1993) found that, while there was no evidence of Asian pupils being bullied more often than white children, they did suffer from name-calling with reference to their colour to a considerable extent.

Signs of a child who is becoming a victim in school include coming home from school in a dishevelled state or without some of his/her belongings; some deterioration in concentration or other aspects of school work; or even a fear of going to school (Crabtree, 1981; Mortimore *et al.*, 1983).

Perry *et al.* (1988) used peer nominations, teacher nominations and self-ratings in a study of victims of peer aggression at school. Their sample consisted of 165 pupils (eighty-three boys; eighty-two girls) aged 9+ –11+ in schools in Florida, USA. The main instrument used to assess children's victimization and aggression was a modified version of the Peer Nomination Inventory (PNI) devised by Wiggins and Winder (1961). This technique required children to mark those in a list of same-sex classmates who fitted specific descriptions of behaviour. Examples of items relating to victimization were:

- he/she gets called names by other kids;
- he/she gets picked on by other kids;
- he/she gets hit and pushed by other kids.

Perry *et al.* (1988) claim well-established validity for the peer nomination scale used in their study, and found a high degree of consensus in the peer groups on the issue of which children were victimized. Objections may be raised to obtaining negative nominations or ratings of peers from children (Malik and Furman, 1993). However, the peer group is probably the most fruitful source of information about which children are victims of bullying, and the use of peer nominations is perhaps more acceptable in the case of research studies undertaken by outside personnel than when teachers question pupils with whom they have regular contact.

On the basis of their research, Perry *et al.* (1988) concluded that about 10 per cent of the sample could be classified as extremely victimized and were mostly rejected by their peers. Their status as victims was stable over a period of three months, and the sustained maltreatment tended to lower the child's self-esteem and raise their feelings of fear, depression and mistrust. Some of the most extreme victims were also among the most aggressive children in the sample; these were among the most disliked members of the group. Perry *et al.* emphasize that aggression is likely to increase if the victim has a history of yielding to an aggressor's demands, and fails to emit signs that normally inhibit aggression towards oneself, for example, signs of intense pain or even threatening facial expressions signalling that one will not be pushed around.

Stephenson and Smith (1989) also found that those children who were both bullies and victims (about 6 per cent of their sample) were rated as being the least popular with other children of all the groups identified in the study. These 'bully-victims' tended to be physically stronger and more assertive than children who were victims but not bullies themselves, and easily provoked as well as provoking others.

In an Australian study, Rigby and Slee (1993) report that while about 20 per cent of a sample of 325 boys and 360 girls said that they would not be friends with children who let themselves be pushed around, 80 per cent said they felt angry when a child is picked on without good reason. This finding provides some grounds for optimism about the use of peer support to help victims of bullying.

Action to Prevent and Reduce Bullying

Identification of Bullies and Victims

It is not easy to identify bullies in school accurately, as incidents of victimization will tend to take place when no adult is close at hand. However, careful observation by teachers and other school staff may help to bring to light even minor cases of bullying and to stop these from escalating by swift action. Bullying often takes place in the playground, where supervision is often more relaxed than in the classroom (Blatchford, 1993), and so playground supervisors can play an important role in the detection of bullying. A bully may be deterred if he/she knows that responsible adults are in a position to observe his/her aggressive acts.

Asking peers to nominate the bullies in their class or other group may be a useful method of identification in research projects which safeguard the anonymity of the respondent, but is not likely to appeal to teachers carrying out their normal duties.

Victims are perhaps somewhat easier to identify than bullies. Parents may notice that their child arrives home with the loss of a cap or scarf or that he/she is reluctant to go to school. A sociometric survey of the class (see chapter 2, pp. 33–4) may be useful in identifying isolated and lonely children at risk of becoming victims and in helping to plan changes in seating arrangements in the classroom.

Assessment

Assessment can take place at two levels — discovering the nature and extent of bullying in a school as a whole, and assessing the needs of individuals who engage in or suffer from, bullying.

Assessing the prevalence of bullying in a school is best carried out through an independent agency, i.e. not the school staff itself, using anonymous questionnaires. A project based at the University of Sheffield, for example, is aiming to show how schools can avail themselves of a service to discover how much bullying takes place, and to base their policies and intervention strategies on this information allied to a knowledge of effective approaches to the eradication of bullying (Smith and Thompson, 1991). Questionnaires designed to assess the nature and extent of bullying in a school include those devised by Arora and Thompson (1987) and Olweus (1989).

At the individual level, both bullies and victims merit detailed assessment in cases of serious bullying, as already described in chapter 3. It is important to ascertain, as precisely as possible, both the nature and context of the bullying episodes; to draw up a profile of the strengths as well as the weaknesses of the children involved; to link the assessment closely to intervention; to involve the parents; and, if necessary, to enlist the aid of the relevant support services, especially the School Psychological Service.

Involving parents in assessment
The contribution of parents to the assessment of children with EBDs has been discussed in chapter 3 (pp. 50–1). Besag (1989) suggest a number of questions that might form the basis for interviewing the parents at school, for example:

> How long have you been aware of the situation?
> Has there been a history of bullying?
> Has there been a change of mood, habit or behaviour recently?
> What effect is the bullying having on the child?

The attitude of both mother and father to the situation needs to be explored, and any factors known to the parents which seem of relevance should be discussed.

The role of the School Psychological Service (SPS) in assessment
The educational psychologist working in the School Psychological Service is well placed to adopt a coordinating role in the assessment of incidents of

bullying (see chapter 3, p. 51 for a general consideration of the contribution of the SPS to the assessment of children presenting EBDs). Educational psychologists can not only help in the assessment of all the individuals involved, but can assist schools in an examination of their policy (if any) towards bullying and of teacher-child relationships within the school.

Intervention Strategies

Intervention in cases of bullying may be considered from two main points of view — taking prompt action as soon as an incident comes to light, and longer-term measures designed to prevent, or at least reduce, the occurrence of bullying in school. Much practical advice is now available to schools in the form of books, pamphlets, in-service training and resource packages and videos (see, for example, Besag, 1989; Elliott, 1991; Smith and Thompson, 1991; Sharp and Smith, 1991; Maines and Robinson, 1991; Skinner, 1992; Tattum, 1993; Tattum and Herbert, 1993; and Tattum *et al.*, 1993). This section summarizes the main measures and procedures that might be considered by schools.

Immediate action
Taking prompt action may involve:

(i)   the teacher and/or the parents talking calmly to the bully, making it clear that bullying is unacceptable, and giving constructive tasks to the bully while possibly temporarily removing some privileges from him/her;

(ii) reassuring the victim that action is being taken to stop the bullying;

(iii) increasing supervision by adults in school and playground, if this is needed;

(iv) using members of the class to support the victim;

(v)   assessing both victims and bullies along the lines previously indicated, and arranging counselling or other forms of help if appropriate, with the assistance of an educational psychologist;

(vi) asking bullies to appear before a school court, to be judged by their peers, with compensation or sanctions in some form possibly being imposed on them (Laslett, 1982; Elliott, 1991). School courts may have some benefits, especially in that they increase pupils' understanding of themselves and others (Brier and Ahmad, 1991). However, they may not be favoured by those who prefer a less formal and more positive approach to bullies (Maines and Robinson, 1991a and 1991b), and are perhaps less appropriate in primary schools than at the secondary stage;

(vii) using groups to help both bullies and victims, as described below.

Group work with bullies and victims
Small groups (say six-eight children) may be set up in school consisting of bullies and victims, together and/or separately. Through such groups, social

skills may be taught, training in relaxation and assertiveness given, and the implications of bullying discussed (Foster *et al.*, 1990; Arora, 1991). Two somewhat different approaches combining work with individuals and with groups have been developed by Pikas (1989) in Sweden, and Maines and Robinson (1991a) in England: these are described below.

Pikas was particularly concerned with treating group or gang bullying among schoolchildren, with the main initial aim of re-individualizing the group members through separate talks, during which their basic fears and reservations about their own behaviour are made conscious and immediate escape is offered. Pikas's Method of Common Concern has attracted a good deal of interest. It involves

(i)   individual talks with three to six suspected bullies carried out consecutively, with ten to twenty minutes allotted for each talk. Bullies are involved first, to protect the victim from being accused of having informed on them;

(ii)   talking to the victim immediately after the above series, which takes about sixty to ninety minutes in all;

(iii)   repeating the talks either with the individuals concerned, or with all those involved assembled as a group, after about a week; and

(iv)   arranging a further follow-up meeting.

Pikas gives specific guidance about the questions to be asked by the therapist, whose main aim is to reinforce the idea that the situation of the victim is something to be concerned about, and to obtain suggestions for action from the bullies themselves. He claims that the method is generally successful and suitable for use by teachers, especially after some training and if they work in conjunction with an educational psychologist. He warns, however, that some teachers find it hard not to try to establish guilt quickly and not to administer reprimands.

Maines and Robinson (1991) assert that the primary focus of any plan to stop bullying should be on the feelings and status of the bully. In their approach, bullies are given the opportunity to acknowledge that there is a problem, to understand the degree of distress suffered, and to feel that their ability to change behaviour is recognized. Maines and Robinson stress the need to avoid labelling through the use of the terms 'bully' and 'victim' in talking to children and young people, though these terms are so much a part of common parlance that it is difficult to see how their complete avoidance can be achieved. They advocate the following procedure for group work with bullies when bullying has been confirmed in school.

(i)   Take down an account from the 'victim' and listen attentively to him/her, noting the feelings expressed and using pictures and/or writing.

(ii)   Convene a meeting of those involved, including any observers — about six to eight people if possible.

(iii) Explain the problem and tell the story of the bullying episode, describing the distress caused.

(iv) Don't attribute blame, but stress that the members of the group are all responsible for doing something about the bullying.

(v) Ask all the members of the group for suggestions about what action to take, without extracting any promises of improved behaviour.

(vi) Arrange to meet each group member alone in about a week's time to find out how things are going.

(vii) Convey throughout the belief that the pupils involved are not 'bad', are capable of kind behaviour and can help the 'victim'.

There are similarities in the procedures advocated by Pikas and Maines and Robinson, but the latter consider that their approach differs from Pikas in three main ways. In the first place, Pikas speaks first to the bullies to prevent the victim possibly suffering further in revenge for 'telling'. The Maines and Robinson plan of campaign takes this risk in exchange for the powerful group influence brought to bear on the problem. Secondly, Pikas speaks separately to each member of a group of bullies, whereas Maines and Robinson rely on group effects. Thirdly, their approach stresses empathy with the victim by telling the bullies how the victim feels.

Longer-term measures
In recent years, not only schools but local education authorities have launched many initiatives in an effort to prevent or reduce the occurrence of bullying in the classroom (Wilkinson and Priest, 1991; Nottingham Education Committee, 1991). These initiatives have been multi-faceted, as is shown below.

(i) Schools have developed a 'whole school' approach to bullying (see chapter 5 for a discussion of this approach to EBDs in general). This has meant raising awareness of bullying and its effects, ensuring that the ethos of the school encourages fairness and cooperation, and establishing an agreed policy for dealing with incidents of bullying. A 'whole school' approach involves pupils, parents and governors as well as all the staff, and ensures that teachers are adequately supported in dealing with behaviour problems (Besag, 1989; Foster *et al.*, 1990).

(ii) Teachers have been encouraged to examine their own behaviour and management style to ensure that they are not themselves providing a model of domineering behaviour. They may be helped in this self-appraisal through in-service courses organized specifically dealing with aspects of bullying. Some LEAs and other organizations (for example, Avon LEA and the Scottish Council for Research in Education) have developed their own packages for use in such INSET courses. Other forms of support for schools and teachers are discussed by Elliott, 1986; Ahmad *et al.*, 1991; and Tattum, 1993.

(iii)   Older pupils have been involved in taking some responsibility for the induction of younger pupils, who may be particularly vulnerable to bullying.

(iv)   The curriculum has been used to provide many opportunities to discuss issues relating to bullying and how both victims and others should respond to it. These opportunities have been given through, for example, personal and social education courses which teach social and coping skills (Gregory, 1992); the use of literature and drama to help children gain better insight into the effects of bullying (see Tattum and Herbert, 1990 for a list of books which stimulate discussion about bullying; Smith and Thompson, 1991 for several contributions on the use of literature and drama for this purpose; and Elliott, 1991); and setting up specific group work projects which encourage a spirit of cooperation and the exploration of feelings and attitudes towards bullying (Maines and Robinson, 1991a and 1991b).

Effectiveness of intervention

It is too early to assess the long-term effectiveness of measures adopted to reduce the prevalence of bullying in schools. However, experience of the nationwide community level campaigns against bullying conducted in Norway since 1983 suggests that, where a school adopted an active programme against bullying, it was measurably successful (Roland, 1989; Olweus, 1992a and 1992b). Certainly both the immediate suffering of victims of bullying and long-term consequences of allowing bullies to continue victimizing others justify vigorous action against bullying. Pre-adolescent bullying may well lead to juvenile delinquency and violence in adulthood (Farrington, 1993; Tattum, 1993). Although this progression is difficult to prevent in some cases, carefully planned intervention by the school and other agencies can do much to guide children who bully towards more positive behaviour in later years (Lane, 1989).

Illustrative Case Studies

The following cases will serve to illustrate some of the points made in this chapter about bullies and victims.

Bullies

Neil

Neil was 8 years old, a big boy with a large frame and somewhat overweight. He was of below average academic ability but achieved success in school sporting activities. He sought attention in class but responded well to praise. His mother was a regular visitor at school: she perceived her son as a victim and regularly commented, 'I've told him, if anyone hits him, he's to hit them back'. Neil's father is not known to the school, as he never visits.

Neil picked on children within his peer group or younger; there had been no reported cases of aggression towards older pupils. His victims were mostly boys, with a few exceptions. He imposed his will on others by physical intimidation, using his size and the threat of his karate hobby to exert his power. He was quickly reduced to tears by figures in authority and was always quick to deny his part in any incident. However, his apparently obedient attitude towards teachers was short-lived once he was out in the school playground, where attacks on other children included punching, pushing and kicking. He acted as an individual, and did not lead or influence any followers. He had gained a 'reputation' with parents, and was perceived by the school as a 'nuisance' rather than posing major problems.

Neil did respond to praise, and this was his year 3 teacher's main strategy. She gave him praise as early as possible in the day and this seemed to set Neil off on the right track, helping to avoid incidents. Once an incident did take place, the cycle of tears, denial and mother's intervention occurred and the outcome tended to be very unsatisfactory. Not all the other teachers agreed with the class teacher's preventative approach despite its success to an extent, as some saw it as favouring the boy unjustifiably.

With the help of the educational psychologist, the school attempted to persuade Neil's mother to change her attitude and to reflect more on the reported incidents. Neil's mother was quick to take offence and could be very threatening in her manner: to her, Neil was invariably the innocent party. She encouraged interviews to be confrontational, and became aggressive, asking for teachers to be disciplined. However, with great patience on the part of the headteacher, teacher and psychologist, Neil's mother was helped towards taking a more realistic view of the situation. The use of 'Why do you think . . . ?' questions proved to be quite successful. After a while, Neil's mother conceded that a different course of action on Neil's part might have been better, and began to speak more reasonably to her son. Her change of attitude helped to reduce the number of incidents of bullying for which Neil was responsible. The school supported the victims, assuring them that action was being taken to stop Neil's bullying.

Pamela

Pamela, aged 10+, was a rarity in her school — an aggressive girl pupil. She exhibited few, if any, behaviour problems in school; was pleasant and helpful to staff; and was well-liked by her teachers. However, the school received reports and evidence of her intimidation of others outside school hours. Pamela's bullying took the form of threats and sanctions against other girls in her age-group. Some physical aggression was reported to the school, but not witnessed by the staff. Pamela had a group of close girl friends who were influential characters in her class and undoubtedly intimidating to some other pupils.

Both the Head and Deputy Head attempted to counsel Pamela about her growing reputation as a bully but, while she appeared cooperative, complaints continued to be received about her and there was talk of police involvement in the case of one parent. This case was particularly difficult because all the incidents took place out of school and the bullying was mostly verbal rather than physical. However, further action was necessary because there was evidence of a loss of self-esteem on the part of some of the victims and because Pamela was in her final year at the primary school.

The school, therefore, (i) discussed the problem with Pamela's parents and the parents of identified victims; and (ii) discussed the effects of bullying in small groups consisting of the bullies and the victims, sometimes separately, at other times together. These steps proved successful, and Pamela had stopped victimizing others by the time she transferred to a large comprehensive school.

Nigel

Nigel, 11 years of age, was the youngest of a family of four boys, all of whom had exhibited behaviour problems in school. He had learning difficulties, but was a keen and competitive sportsman. Nigel was recognized as having a 'short fuse' and, when in a temper, turned on pupils and staff alike. Many of the bullying incidents which took place were directed against pupils whom he thought were spoiling a game of soccer, affecting his performance or criticizing his play. Nigel's whole family had a reputation for violence and many children feared Nigel with good cause. He himself was hero-worshipped by a small group of his peers, all of whom had learning difficulties, and who were carefully avoided by most of the class but were a source of fear to many sensitive pupils and a problem for most staff. Nigel had the additional power of his older brothers' support, and while this was confined to out-of-school attacks, the victims were often pupils from the school.

This was a particularly difficult case, since Nigel had long been labelled as a behaviour problem, and perceived in a negative light by his teachers. His values were opposed to those of the school, but in line with those of his family. No success had resulted from trying to involve his parents, as they saw aggression as natural and vital for survival. However, the school invited the educational psychologist to help in this case, mainly in order to oversee Nigel's transition from primary to secondary school. Little progress was possible in the short time available while Nigel was at primary school, but the educational psychologist was able to encourage the staff to be as positive as possible towards Nigel, and used Pikas's Method of Common Concern with the bullies and some of the victims.

Victims

Martin

Martin, aged 10 years, and his younger sister Simone began attending school X during his fourth year of junior school and her second. Simone settled down quickly and proved a happy, confident and popular child while Martin remained a loner for some time, failing to fit into his new peer group. Martin was not a success either scholastically or in sporting activities; he was pale and looked lethargic, although he was pleasant in one-to-one conversations. Although he took some time to settle down in his new school, it was some months after his arrival that he became the victim of bullying. The bully was a boy named *Hugh* in the same class who was often in trouble for anti-social behaviour. Hugh made physical threats against Martin and actually moved towards him in a threatening manner which sent the victim scurrying out of his way.

This situation was first brought to the school's attention by Martin's mother following an incident on the way home from school. Hugh had lunged towards Martin causing him to run out into the road, where a car only narrowly missed hitting him. The incident was witnessed by other parents, who reported it to Martin's mother. When she questioned the boy about the incident, he told her of the threats during school time.

When the school staff were notified, certain measures were taken. These included:

(i)   speaking to Hugh. He denied actual violence (which he had not been accused of), and claimed that anything else was Martin's just being a baby. He showed no obvious remorse;

(ii)   daily interviews with Martin. In the short term he was spoken to in private each day prior to going home. He seemed to find enormous comfort in knowing that adults were keeping a close eye on him; and

(iii)   raising the issue of bullying with the whole class. Without naming anyone, it became evident that several children were aware of the situation. Two pupils took to championing Martin. Both were sensible boys unlikely to involve themselves in physical confrontations, and Martin was delighted to be their 'friend'.

Martin's mother was kept informed and was asked to let the school know of any further incidents. Staff felt dissatisfied with Hugh's response and there was a general belief that he might transfer his attention elsewhere. Martin remained visibly nervous in Hugh's presence and sought reassurance from staff and other pupils. However, he maintained that he was now happy in school, and his mother confirmed this.

Denise

Denise, 11 years of age and in her final year of primary schooling, was a very distinctive child with long curly dark hair, vivid blue eyes and a seemingly endless wardrobe. Denise loved to perform and carried a 'dramatic' approach into everyday life. She was of average ability but contributed in an all-round way to school life. For example, she played the recorder, was in the netball team, and was a responsible monitor.

In the last year at her primary school, she became the victim of bullying by two other girls in her class acting together, with a third girl collaborating on their directions. The three bullies were not considered to be a problem in any other area of their schooling. Indeed, as it became known that they had bullied Denise there was considerable disbelief among staff. Denise's mother came to the school in a state of great distress to explain what had been happening. The school was entirely unaware of the situation, although it had been noticed that Denise often felt unwell during the day and had asked to go home on several occasions: this had been attributed to her approaching puberty.

Denise's mother stated that the girl had been 'sent to Coventry' by these girls and their group of friends; notes of a cruel kind had been put in her desk accusing her of being a 'tart'; she had been the victim of name-calling at a distance, and a whispering campaign had begun which Denise found intolerable.

The Headteacher was shocked at the extent of the bullying and saw the two alleged bullies immediately. Neither girl denied being involved. Both claimed to dislike Denise intensely but were upset that their actions had caused the Headteacher to be angry with them. He explained that they did not have to befriend Denise, but that they must conform to certain standards of behaviour even towards those whom they did not actively like. The next day the mothers of the two girls arrived at school unexpectedly and promised their full support. They were cross with their daughters and ashamed of their behaviour, but both described Denise as being 'an oddity' who 'brought a lot of it on herself'.

Denise's mother was quite dissatisfied with the school's action. She felt that the situation was serious enough to warrant the girls' suspension. The Head tried hard to reassure her, but she was evidently left with the impression that the girls had 'got away with it'. An informal contract was drawn up (in writing but unsigned) to the effect that:

(a) Denise would report any incidents immediately;
(b) the two girls would be reminded about behaving positively, on alternate days;
(c) staff would keep a closer watch on the girls at break and other appropriate times;
(d) the class would be cautioned regarding name-calling and other forms of taunting others; and
(e) Denise would be interviewed in private on a weekly basis.

This worked well for a week and then Denise's mother returned to the school in a very angry mood. She felt that Denise was hiding the truth from the staff and that the bullying had become more sophisticated and harder to detect. The school had no evidence of this whatsoever. Denise's mother perceived examples everywhere, alleging that her daughter was being stared at during assembly (difficult to avoid as she was part of the orchestra), she had been called 'mermaid' by a boy in the class (she would not accept that this could be a compliment); and other parents had 'heard things'.

The Head reiterated his satisfaction with what had been achieved and promised the school's continuing support for Denise. He did not consider that anything more was called for or could be justifiably undertaken. Denise reported good and bad days, and was helped to understand that some behaviour of her classmates did not amount to bullying and could not be entirely eradicated. She remained highly sensitive to perceived slights but became much happier. She recognized that the bullies had learned a lesson but believed them to be controlling other pupils' behaviour; although there was no evidence of this. Her mother, on the other hand, had written a formal letter of complaint to the school governing body and had already sought a preferred placement for Denise at the secondary level, to prevent her from attending the comprehensive school in her locality.

Overview

Bullying in school in its varied forms, physical and psychological, causes its victims considerable distress. It is sufficiently common in middle childhood as to arouse widespread concern among teachers, parents and professional agencies. Several surveys have suggested that at least 20 per cent of pupils in junior or middle schools are involved either as bullies or victims. Bullies are mostly assertive and physically strong, but some are lacking in self-confidence. Victims are usually anxious and socially ineffective, with poor self-esteem and a low status in the peer group, but some may be provocative and seem to be inviting aggressive acts against them. There are links between bullying and a child's temperament and physique, as well as his/her situation in school, home, playground and street. The association between aggression and rejection seems to be especially strong round about 9–10 years of age.

It is important to take swift and firm action to intervene when bullying, however mild, is identified. Both bullies and victims may benefit from being assessed comprehensively with a view to meeting any special needs that they may have, but short-term measures focussing on reassuring the victim and making it clear to the bully that his/her behaviour is unacceptable are likely to have an effect. Increased supervision in the playground and elsewhere may be required, and various strategies have been developed for group work with bullies and victims. In the longer term, a 'whole school' approach to bullying, which involves pupils, all school staff, parents and governors as well as the wider community, is likely to contribute to the prevention, or at least the reduction, of incidents of bullying at school.

Chapter 11

Withdrawal, Anxiety and Depression

The ability to interact with others, adults or children, in a positive, productive way is important for an individual's intellectual development and emotional well-being. Skills in initiating conversation, in joining in activities coopera-tively, in sharing responsibility, in having fun with others and in being able to ask for help when required enable individuals to be positive rather than negative in their dealings with others and to feel comfortable in group set-tings. Some children are, of course, more positive (or pro-social) than others. However, when children consistently pull back from contact with others and so fail to take full advantage of the learning and social opportunities available to them, they can be considered to have emotional and behavioural difficulties which require help just as much as aggressive, disruptive children. It is the latter who often dominate the classroom but withdrawn, anxious or depressed children must also cause teachers concern.

The size of the problem they present is difficult to quantify. As pointed out in chapter 2 (pp. 24–5), while more boys than girls show anti-social behavi-our, inhibited, internalized behaviour tends to be slightly more common in girls. Many children with EBDs, too, present a mixed pattern of externalized and internalized behaviour problems. Further, teachers and parents may well differ in their identification of these children. Quiet, subdued behaviour is not always seen as unacceptable. Indeed, only recently has it been recognized that fairly young children can suffer from depression (Gotlib and Hammen, 1992) or that shyness may inhibit effective academic performance (Zimbardo, 1977).

Shyness and Withdrawal

Most people have felt shy in some social situation at some time in their life. The acceptance of the term in common parlance may, however, serve only to complicate any attempt to define it, quantify it or estimate its effects on individual functioning. There is considerable truth in the statement that 'shy-ness is a fuzzy concept' (Asendorpf, 1986). After reviewing the literature on the concept, Van der Molin (1990) concluded that there was still no agreed definition of shyness and 'that the individual is the most reliable expert on his or her own shyness' (p. 258). There may be justification for this conclusion but it does present difficulties for any teacher wishing to help a shy child. To ask children directly if they feel shy and if their shyness affects their response to school in any way may well merely exacerbate the situation.

Yet shyness can be inhibiting, especially when it restricts the exercise of the pro-social skills already mentioned. The difficulties surrounding the definition of the condition and its implications for individual well-being cannot be an excuse for lack of action on the teacher's part. Possible strategies which could help will be discussed later in this chapter. In the meantime, it can be reiterated that if children (and adults) feel that there is a discrepancy between the way they are behaving and the way they would like to react, their self-esteem is likely to be low (Lawrence, 1988). To avoid such negative feelings, children may lower their expectations of themselves and accept a lower level of performance or social interaction than they are capable of, or may try to avoid further feelings of failure by withdrawing from the situation in which they feel their self-esteem to be threatened (see chapter 1, pp. 3–7).

Lawrence and Bennett (1992) point out that shy individuals may have particular problems when their performance is being assessed. In the traditional, essay-type examination or the written test, they may be able to perform as well as their peers, provided they can contain their feelings of possible failure. But 'oral work, abilities concerned with working in groups and effective self-presentation could place the shy individual in a disadvantaged position' (p. 261). While their findings were based on pupils aged 11 to 18, there would seem to be a strong possibility that they would also apply to a younger age group. They also add that 'shyness is a neglected and relatively unrecognised special need which handicaps the shy at crucial points and in important aspects of their educational careers' (p. 261).

Withdrawn children may be more easy to identify with some confidence than shy children. Their lack of participation is more marked and more pervasive and they may fail to respond appropriately as individuals and as members of groups. Where their response is particularly inappropriate, they may even be considered to have autistic tendencies.

Autism is a severe condition (see for example, chapter 2), which is unlikely to be encountered by teachers of children in the middle years of their ordinary schooling, as it could be expected that help will have been offered earlier in separate provision. Extremely withdrawn children, however, may show reluctance to make any kind of eye contact with other children or adults, may shrink from any form of physical contact and fail to form relationships. They may never initiate any dialogue and respond only briefly (if at all) to attempts to communicate with them. Some of these reactions could be seen as nearly autistic and are very likely to interfere with educational progress and emotional development. Even a highly intelligent child who 'lives in a world of his/her own' and does not seem to need the companionship of classmates may be missing opportunities for emotional and social development which could detract from his/her achievements in the future.

Two children, Margaret and Beth, can be looked at briefly. *Margaret* at 8 years of age was noticeably isolated from her peers and had been so for a number of years. She had a history of physical abuse, although that situation had been resolved. She seldom communicated with anyone and then only in a scarcely audible whisper. The school was well aware of the problem and of the fact that Margaret showed occasional outbursts of temper when she could be physically aggressive towards other children. It was extremely difficult for her teacher to know how far Margaret was responding to any programme of work and also whether or not she should push her towards lesson objectives. It is probably true to say that her teacher worried quite considerably about Margaret but did very little as a result of her concern in case matters were made worse rather than better.

Beth, slightly younger than Margaret, was in a special class for pupils with learning difficulties along with her older sister, *Anne*. Beth relied totally on Anne to communicate for her and only existed in Anne's shadow. The school, feeling that it might be in Beth's interests to be separated from Anne for some time, arranged her integration into an ordinary class for certain lessons. The experience revealed that Beth's learning difficulties were not as severe as had been thought. While she remained very silent, Beth showed that she could understand the content of ordinary class lessons and retain it over time. Further integration was planned. Anne, however, was not happy about the loss of her domination over her sister (who was now shown to be considerably brighter than she was) and their mother complained of growing tension between them at home.

Withdrawn children such as these are difficult to reach and, perhaps because this is so, teachers may offer them little by way of help although being by no means unaware of their problems (Laing and Chazan, 1987). Unlike shy children, who may want to join in but feel self-conscious about doing so, withdrawn children may prefer to stand aside from life in school or at home. They are, therefore, more difficult to help as, whatever strategies are used, their problem is not ineptness or faulty socialization but arises from their total personality and is very much part of their self-picture. Until they feel the need to change their view of themselves, as happened to Beth when her whole experience of school was altered, well-meaning intervention from adults may be ineffective.

Fear and Anxiety

'Fear' is the term generally used in referring to the response to specific stimuli perceived as threatening, while anxiety tends to indicate a less focussed state of distress or discomfort, a response to a subjective rather than an objective danger. However, a clear-cut distinction between fear and anxiety is not easy to maintain. Fear and anxiety should not be regarded only as distressing and harmful emotions: a certain amount of anxiety is necessary for survival and for taking precautions against dangers, as well as for producing positive action from individuals in some situations.

Shy children are often fearful children and withdrawn children may be highly anxious. It is, therefore, difficult to discuss the content of this section separately from the previous one. Childhood fears are common. Just as many very young children are shy when faced with unfamiliar situations, so they may be afraid of them. Their level of cognitive development may enable them to realize that there is potential danger in a new situation, while at the same time they may feel that they are unlikely to be able to control that situation. Such an explanation would account for the changes in the focus of children's fears as they grow and develop: what they at one time feared can be taken in their stride later on. Studying fear in American and Australian children aged 7 to 16 years, Ollendick *et al.* (1989) found five clusters of fears: fear of failure and criticism; fear of the unknown; fear of injury and small animals; fear of danger and death; and medical fears. A subsequent study by Ollendick *et al.* (1991) found British school children to be very similar in their reported fears, with girls reporting a higher level of fears than boys.

Perhaps because of the similarity of results from various studies like these, it has been argued that there is a strong genetic component in fear reactions. Where fears continue to be shown at age-inappropriate times or appear to be extreme (even if appropriate), a social/environmental component may well also be involved. Thus, many adults who report fears which they had when younger, such as of moths, birds or cats, can often point to the occasion which seemed to trigger off the fear. They frequently admit, too, that they retain at least a strong dislike of the 'trigger', even if they manage to control earlier panic reactions as they grow older. Presumably it is the 'learned' component in fears which can be modified through later experience.

Anxiety, like fear, reflects the individual's concern over his/her ability to exercise some form of control over impending events. It can be seen in very young children when they are uncertain where the focus of their attention — often the mother — is. If they experience this feeling of uncertainty frequently, either because of the principal care-giver's absence or because of rejection, they may well reflect their anxiety in their behaviour. They may have learned not only helplessness (Dweck and Repucci, 1973; Seligman, 1975) but also hopelessness. This may lead them to become listless, apathetic and depressed; to shut themselves away from contact with others as it has proved painful to them in the past; or to show aggression, physical or verbal, towards those around them. Like fear, anxiety is common in both children and adults. It is when it exists in an extreme form that emotional and behavioural difficulties accompany it. The individual then behaves in such a way as to avoid or minimize the impact of the situations which he she feels threatening.

Toby at 9 years of age still found reading and written work very difficult. He was a child in foster care who had a history of neglect at home. This had led to his being taken into care but he proved to be quite a problem to those concerned about him. His immediate reaction to new situations or those he distrusted was aggressive over-activity. He was restless, inattentive, unable to share or wait his turn, given to punching and kicking and would run away if rebuked. He was not unintelligent but fairly frequent changes of school and his unsettled behaviour when in class meant that his progress in the basic skills was poor, although he could cope well orally with money. Whenever reading or written work was called for, upheaval would ensue. Because he spent most of the time in which reading was involved either in confrontations with the teacher or in the headteacher's room, he very effectively hid the fact that the work set was beyond him. Because reading was involved more and more as he moved up the school, his behaviour was becoming increasingly difficult. It is true that there was much more to Toby's problems than his low reading ability but the anxiety this generated in him made matters very much worse.

Depression

Links have been shown to exist between fearfulness and anxiety, and between anxiety and depression (Ollendick *et al.*, 1991). These findings would imply that fearful individuals may at times be overly anxious but are no more prone to depression than anyone else. It is, therefore, appropriate to consider depression separately, bearing in mind, however, that anxiety and depression are related.

It is only fairly recently that depression has been recognized in children. It would appear to affect only a minority of children prior to adolescence, at which time the incidence of depression increases sharply, especially in girls, although currently there seem to be more young men showing depressive symptoms than previously. In childhood, depression may not be directly expressed, say in frequent weepiness, but may be revealed in 'depressed mood, reduced pleasure from activities, weight and sleep disturbance, psychomotor agitation or retardation, fatigue, feelings of worthlessness or guilt, impaired concentration or decision-making and thoughts relating to death' (Kennedy *et al.*, 1989, pp. 561–2). Perhaps, not surprisingly, interpersonal difficulties and low academic achievement are also to be found, both resulting from the depressive state and contributing to it.

Why some children become depressed while others who appear to suffer similar stresses do not, is not clear. It may be that there is 'an underlying vulnerability of a biological or psychological nature' (Gotlib and Hammen, 1992, p. 26). Depressive symptoms have also been linked to lower social status on the part of the family and to neglect or rejection within the family. Where mothers themselves are depressed, they may be negative or unresponsive towards their children. They may also feel unable to protect their children from ordinary life stresses or to help them to cope with these. For whatever reason, depressed children hold extremely negative views of themselves and others, anticipate failure and often experience it at school and at home. Where the condition is extreme, they will probably have to receive clinical help outside of school, with staff in school cooperating in a supportive role.

Factors Associated with Negative Affect

At Home

Negative emotional interactions which have been sustained over a number of years, especially the early, formative years, affect the self-picture which a child develops. Frequent maternal criticisms or maternal rejection have been shown to be related to persistent behavioural disturbance, depressive disorder in particular (Gotlib and Hammen, 1992). Parental mental health is, thus, all important. Children seem to be able to cope with occasional outbursts of irritability or criticism from adults but persistent hostility compounds other problems and seriously affects children's emotional development.

It must also be remembered that, in the early years, children model their behaviour on what they see in those who are caring for them. Their main focus of attention is on the home. If, therefore, they see at home shy, fearful or timid behaviour as the usual reaction to events, their behaviour is likely to reflect this. As their focus widens, say when they join a playgroup or enter school, the inhibited behaviour may remain typical for them, may then come to be expected of them and so be reinforced.

At School

If, as a result of parental criticism or hostility, a child forms a view of him/ herself as unlovable, incompetent and worthless, there must be a danger that such a view will extend to school performance. The importance of high self-esteem in academic achievement has long been established (Coopersmith, 1967). Low self-esteem, with all its implications for response to the educational programme, considerably lowers expectations, both the child's and the teacher's. It could be suggested that there are two occasions when lowered expectations are particularly damaging:

(i) *transfer and change*: When faced with a new situation which demands reorganization of interpersonal relationships, children with negative affect feel additional stress to that which is common at such a time. Entry to a new school or transfer to the secondary school is particularly hard for them. It may be that at the secondary stage, with frequent changes of teacher, they have more chance of meeting someone to whom they can relate. It is perhaps more likely that the secondary organization enables them to slip unnoticed through the school day or offers opportunities to absent themselves altogether;

(ii) *testing*: Again, it is commonplace for anxiety to be generated by testing. Buss (1986) distinguishes between 'fearful shyness' (generated by novelty, intrusion and social evaluation) and 'self-conscious shyness' (resulting from excessive socialization training when children

177

have been frequently criticized and admonished). Both forms of shyness may combine when children are being assessed. They not only feel they are being evaluated but they also feel that they cannot meet the demands of the situation. The amount of test anxiety generated, therefore, is considerable especially, as has been mentioned earlier in this chapter, if the assessment involves open comparison of individual performance with that of others. Sarason and Sarason (1986) point out that test anxiety generates high cognitive interference (i.e., time-wasting, compulsive behaviour; high levels of task-irrelevant thoughts; and self-preoccupation).

At Home and School

The distorting effect which negative views of the self have on performance in school is likely to affect all interpersonal relationships. Children who lack pro-social skills are not necessarily actively disliked; they may rather be overlooked or ignored as they do little to establish or maintain contact. But the lack of pro-social skills and of opportunities to develop them in interaction with other children and adults is an important factor in the persistence of negative affect and poor academic performance, as well as inadequate social response. Such children are not at ease either at home or in school, although they may cope fractionally better in one situation than in the other. When both home and school unite in criticism of a child's performance or behaviour, the effect may be to exacerbate the negative feelings rather than inculcate a more positive approach.

How Can these Children be Helped?

As children grow older, the focus of their uncertainties changes but their negative reactions to what they presently find they cannot cope with may remain and become even more entrenched. Studies of children (for example, Richman *et al.*, 1982) have shown a decline in the overt expression of fear between the ages of 3 and 8 years but an increase in anxiety. Those who were highly fearful remained so two years later, as Spence and McCathie found in their study of children between 8.5 and 10.5 years. There would seem, therefore, to be considerable grounds for arguing that teachers, however difficult they may find it, should attempt to help unforthcoming and underreacting pupils as far as they can towards a more positive adjustment.

Behaviour Management

To be afraid of strange or threatening situations is natural and, indeed, sensible. Children who show extreme reactions, however, may benefit from strategies aimed at modifying their behaviour so as to bring it nearer to the normal range. The principles and approaches of behaviour management are to be found in chapter 5 (pp. 80–1) and any of these can be adapted for use in cases of negative affect. Of particular interest is the 'desensitization' approach (Herbert, 1981), which tries to reduce the strength of the adverse emotions aroused.

There are two ways in which desensitization can be attempted. The first strategy is to bring the fearful or anxious individual into contact with whatever triggers off the extreme reaction, but only after ensuring that the trigger is minimally threatening. Thus, someone who is too afraid to go out of the house could be encouraged to look out of a window, then perhaps to go to the front door, to open it, to go to the front gate and then on to the street, all with support and encouragement over quite a long period of time. Defusing the threatening situation in this way takes time but it has to be remembered that the fear (or anxiety) may have been established over many years and a new way of behaving cannot necessarily be learned instantaneously.

The second technique involves linking the adverse trigger to something which the individual does not fear or even enjoys. The two are linked to begin with in a rather remote way (for example, by keeping the trigger at the other end of the room or outside the window) while the individual concerned is playing, eating or whatever. Gradually, the source of the problem is brought nearer and nearer. Particular care must be taken to plan this strategy very carefully and sensitively. Otherwise, the adverse reaction may become linked to the enjoyable event instead of the other way around, and another trigger for fear or anxiety be added rather than the original one being eliminated.

Social Skills Training

A description of social skills training has already been given in chapter 5. Where social ineptness is mainly the result of lack of knowledge or lack of experience of how interactions can be initiated and sustained, opportunities to discuss and practise appropriate strategies are likely to be beneficial. When such opportunities are provided in a non-threatening, supportive atmosphere, involving perhaps the whole class, children who have particular difficulties in this area can see that others are not without their problems and can experience possible solutions to these problems. As Stott (1966) pointed out many years ago, children showing inhibited behaviour may be defensive 'against anybody or anything strange, not against affection in general' (p. 154). Helping them to overcome their lack of responsiveness by giving them access to discussion, group work and carefully selected activities can be successful.

For some children, however, social skills training is not productive. These children may not be as proficient in pro-social skills as they could be, but their lack of proficiency arises from their preference not to be part of a group. They choose to be isolated rather than companionable. Self-sufficiency is an admirable trait provided it does not become self-centredness. Such children might, however, benefit from encouragement towards finding greater satisfaction in social interaction than they do at present. Teachers have to know their pupils well enough to be able to appreciate individual differences in the degree to which they need to be outgoing and to judge what are effective social interactions in each case. The same social skills training programme given to all class members with the expectation that all will achieve similar objectives is not realistic. Some children require considerable support to reach the objectives set while others may be perfectly happy with more modest objectives.

Yet other children may need more help than social skills training programmes can offer. Toby could not make satisfying relationships. His defensiveness and unresponsiveness towards those around him were more deep-seated than lack of knowledge as to how he should behave. Both he and Paul, whose case is discussed later in this chapter (pp. 186–7), are examples of children for whom social skills training would do no harm but who really require individual, possibly fairly lengthy, therapeutic help.

Interpersonal Approaches

The establishment of a good, working relationship between an individual child and an adult should prove helpful. However, it is often the case that the difficulties children experience in interpersonal relationships are not so evident in 'one-to-one' situations. Their problems really lie in making contact in groups, whether the family, the neighbours or the school class. Help may be more productive, therefore, if it involves experience of interacting with others.

Some children may require clinical help outside of school but for others support can be offered within the classroom. Sociometric techniques were described in chapter 2. The results from such investigations can be used constructively by teachers to form small groups in which shy, withdrawn or anxious children may be most likely to be successful participants. Care has to be taken to ensure that all those involved have been helped towards acquiring the social skills necessary for groups to work (see chapter 5, pp. 81–5). Nor is it enough just to arrange that no children will be left out of groupings. Teachers have to consider very carefully where to place children who are poor in pro-social skills and what their role in the group will be so that they can feel a sense of achievement. Depressed children are especially difficult to place as it is only too easy to expect little of them, both intellectually and socially.

Familiarity with working in groups helps underreacting children who are inhibited by new situations. Teachers have also to consider, however, how frequently the group membership should be changed. While it may be of no benefit to vulnerable children to keep them in a group when the experience is clearly not productive, changing group membership around too often may simply make matters worse. Perhaps the best solution is for teachers to use group work only when they are sure that more can be gained from this form of organization, including the acquisition and practice of interactive skills, than could be derived from class or individual work. The groups should always be structured and changed to maximize as far as possible the contribution of each member.

Enhancing Self-esteem

If, for whatever reason, children adopt a lowered view of their capabilities and characteristics, they are likely to find little satisfaction in living down to their depressed expectations. If others also expect little of them, a downward spiral of reduced achievement and increased hopelessness is initiated and self-esteem is damaged.

Sarason and Sarason (1986), writing about anxious children, suggest three strategies for enhancing self-esteem in children:

(i) *offer experience of social success*: Achieving a carefully selected objective in a group or class setting can begin to alter children's views of themselves and the views others have of them. If repeated, the enhancement of self-worth becomes more and more marked;

(ii) *increase children's belief in themselves*: At the primary stage, children are unsure of their abilities, physically, socially and cognitively. Erikson (see Maier, 1969) sees the years from 7–11 as the time when children acquire a sense of their own competence, indeed of their ability to succeed in comparison with their peers. Failure makes them feel inferior and this feeling in its turn adds to their anxiety or their withdrawal from situations in which they might again fail;

(iii) *teach interactive skills*: This strategy has already been discussed. Sarason and Sarason (1986) stress the importance of being able to attend to others; of maintaining appropriate eye contact; and of avoiding negative messages in the body language used.

They stress the importance of the teacher in reducing anxiety in children, pointing out that it is potentially harmful to some children when too much emphasis is placed on achieving high standards of work in the classroom. 'In the case of the anxious child, we feel that the teacher's response to an inadequate performance must avoid reinforcing the attitude that failure and being personally liked and accepted are in any way related' (p. 273). This point of view should not be taken to mean that work of a poor standard should simply be accepted. The argument is that there is more to interpersonal relationships than academic achievement, important though that is. If children can feel secure, valued for the contribution each can make and challenged by work which has been carefully chosen for them, they are much more likely to cooperate in the learning process than if they are nagged, belittled or ignored.

Cognitive-behavioural Counselling

According to Trower *et al.* (1988), an individual's emotional outlook and his/her behaviour are determined by how she/he thinks. They propound an ABC model where A is the activating event, B indicates the beliefs which the individual holds about this event, and C is the consequence of this thinking about the event. If the individual's thinking is negative or unrealistic, the consequent reactions, whether emotional or behavioural, are likely to indicate upset. Altering the negative or unrealistic thinking will change B and hence C.

The counselling offered does not need to be only an encouragement to talk the problem out. In fact, Trower *et al.* stress the behavioural aspect of their suggested therapy. They see practical tasks as being the catalyst for changing self-defeating beliefs. These tasks can cover a wide spectrum, not just those connected with the particular aspect of learning being undertaken at the time. They could involve out-of-class activities which are suitable to the children's age and abilities. Whatever is chosen must be capable of successful completion by the children who are being helped.

It is sometimes difficult for the teacher to be sure that the task chosen is both sufficiently challenging and capable of successful completion. A simple example can illustrate the difficulty. Suppose children are asked to collect four different kinds of leaves in the autumn. What is success in such a task? Finding the leaves? Bringing them to school? Displaying them on the wall? What message is received by children who only find three different kinds and these the same as everyone else's? What about those who forget to bring them in or whose mother threw them away because she thought they were rubbish? What is the reaction of those who hang back and whose leaves are not displayed? Teachers who use practical tasks as the basis for changing negative thinking have themselves to think very carefully about all the implications of the task set and make sure that all of those involved can achieve an outcome they can be satisfied with. An emphasis on positive thinking, however, is always a useful one to maintain.

Encouraging Cooperative Play

It is very unfortunate if children's experiences outside of the classroom act against teachers' efforts to improve social development in class. It is to be hoped that the interpersonal skills encouraged within classrooms will transfer to the playground so that any enhanced status will be reinforced by socially successful experiences not organized by adults. Rubin and Pepler (1980) stress the importance of play at all stages to social and cognitive development. They argue that it is in play that children acquire perspective-taking skills (for example, realizing that others see things differently; seeing situations from the other person's point of view).

For children in the middle years of schooling, teacher participation in play cannot be implemented in the way that such a partnership is possible with younger children. It may be possible, however, for the teacher to:

(i)   observe unobtrusively what is happening to certain children in the playground;

(ii)   build on a tentative friendship established in the classroom by suggesting a cooperative activity outside;

(iii)   demonstrate to other children that the isolated child has useful skills so that they accept him/her more readily in other settings.

While these approaches to the problem of solitariness may work for shy, anxious or fearful children, those who are withdrawn or depressed may have no inclination at all to be with others and, indeed, may find being in the playground quite difficult to take. One suggestion which could be made in these cases is that teachers could look at the total situation in school and consider whether certain rules, for example, not being in the classroom or the library except at specific times, could be adjusted to accommodate children with interpersonal difficulties. It may be that they will in time and with encouragement come to establish relationships with another child who also prefers to be out of the clamour of the playground, or begin to take on responsibilities inside the school building which might give them status in the eyes of the rest of the class. The ultimate aim must be that they join in playground activities to some extent but the way to that aim has to be carefully considered by the whole staff.

Negative feelings towards school or home or both do not always result in inhibited behaviour in school of the kind which has been discussed so far. Fearful and anxious children may, of course, absent themselves from school, especially when lessons they dread are known to be timetabled or when they believe that other children will bully them or when they are terrified or resentful of a teacher. Some children, however, refuse to go to school when there is no immediately obvious reason for such a reaction. Paul was one of these and his case will be discussed after a review of the condition itself.

School Refusal

School absenteeism, whatever its cause, almost inevitably has adverse long-term effects on academic progress and social development. Teachers and educational psychologists, therefore, are right to be concerned about pupils whose refusal to go to school is associated with severe emotional upset. School refusal of this kind occurs relatively infrequently, but is a complex problem which can be differentiated in several respects from truancy (see chapter 2), even if both terms are used to refer to a wide range of individuals in a variety of situations. Children considered to fall into the category of 'school refusers' rather than that of 'truants' do not attempt to hide their absence from school from their parents, but stay at home; show signs of severe emotional disturbance, often of a phobic nature; cannot bring themselves to go to school in spite of persuasion or threats; and act on an individual basis rather than in collaboration with other children (Hersov, 1977; Kahn *et al.*, 1981).

School refusal may be part of a more widespread emotional disorder such as depression, or may be associated with a general withdrawal from the outside world perhaps resulting from schizophrenia, rather than being directly related to the school situation (Rutter, 1975). In this section, the discussion will focus on children with a phobia of school who do not seem to be depressed or psychotic. School phobia effects boys and girls equally and may occur at any stage of schooling, though major peaks have been found at the ages of 5–6, 11–12 and 13–14 years (Blagg, 1987).

Symptoms of School Phobia

Typically, the child suffering from school phobia shows signs of extreme anxiety or panic when the time for going to school comes, or when going to school is discussed at home; is unable to leave home; and may complain of stomach pains or other ailments, or actually vomit. Very often, once the pressure to attend school is removed, the emotional and physical symptoms disappear (Hersov, 1977). In most cases, the child is well-behaved at home and school, and not in any way delinquent.

Causative Factors

It is important to assess the factors underlying the problem as comprehensively as possible, and normally an educational psychologist and a child psychiatrist are called in. Because of the wide range of individuals and contexts involved, it is often difficult to ascertain with any certainty the specific factors which are contributing to a case of school phobia. Some clinicians stress separation anxiety as a frequent cause, where an immature and dependent child is afraid to leave home and mother, who is herself usually overprotective (Stafford-Clark and Smith, 1983). Other family situations which have been considered as possibly relating to school phobia include the loss of a loved relative; marital disharmony; or particular patterns of relationships in the home, such as an overindulgent mother and a passive father (Hersov, 1977).

Sometimes, the fear of school appears to be irrational and inappropriate, for example, when the child is well-adjusted at school, making good progress and with no complaints about school. However, underlying the child's fears, if not completely explaining them, there may be evidence of a dislike of certain teachers, experience of being bullied, or anxiety about failure in some aspects of school work (Galloway, 1985a; Blagg, 1987). As the child may be reluctant to talk about school, and as fears about school may be imaginary as well as real, diagnosing the problem is fraught with difficulties. Further, the factor which seems to trigger off the phobia (the precipitating factor), such as a reprimand in class or a bout of illness, may serve to distract attention from predisposing factors such as family tensions or unsatisfactory peer relationships at school.

Treatment

A variety of strategies have been employed in the treatment of school phobia, depending partly on the theoretical orientation of the professionals involved in the intervention and partly on the nature of the case. In some instances, the emphasis is put on improving relationships within the family, through psychotherapy or counselling, prior to attempting a return to school; in others, the focus is on an immediate or gradual return to school, helped by the use of behaviour modification techniques such as desensitization (see p. 179). Admission to hospital is a possibility in cases proving resistant to treatment, though this removes the child further from normal home and school life. Kahn *et al.* (1981) stress the need for a multidisciplinary approach, with attention given to the child, family and school (see also Hersov and Berg, 1980).

The Rapid Treatment Approach to school phobia, described by Blagg and Yule (1984), illustrates how a combination of strategies, based on a flexible behaviourist approach, can be used in solving the problem of school phobia. These strategies, coordinated by an educational psychologist, include,

(i)   establishing good relationships with the child, family and school;
(ii) attempting to clarify the real or imagined events that have caused anxiety;
(iii) desensitizing the child, and if necessary the parents and teachers, through a variety of techniques including discussion, humour, role-playing and emotive imagery;
(iv) confronting the feared situations through forced school attendance;
(v)   dealing with home and school-related factors through appropriate advice based on behaviour modification principles; and
(vi) negotiating any areas of change required with the school and family.

Actually persuading the child to return to school may not be easily achieved, and much support will be needed. A suitable escort may be required in the early stages, and in some cases the child may be willing to attend a different mainstream school, a special school or special unit, but not his/her usual school. A carefully graded return to school may be helpful, for example first going as far as the school gates, then spending a short time in the headteacher's room, and later going part-time into the classroom before a full return proves possible. It seems important to keep the child in a school-like atmosphere whenever feasible, rather than allow him/her to remain in isolation at home for a lengthy period, even if home-teaching is provided. However, objections have been voiced to any element of compulsion in returning the child to school (Knox, 1990).

Outcome

The outcome for school phobics in the 7–11+ age range is usually good, provided that the problem is dealt with at an early stage and that treatment is not hampered by long-term or complex difficulties in the family (Galloway, 1985a). Even though successes have been reported in the case of older children, school phobia arising in secondary schools tends to be less easy to treat than at the primary stage, and the outcome is more variable (Blagg, 1987). Prolonged absence from school may well have serious implications for adjustment in adult life.

Illustrative Case Study

The following case study will help to illustrate many of the points made above.

Paul, an only child, was just over 11 years of age, in his last year at primary school, when he refused to go to school. Over the preceding months, he had become increasingly reluctant to attend, saying that he felt unwell and often being sick when he got up. He showed signs of extreme anxiety whenever school was mentioned. Both parents were very concerned and spent time trying to discover a medical reason for Paul's condition. The school did not report any problem with him when he was there. Paul had attended the same, fairly small, country primary school since he was 5 years old, and was making good progress. There had been no significant changes of staff recently.

Paul was quite a large boy for his age, and somewhat plump. While not very outgoing or talkative, he appeared to fit in at school and had friends in the playground. At home, because of where he lived, he was rather isolated from other children of his own age, but did meet them occasionally at weekends. His parents appeared to get along reasonably well.

When no medical explanation for Paul's problems could be found, the school insisted that an educational psychologist be involved. Initially, this move met with resistance: the parents did not want the intervention and Paul was uncooperative, being reluctant to say anything. However, the situation gradually improved, and both the boy and his parents began to open up. It transpired that the apparently problem-free picture of relationships at home and school concealed a number of difficulties that may well have contributed to Paul's anxiety state. At home, there was tension between the parents, following an incident when the father had become involved with another woman. The mother tended to be somewhat domineering and overprotective, and was clinging more to the boy now that the marriage was in some jeopardy. The father was rather passive, inclined to be cooperative, but not challenging his wife in her initial resistance to help from a psychologist for Paul. At school, Paul had recently experienced some bullying and teasing in class, particularly on account of his weight.

Treatment strategies included (i) keeping Paul occupied with work sent from school, which was conscientiously completed; (ii) helping Paul to return to school in carefully planned stages; (iii) discussing with Paul, the parents and the school ways of dealing with the bullying and teasing at school; (iv) attempting to improve Paul's social adjustment through group play therapy at the local Child Guidance Centre; and (v) helping the parents towards better relationships with one another and with Paul.

Everyone concerned cooperated well with the intervention programme, and over time the outcome was reasonably successful. Paul returned full-time to his school after some weeks, and later made a satisfactory transition to secondary school. The educational psychologist continued to give support to the boy, the primary and secondary schools which he attended, and the family over a considerable period.

Overview

Individuals who are prone to depression construe the world negatively; have an inadequate self-image; believe others hold adverse views of them; lack responsiveness to others; feel unable to attain desired goals; and cope badly (Gotlib and Hammen, 1992). While varying in the degree to which these feelings and beliefs are experienced, children who are shy, fearful, anxious and withdrawn are also liable to display in their behaviour that they, too, suffer similar reactions to demands made upon them.

Teachers, therefore, cannot afford to neglect children who appear inhibited in social interactions. Because they seldom draw attention to themselves in class, it does not mean that they are content there or that they are achieving what they are capable of. As pointed out by Ollendick *et al.* (1991), although many childhood fears and anxieties may be transitory, highly fearful and anxious children may have persistent negative feelings about themselves and do need help and support. Teaching approaches and activities which promote successful social interaction and enhance children's self-esteem could be useful for all class members and especially for those with negative affect. Examples of practical programmes in personal and social education can be found in Hollin and Trower, 1986; McNiff, 1986; and Ryder and Campbell, 1988. Many of their suggested approaches can be incorporated in the normal school programme as the personal and social skills they are intended to develop are often part of the content of the National Curriculum as well as enabling its objectives to be achieved effectively.

Chapter 12

Conclusion

Throughout this book, the reader will have found that each chapter ends with an overview. The purpose of this final chapter is not, therefore, to draw together what has already been written but rather to comment on some of the main points which arise out of the previous chapters. Five points have been selected for this purpose:

1   the effectiveness of identifying pupils as having EBDs;
2   the implications of the National Curriculum for these pupils and vice versa;
3   the dilemma facing schools with regard to pupils with EBDs;
4   the dilemma facing parents with regard to children with EBDs;
5   the possible effects of recent legislative changes.

What's In a Name?

To identify and label a category almost inevitably implies that there is a common understanding of at least the essentials of the objects or conditions so named. If no consensus exists, then discussion of the concept makes little progress with regard to any action to be taken. How far is the label 'emotional and behavioural difficulties' meaningful and/or useful?

Teachers say they know which of their pupils cause concern over behaviour. However, there is a range of behaviour in this category which is so wide as to make it difficult for different raters (parents or teachers, for example) to agree on whether or not any individual has emotional or behavioural difficulties. Does being awkward or unforthcoming in class or at home justify the label? How awkward does the child have to be? or how unforthcoming? Judgments begin to be relative and situation-specific. Howard (1992) says that the EBD label '. . . is subjective not objective, relative not immutable, as concerned with classroom management and the curriculum as with problems with the pupil or his/her background' (p. 392).

Would it help teachers if the label were changed? Sutton (1993), for example, proposes three categories of difficulties: central, peripheral and functional. Central difficulties imply an underlying, neurological malfunctioning which may range from mild to profound. Peripheral difficulties involve physiological, developmental problems, again varying in degree, which interact with any social problems which exist. In children with functional difficulties, the physiological mechanisms are intact but there is failure to learn or to progress. Examples of functional difficulties would be 'glue ear' (i.e., temporary hearing loss which makes it difficult for children to grasp the early stages of reading); lack of support for learning in the home; inability to concentrate which has no physiological basis. Emotional and behavioural difficulties, however, could be placed in all three categories (see chapter 3).

Nevertheless, although there may be no firm agreement among the adults concerned as to what constitutes emotional and behavioural difficulties, the use of that label does allow discussion to take place, 'whole school' policies to be set up and individual programmes planned. Careful observation and recording of incidents enable constructive action to be taken and these helping strategies are more important than precision in the label.

In respect of offering help, Halliwell and Williams (1993) describe a useful approach to identification and assessment called 'Pathways'. This could be implemented in middle childhood in any situation which causes teachers concern. The three steps they advocate entail obtaining a full picture of any difficulty; working out a plan of action in collaboration with the child and the parents; and reviewing the plan and its possible revision or extension. 'Parents, pupils and staff are involved early on as equals in the actions within Pathways' (p. 181). Good record-keeping enables decisions to be taken, and action to be planned and reviewed. Children are not specifically labelled but rather the pressures which they are under at home or in school are identified, the effect of their behaviour on their development is noted and a cooperative way forward is attempted. The help offered becomes the important consideration rather than the label attached.

The National Curriculum

The intentions of the National Curriculum are admirable. The aims of balance, breadth, relevance and progression which it strives to attain can only be of benefit to all pupils and their teachers. The major worries which teachers have about it centre on the accompanying legislative framework. They feel that their professional freedom has been curtailed because of pressures on them for their pupils to reach certain levels in specific areas, the levels attained then being used for interschool comparison and competition. Making changes to the content of the Curriculum may not, therefore, address the teachers' worries if they still feel that judgments are being made on the assumption that all pupils respond in a uniform way to any educational programme.

Blyth (1984) points out that, national planning notwithstanding, each individual learner constructs his/her own version of the curriculum, differing from that of the other pupils in the same class on the twin bases of performance and of engagement. These two could perhaps be combined into the notion of 'what children get out of any educational experience'. Thus, there are those who perform well despite emotional difficulties or low personal involvement: there are those who are willing and involved but whose performance is disappointing; and there are those who see little of relevance in what they are doing but who perform adequately. There are as many individual variations in performance and in engagement as there are pupils and to ignore this fact is unhelpful.

Some pupils with EBDs may spend little time interacting with the National Curriculum. Their own concerns dominate their reactions and they may, therefore, deliberately or inadvertently, pose a threat to the teacher. Lessons are not seen as going well when some class members make little progress. Ignoring the difficulties in behaviour or development which these pupils have exacerbates the situation and may lead to the breakdown of the programme by absorbing too much of the teacher's time and energy and disrupting the learning of other pupils. If the National Curriculum cannot be considered apart from the legislative framework in which it is embedded, then some pupils with EBDs are often not being helped to develop through it and may become a source of additional stress to an already pressured teacher. Of course, it should be remembered that not all pupils with EBDs make little educational progress; some do well in their school work and others may find relief in academic challenges.

The content demands of the National Curriculum are considerable for teachers and pupils. Is there sufficient time left for opportunities to be provided for personal and social education? Earlier in this book, it was suggested that activities aimed at extending social skills would help many pupils in middle childhood, not only those with difficulties in interpersonal behaviour and relationships. It is possible to incorporate these activities in the teaching of core or foundation subjects but teachers may not always be willing to devote to them the time that they undoubtedly take. The same could be said for the construction and implementation of any individualized, differentiated programme.

The review of the National Curriculum carried out by Sir Ron Dearing (SCAA, 1994) offers possibilities for overcoming some curricular difficulties once its recommendations are implemented. The proposed reduction of both content and national assessment should give more opportunities for teachers to differentiate their programme. Systems of moderated teacher assessment are to be developed to maintain national standards without being too time-consuming. Easing pressures on teachers in these ways are intended to increase their teaching time and so children benefit. The broadening of the NC levels ought to help in particular those with any form of learning difficulties, as work at an appropriate level can now be more easily arranged, with parental cooperation being sought when curricular objectives specific to a particular pupil are set.

The question still remains as to whether behavioural change and emotional development can be fully provided for in mainstream schools today, with dwindling teacher support and school resources. It would be unfortunate for all concerned if teachers were to find themselves unable, because of bureaucratic or financial constraints, to build on their current interest in, and concern for, pupils with EBDs, especially in the middle years of schooling. Efforts to help can be particularly productive in those years.

The School's Dilemma

Handing over financial control to each individual school is quite a good idea in theory. In practice, for primary schools which are often fairly small in numbers, it has led in some cases to economies in the very areas of support which could benefit pupils with EBDs and their teachers. As has been noted earlier, some local authorities continue to provide behavioural support teams and point to the benefits these produce. In other authorities, the support and advisory services have been reduced and their purpose changed to administration or monitoring instead of actually working in the classroom with children in need.

Newton (1992) discusses the ways in which giving financial control to individual schools has altered requests for support from outside. Schools are now:

(i)   concentrating on statemented children whose needs have to be met, and pupils with EBDs are seldom statemented at the moment;

(ii)   abandoning differentiation as too time-consuming for class teachers; and

(iii)   favouring withdrawal of pupils whose progress is out of step with the majority of the class members.

While not perhaps so marked as at the secondary stage, these changes are beginning to be seen at the primary stage as well. Furthermore, if schools have to pay for additional support, they may well feel (or even be encouraged to feel) that they have a right to say what form the support should take. Integration in mainstream classes may simply prove to be unattainable financially, however inappropriate such a yardstick may be. Again, there may not be enough money to pay for a teacher to run a separate special class and the pupils may be placed in the mainstream with no extra within-school support. This is indeed a dilemma.

Is the answer curriculum exception or even exclusion of pupils whose behaviour causes teachers concern? It is ironic that both of these are effective. As pointed out earlier in this book, both relieve the teacher of the focus of his or her concern. They may also offer some financial advantage (see chapters 8 and 9). Excepting pupils from part of the curriculum is, however, only a short-term solution in most instances and may eventually create more difficulties for the teacher than it alleviates, as indeed does exclusion. The pressure is on schools, therefore, to contain their pupils, for example by publishing exclusion and truancy rates; by transferring the pupils' share of funding to home tuition services; and by reducing the school's ability to refuse to accept any pupil on to the roll. Here is another dilemma for the school as the pressure applied by parents or the local authorities for a child to be admitted may in turn provide the reasons for his/her exclusion.

It is probably true to say that the effect of recent changes in the expectations which government and the general public have of schools has often been detrimental to pupils with special educational needs. It may even be the case that pupils with EBDs will be most adversely affected as they are not always recognized as having special needs and some do not have learning difficulties. Only a 'whole school' policy covering behaviour, discipline and exclusions, as well as continuing goodwill on the part of school staff, may be able to counteract negative trends and offer positive ways out of some of the dilemmas which schools face.

The Parents' Dilemma

It is only too easy to say that there are now recognized to be three parties in any educational partnership — school staff and governors, parents and the pupils themselves. In an ideal situation, all would be pulling together and contributing equally. The reality is often different, especially when emotional and behavioural difficulties are the cause for concern. When these are extreme, teachers may feel blocked in their endeavours; parents may not see what they can do about classroom behaviour; and children may find little of relevance or support either at school or at home. Even in relatively minor instances of behavioural or emotional difficulties, the balance hoped for between all three parties can be upset. When this happens, it is often the parents who come off worst as:

(i)   they are non-professionals and thereby likely to be 'disempowered' in discussions with professionals;

(ii) they are seen as having ultimate responsibility for their children and, therefore, open to blame when things go wrong;

(iii) for a whole variety of reasons, they may not be as effective as they might be in their parenting role.

They are faced, therefore, with not one dilemma but many. They are under pressure to cooperate with teachers and other professionals but often do not fully understand what they are supposed to be doing or actually incapable of implementing any programme. If they are concerned about their child's school experience, they may find staff unable to find the time to discuss this with them as fully as they would like when they go to school; if they do not go to school, they may be thought of as uninterested or lacking in cooperation.

If they tackle their child about the situation he/she may complain about being nagged or 'picked on'; if they say nothing, their child may think they do not care enough to bother about what he/she does. It may be not so much a partnership as a minefield.

Before a partnership can even begin to be envisaged, informal non-judgmental contacts need to be established with professionals. Parents have to feel that the professionals involved will listen to them and try to understand what lies behind what they are saying. Parents need to be helped, if necessary, to communicate and to know their rights and responsibilities. The dangers inherent in failing to achieve real contact are well demonstrated by Armstrong and Galloway (1992) in their descriptions of how the parents viewed the assessment process in the cases of three boys with EBDs. No-one was really satisfied with the outcome and it is questionable how far the boys were helped. The main problem seemed to be that the parents felt the professionals had made up their minds about each case before the parents' point of view (or, indeed, the child's) had been considered properly.

Various local authorities, including Avon (Broomhead and Darley, 1992), have developed schemes to inform and support parents and these are undoubtedly helpful. There is still concern, however, that some of the very parents who most need such information and support may not be reached by the schemes any more than they are reached by school-based initiatives, such as parents' evenings or open sessions. Because of the nature of their child's problem, whether it takes the form of externalized or internalized behaviour difficulty, these parents may be reluctant to become involved in situations which they see as basically hostile to their current practice. Not all parents of pupils with EBDs fall into this category, of course, but some do. The way forward would appear to be to reiterate the importance of good, close relationships between school and home, built up from the earliest years in school and sustained in the middle years of schooling as vital to success.

Recent Legislative Changes

Recent trends in legislation with regard to special educational needs in the UK have emphasized mainstream responsibilities and parental involvement. Thus, the 1993 Education Act (DFE, 1993a), which contains a whole section on special needs, widens statutory regulations to include mainstream pupils who need help but who do not have any official 'statement' of their needs. Schools now have to document their policy for helping these children and parents should be aware of this policy. Procedures for obtaining help should be known to teachers, parents and children. Does a policy of this kind, which should benefit those with EBDs, overcome the worries expressed in previous sections of this chapter? Obviously, only time will tell but it has to be said that the production and availability of any document does not necessarily mean its full implementation in every case. Pupils, parents and teachers may still fail to obtain the support they need.

When children are identified and assessed as in need of help — and the steps to be taken in such identification and assessment are now clearly spelt out (Draft Code of Practice, DFE/WO, 1993) — then help should be readily and fairly rapidly offered. There are financial implications here and if these are not met in the school's budget, any help provided may well not be adequate. There are also responsibilities on other agencies, such as social services departments, area health authorities and school psychological services. Again, the query has to be raised as to their ability to fulfil what is expected of them within the time limits set and the money available.

On the whole, recent legislation and associated government guidelines do not often specifically consider pupils with EBDs, except when dealing with exclusions. When they do, they make a number of interesting points some of which are general and some specific to behavioural and emotional problems.

(i)   Schools have to consider how to support the parents of pupils with special needs, presumably including EBDs.

(ii)   Pupils should be involved as far as possible in their own assessment.

(iii) Requests for help from outside agencies should be backed up by evidence of the nature of the problem accumulated over time and giving 'clear, recorded examples' of the behaviour which is causing concern.

(iv)   The definition of what constitutes cause for concern is wider than that often given now. It includes depression, eating disorders and 'difficulties in establishing and maintaining balanced relationships with his or her fellow pupils or with adults' (Draft Code of Practice, DFE/WO, 1993, III, 44).

(v)   Preventative and supportive action on the part of schools is emphasized with the underlying cause of the difficulties being seen as 'a significant delay in the development of life and social skills' (*ibid*). This is still, of course, a relative, subjective judgment.

Parents now have two further rights which they can exercise if they feel that their child is in difficulty and the school is unwilling to offer additional support. In the first instance, they can change the child's school by arranging a preferred placement if there is room in the school of their choice. In the second place, they can ask for a 'statement' of their child's needs to be drawn up. Provided such a request is reasonable and backed up by evidence of its appropriateness, the statement has to be completed within specified time limits. The parents themselves must be involved at all stages, including decisions as to school placement. If a school is named in a statement, the child must be admitted if at all possible. Additionally, parents have the right of appeal against any part of a statement which seems to them to misrepresent their child's case.

Taken in conjunction with the Children Act, 1989, both the 1993 Education Act and the Code of Practice, 1994, tighten up considerably procedures for offering help to those identified as in need of it and their parents. Much of the guesswork is removed so that schools have reasonably clear guidance on how to find out which children need help, what help can be given and by whom. Education 'otherwise than at school' is also considered with proposals for the setting up of Pupil Referral Units for those excluded for any length of time from school.

It will never be possible to legislate for each specific case. Loopholes will remain and may be exploited. For example, schools may have to admit certain pupils with EBDs but that does not necessarily mean that they will be successful with them. Exclusion rates could rise; special classes could be formed, with possible detrimental effects from being labelled as such; parents may continue to feel unwelcome or pressurized into decisions they do not wish or do not understand; pupils may not be articulate about their views; relationships between pupils or between pupils and staff members may remain unhappy. Above all, if the legislation is not backed up with the financial resources necessary to bring it into reality fully and easily, it may fare no better than that which it replaces.

What has been said may appear to be unduly negative. The concerns of recent legislation and other directives were intended to be positive. Giving substance to the curriculum provided; offering clear directions as to how learning and behaviour difficulties can be identified, assessed and helped; involving parents in their child's school; and increasing their responsibilities in the running of the school through representation on the governing body are all progressive intentions. But can the opportunities be fully grasped?

Legislation is one way forward from the 'pedagogic poverty of provision' (Sutton, 1993) which is often the fate of pupils with emotional and behavioural difficulties. Another way is to become more informed about the nature of these difficulties, their causation and their treatment. It would also help to know more about how many pupils are likely to be involved at different ages and how far they can be successfully helped.

Existing research shows what can be done and highlights considerable areas where more work is required (Chazan, 1993). O'Shea and O'Shea (1989) point in particular to the need for research into how effective remedial programmes are for those with EBDs, which pupils can be helped by them and how teachers can be supported to carry out these programmes (or other preventative measures) in the mainstream. Teachers sometimes feel that research has an 'ivory tower' location; tackling emotional and behavioural difficulties effectively could not be more practical.

Discussion of emotional and behavioural difficulties is often bedevilled by the conscious or unconscious assumptions which are made about many aspects of them. All who come into contact with pupils with EBDs should be aware of the need for:

(i)   an open mind but not an empty one. Current understanding of the causation of EBDs and how they can best be alleviated may not be complete but it does provide possible guidelines for action;

(ii) cooperation. School staff, parents, other professionals and pupils —
especially the pupils presenting the difficulties — need to be genuinely involved if any help is to be effective;

(iii) a concerted approach to any difficulties within the school itself. The
whole school has to know about the agreed policy on behaviour
and discipline, as do the parents. To work properly, a school policy
cannot be imposed in an arbitrary fashion. It must be agreed by all
parties to the contract and carried out with consideration and care.

The acquisition by pupils in the middle years of schooling of social and
life skills must be one of the main aims of their education and is essential for
their future development. The long-term effects of doing nothing about
emotional and behavioural difficulties are, therefore, considerable. So, too,
are the benefits from resolving these difficulties.

References

ACHENBACH, T.M. and EDELBROCK, C.S. (1983) *Manual for the Child Behaviour Checklist and Revised Behaviour Profile*, Burlington, VT: University of Vermont Department of Psychiatry.

ACHENBACH, T.M. and EDELBROCK, C.S. (1986) *Manual for the Teacher's Report Form and Teacher Version of the Child Behaviour Profile*, Burlington, VT: University of Vermont Department of Psychiatry.

ACHENBACH, T.M., McCONAUGHY, S.H. and HOWELL, C.T. (1987) 'Child/adolescent behavioural/emotional problems: Implication of cross-informant correlations for situational specificity', *Psychological Bulletin*, 101, 2, pp. 213–32.

ACHENBACH, T.M., VERHULST, F.C., BARON, G.D. and ALTHAUS, M. (1987) 'A comparison of syndromes derived from the Child Behaviour Checklist for American and Dutch boys aged 6–11 and 12–16', *Journal of Child Psychology and Psychiatry*, 28, 3, pp. 437–53.

ACKLAW, J. (1991) 'An educational psychologist's response to the Education Reform Act', *Newsletter of Association for Child Psychology and Psychiatry*, 13, 6, pp. 3–9.

ADVISORY CENTRE FOR EDUCATION (ACE) (1992a) 'Exclusions', *ACE Bulletin*, 45, pp. 4–5.

ADVISORY CENTRE FOR EDUCATION (ACE) (1992b) 'Exclusions', *ACE Bulletin*, 47, pp. 4–5.

AHMAD, Y. and SMITH, P.K. (1990) 'Behavioural measures: Bullying in schools', *Newsletter of the Association for Child Psychology and Psychiatry*, 12, 4, pp. 26–7.

AHMAD, Y., WHITNEY, I. and SMITH, P.K. (1991) 'A survey service for schools on bully/victim problems', in SMITH, P.K. and THOMPSON, D. (Eds) *Practical Approaches to Bullying*, London: Fulton.

AINSCOW, M. (Ed.) (1991) *Effective Schools for All*, London: David Fulton.

ALEXANDER, R. (1992) *Policy and Practice in Primary Education*, London: Routledge.

ALGOZZINE, B., MAHEADY, L., SACCA, K.C., O'SHEA, L. and O'SHEA, D. (1990) 'Sometimes patent medicine works: A reply to Braaten, Kauffman, Braaten, Polsgrove and Nelson', *Exceptional Children*, 56, 6, pp. 552–7.

ANDERSON, E.M. (1973) *The Disabled Schoolchild: A Study of Integration in Primary Schools*, London: Methuen.

ARMSTRONG, D. and GALLOWAY, D. (1992) 'On being a client: Conflicting perspectives on assessment' in BOOTH, T., SWANN, W., MASTERTON, M. and POTTS, P. (Eds) *Policies for Diversity in Education*, London: Routledge and the Open University.

ARONSON, E., BLANEY, N., STEPHAN, C., SIKES, J. and SNAPP, M. (1978) *The Jig-saw Classroom*, London: Sage.

ARORA, C.M.J. and THOMPSON, D.A. (1987) 'Defining bullying for a secondary school', *Education and Child Psychology*, 4, 3/4 pp. 110–20.

ARORA, T. (1991) 'The use of victim support groups' in SMITH, P.K. and THOMPSON, D. (Eds) *Practical Approaches to Bullying*, London: David Fulton.

ASENDORPF, J.B. (1986) 'Shyness in middle and late childhood' in JONES, W.H., CHEEK, J.M. and BRIGGS, S.R. (Eds) *Shyness: Perspectives on Research and Treatment*, New York: Plenum Press.

ASENDORPF, J.B. (1990) 'Beyond social withdrawal: Shyness, unsociability and peer avoidance', *Human Development*, 33, pp. 250–9.

ASHER, S.R., PARKHURST, J.T., HYMEL, S. and WILLIAMS, G.A. (1990) 'Peer rejection and loneliness in children' in ASHER, S.R. and COIE, J.D. (Eds) *Peer Rejection in Childhood*, New York: Cambridge University Press.

ASHLEY, J. (1987) 'The beginnings of outreach work and behavioural support in Oldham', *Maladjustment and Therapeutic Education*, 5, 3, pp. 30–4.

ASHTON, P. (1981) 'Primary teachers' approaches to personal and social behaviour' in SIMON, B. and WILLCOCKS, J. (Eds) *Research and Practice in the Primary Classroom*, London: Routledge and Kegan Paul.

ASHTON, P., KNEEN, P., DAVIES, F. and HOLLEY, B.J. (1975) *The Aims of Primary Education: A Study of Teachers' Opinions*, London: Macmillan for the Schools Council.

ATKIN, J., BASTIANI, J. and GOODE, J. (1988) *Listening to Parents*, London: Croom Helm.

AUDIT COMMISSION/HMI (1992) *Getting in on the Act: Provision for Pupils with Special Education Needs — The National Picture*, London: HMSO.

AUERBACH, J.G. and LERNER, J.G. (1991) 'Syndromes derived from the child behaviour checklist for clinically referred Israeli boys aged 6–11: A research note', *Journal of Child Psychology and Psychiatry*, 32, 6, pp. 1017–24.

BADGER, B. (1985) 'Behavioural surveys — some cautionary notes', *Maladjustment and Therapeutic Education*, 3, 2, pp. 4–11.

BADGER, B. (1992) 'Changing a disruptive school' in REYNOLDS, D. and CUTTANCE, P. (Eds) *School Effectiveness*, London: Cassell.

BAKER, C., DAVIES, N. and STALLARD, T. (1985) 'Prevalence of behaviour problems in primary school children in North Wales', *British Journal of Special Education*, 12, 1, pp. 19–26.

BALE, P. (1981) 'Behaviour problems and their relationship to reading difficulty', *Journal of Research in Reading*, 4, 2, pp. 123–35.

BARKER, P. (1986) *Basic Family Therapy*, 2nd edn, London: Collins.

BARNES, D. and TODD, F. (1977) *Communication and Learning in Small Groups*, London: Routledge and Kegan Paul.

BARNSLEY SPECIAL EDUCATION TEAM (1981) 'A team approach to disruption', *Special Education/Forward Trends*, 8, 1, pp. 8–10.

BARTLETT, D. and PEACEY, N. (1992) 'Assessments and issues for 1992', *British Journal of Special Education*, 19, 3, pp. 94–7.

BARTON, L. and SMITH, M. (1989) 'Equality, rights and primary education' in ROAF, C. and BINES, H. (Eds) *Needs, Rights and Opportunities*, London: Falmer Press.

BASINI, A. (1981) 'Urban schools and "disruptive" pupils: A study of some ILEA support units', *Educational Review*, 33, 3, pp. 191–207.

BENNETT, N. and CASS, A. (1989) *From Special to Ordinary Schools*, London: Cassell.

BENNETT, P.L. (1992) 'An introduction to the Children Act 1989', *Educational Psychology in Practice*, 7, 4, pp. 202–6.

BESAG, V.E. (1989) *Bullies and Victims in Schools*, Milton Keynes: Open University Press.

BIOTT, C. (1987) 'Co-operative group work: Pupils' and teachers' membership and participation', *Curriculum*, 8, 2, pp. 5–14.

BIRD, C., CHESSUM, R., FURLONG, J. and JOHNSON, D. (1980) *Disaffected Pupils*, London: Brunel University, Educational Studies Unit.

BLACK, D. (1992) 'Working with children of dying parents' in KAPLAN, C. (Ed.) *Bereaved Children*, Occasional Paper No. 7, London: Association for Child Psychology and Psychiatry.

BLAGG, N.R. (1987) *School Phobia and its Treatment*, London: Croom Helm.

BLAGG, N.R. and YULE, W. (1984) 'The behavioural treatment of school refusal: A comparative study', *Behaviour Research and Therapy*, 22, pp. 119–27.

BLANZ, B., SCHMIDT, M.H. and ESSER, G. (1991) 'Familial adversities and child psychiatric disorders', *Journal of Child Psychology and Psychiatry*, 32, 6, pp. 939–50.

BLATCHFORD, P. (1993) 'Bullying in the playground' in TATTUM, D. (Ed.) *Understanding and Managing Bullying*, London: Heinemann.

BLOOM, B.S. (1971) 'Mastery learning' in BLOCK, J.H. (Ed.) *Mastery Learning*, New York: Holt, Rinehart and Winston.

BLYTH, W.A.L. (1984) *Development, Experience and Curriculum in Primary Education*, London: Croom Helm.

BOIVIN, M. and BEIGIN, G. (1989) 'Peer status and self-perception among early elementary school children: The case of rejected children' *Child Development*, 60, 3, pp. 591–6.

BOOTH, T., POTTS, P. and SWANN, W. (1986) *Preventing Difficulties in Learning*, Oxford: Basil Blackwell.

BORG, M.G. and FALZON, J.M. (1990) 'Teachers' perceptions of primary schoolchildren's undesirable behaviours: The effects of teaching experience, pupil's age, sex and ability stream', *British Journal of Educational Psychology*, 60, 2, pp. 220–6.

BOULTON, M.J. and UNDERWOOD, K. (1992) 'Bully/victim problems among middle school children', *British Journal of Educational Psychology*, 62, 1, pp. 73–87.

BOWERS, T. (1984) *Management and the Special School*, London: Croom Helm.

BOWERS, T. (Ed.) (1987) *Special Educational Needs and Human Resource Management*, London: Croom Helm.

BOYLE, M.H. and JONES, S.C. (1985) 'Selecting measures of emotional and behavioural disorders for use in general populations', *Journal of Child Psychology and Psychiatry*, 26, 1, pp. 137–60.

BRAATEN, S., KAUFFMAN, J.M., BRAATEN, B., POLSGROVE, L. and NELSON, C.M. (1988) 'The Regular Education Initiative: Patent medicine for behavioural disorders', *Exceptional Children*, 55, 1, pp. 21–7.

BRIER, J. and AHMAD, Y. (1991) 'Developing a school court as a means of addressing bullying in schools' in SMITH, P.K. and THOMPSON, D. (Eds) *Practical Approaches to Bullying*, London: David Fulton.

BROOKS, R.B. (1984) 'Success and failure in middle childhood: An interactionist perspective' in LEVINE, M.D. and SATZ, P. (Eds) *Middle Childhood: Development and Dysfunction*, Baltimore, MD: University Park Press.

BROOMHEAD, R. and DARLEY, P. (1992) 'Supportive parents for special children: Working towards partnership in Avon' in BOOTH, T., SWANN. W., MASTERTON, M. and POTTS, P. (Eds) *Policies for Diversity in Education*, London: Routledge and the Open University Press.

BROWN, A.L. and DeLOACHE, J.S. (1983) 'Metacognitive skills' in DONALDSON, M., GRIEVE, R. and PRATT, C. (Eds) *Early Childhood Development and Education*, Oxford: Basil Blackwell.

BULL, S.L. and SOLITY, J.E. (1987) *Classroom Management: Principles to Practice*, London: Croom Helm.

BURDEN, R. and HORNBY, T.A. (1989) 'Assessing classroom ethos: Some recent promising developments for the systems oriented educational psychologist', *Educational Psychology in Practice*, 5, 1, pp. 17–22.

BURN, M. (1964) *Mr. Lyward's Answer*, London: Hamish Hamilton.

BURNS, R. (1982) *Self-concept Development and Education*, Eastbourne: Holt, Rinehart and Winston.

BUROS, O.K. (Ed.) (1965) *Sixth Mental Measurements Yearbook*, Highland Park, NJ: Gryphon Press.

BUSS, A.H. (1986) 'A theory of shyness' in JONES, W.H., CHEEK, J.M. and BRIGGS, S.R. (Eds) *Shyness: Perspectives on Research and Treatment*, New York: Plenum Press.

BYNNER, J.M. (1972) *Parents' Attitudes to Education*, London: HMSO.

CALDERHEAD, J. (1984) *Teachers' Classroom Decision Making*, London: Holt, Rinehart and Winston.

CALLIAS, M. and RICKETT, J. (1986) 'School and clinic work together', *British Journal of Special Education*, 13, 3, pp. 97–101.

CAMPION, J. (1985) *The Child in Context: Family-systems Theory in Educational Psychology*, London: Methuen.

CAREY, W.S. and MCDEVITT, S.C. (1989) *Clinical and Educational Applications of Temperament Research*, Amsterdam/Lisse: Swets and Zeitlinger.

CARPENTER, J. and TREACHER, A. (1989) *Marital and Family Therapy*, Oxford: Basil Blackwell.

CARROLL, H.C.M. (Ed.) (1977) *Absenteeism in South Wales: Studies of Pupils, Their Homes and Their Secondary Schools*, Faculty of Education, University College of Swansea.

CARTLEDGE, G. and MILBURN, J.F. (Eds) (1980) *Teaching Social Skills to Children*, New York: Pergamon.

CHASTY, H. and FRIEL, J. (1991) *Children with Special Needs: Assessment, Law and Practice — Caught in the Act*, London: Jessica Kingsley.

CHAZAN, M. (1970) 'Maladjusted children' in MITTLER, P. (Ed.) *The Psychological Assessment of Mental and Physical Handicaps*, London: Methuen.

CHAZAN, M. (1985) 'Behavioural aspects of educational difficulties' in DUANE, D.D. and LEONG, C.K. (Eds) *Understanding Learning Disabilities: International and Multidisciplinary Views*, New York: Plenum Press.

CHAZAN, M. (1989) 'Bullying in the infant school' in TATTUM, D.P. and LANE, D.A. (Eds) *Bullying in Schools*, Stoke-on-Trent: Trentham Books.

CHAZAN, M. (1993) 'Integration of students with emotional and behavioural difficulties', *European Journal of Special Needs Education*, 8, 3, pp. 269–88.

CHAZAN, M., COX, T., JACKSON, S. and LAING, A.F. (1977) *Studies of Infant School Children, Vol. 2: Deprivation and Development*, Oxford: Basil Blackwell (for Schools Council).

CHAZAN, M., LAING, A.F. and JACKSON, S. (1971) *Just Before School*, Oxford: Basil Blackwell for the Schools Council.

CHAZAN, M., LAING, A.F., JONES, J., HARPER, G.C. and BOLTON, J. (1983) *Helping Young Children with Behaviour Difficulties*, London: Croom Helm.

CLARK, M.M. (1988) *Children Under Five: Educational Research and Evidence*, New York: Gordon and Breach.

CLARKE, A.D.B. and CLARKE, A.M. (1984) 'Constancy and change in the growth of human characteristics', *Journal of Child Psychology and Psychiatry*, 29, 2, pp. 191–210.

CLARKE, M. (1990) *The Disruptive Child*, Plymouth: Northcote House.

COHEN, L. (1976) *Educational Research in Classrooms and Schools*, London: Harper and Row.

COIE, J.D. and DODGE, K.A. (1983) 'Continuities and changes in children's social status: A five-year longitudinal study', *Merrill-Palmer Quarterly*, 29, pp. 261–82.

COIE, J.D., DODGE, K.A. and KUPERSMIDT, J.B. (1990) 'Peer group behaviour and social status', in ASHER, S.R. and COIE, J.D. (Eds) *Peer Rejection in Childhood*, Cambridge: Cambridge University Press, pp. 17–59.

COLLINS, W.A. (1984) *Development During Middle Childhood: The Years from Six to Twelve*, Washington: National Academy Press.

CONNERS, C.K. (1973) 'Rating scales for use in drug studies in children', *Psychopharmacology Bulletin* (special issue) on *Pharmacotherapy of Children*.

CONNOR, M.J. (1991) 'Diet and performance in children', *Educational Psychology in Practice*, 7, 3, pp. 131–9.

COOLING, M. (1974) Educational Provisions for Maladjusted Children in Boarding Schools, MEd. thesis, University of Birmingham.

COOPER, P. (1989) 'Emotional and behaviour difficulties in the real world: A strategy for helping junior school teachers cope with behaviour problems', *Maladjustment and Therapeutic Education*, 7, 3, pp. 178–84.

COOPERSMITH, S. (1967) *The Antecedents of Self-esteem*, San Francisco, CA: W.H. Freeman & Co.

COPELAND, I., AYLES, R., MASON, H. and POSTLETHWAITE, K. (1993) 'LEA support for SEN pupils: Two years on from the 1990 SENNAC survey', *Support for Learning*, 8, 2, pp. 43–9.

COUGHLAN, S. (1994) 'Remote control on violence', *Times Educational Supplement*, 15 April 1994, Section 2, p. 25.

COX, T. (1978) 'Children's adjustment to school over six years', *Journal of Child Psychology and Psychiatry*, 19, 4, pp. 363–71.

CRABTREE, T. (1981) *An A-Z of Children's Emotional Problems*, London: Hamish Hamilton/Elm Tree Books.

CRAIG, I. (Ed.) (1990) *Managing the Primary Classroom* (2nd edn), Harlow: Longman.

CROLL, P. and MOSES, D. (1985) *One in Five: The Assessment and Incidence of Special Educational Needs*, London: Routledge and Kegan Paul.

CROSS, J. and GODDARD, S. (1988) 'Social skills training in the ordinary school setting', *Educational Psychology in Practice*, 4, 1, pp. 24–8.

CULLINGFORD, C. (1984a) *Children and Television*, Aldershot: Gower.

CULLINGFORD, C. (1984b) 'The battle for schools: Attitudes of parents and teachers towards education', *Educational Studies*, 10, pp. 113–9.

CURTIS, A. and HILL, S. (1978) *My World: A Handbook of Ideas*, Windsor: NFER/Nelson.

CYSTER, R., CLIFT, P.S. and BATTLE, S. (1979) *Parental Involvement in Primary Schools*, Windsor: NFER.

DAVIE, R., BUTLER, N. and GOLDSTEIN, H. (1972) *From Birth to Seven*, London: Longman.

DAVIES, J.D. and DAVIES, P. (1989) *A Teacher's Guide to Support Services*, Windsor: NFER-Nelson.

DAVIES, J.D. and LANDMAN, M. (1991) 'The National Curriculum in special schools for pupils with emotional and behavioural difficulties: A national survey', *Maladjustment and Therapeutic Education*, 9, 3, pp. 130–5.

DAVIES, L. (1984) *Pupil Power: Deviance and Gender in School*, Lewes: Falmer Press.

DAWSON, R.L. (1980) *Special Provision for Disturbed Pupils: A Survey*, London: Macmillan.

DAWSON, R.L. (1982) 'What concerns teachers about their pupils?', *Journal of Association of Educational Psychologists*, 8, 1, pp. 37–40.

DELAMONT, S. (1980) *Sex Roles and the School*, London: Methuen.

DEN BOER, K. (1990) 'Special education in the Netherlands', *European Journal of Special Needs Education*, 5, 2, pp. 136–49.

DEONNA, T. (1993) 'Cognitive and behavioural correlates of epileptic activity in children', *Journal of Child Psychology and Psychiatry*, 34, 5, pp. 611–20.

DEPARTMENT FOR EDUCATION (1992a) *Special Education Needs: Access to the System*, London: DFE.

DEPARTMENT FOR EDUCATION (1992b) *Exclusions: A Discussion Document*, London: HMSO.

DEPARTMENT FOR EDUCATION (1992c) *Reports on Individual Pupils' Achievements (Circular No. 14/92)*, London: DFE.

DEPARTMENT FOR EDUCATION (1993a) *Education Act 1993*, London: HMSO.

DEPARTMENT FOR EDUCATION (1993b) *'Pupils with Problems' (Draft Circular 1): Pupil Behaviour and Discipline*, London: DFE.

DEPARTMENT FOR EDUCATION (1993c) *'Pupils with Problems' (Draft Circular 2): The Education of Children with Emotional and Behavioural Difficulties*, London: DFE.

DEPARTMENT FOR EDUCATION/WELSH OFFICE (1993) *Education Act 1993: Draft Code of Practice on the Identification and Assessment of Special Educational Needs — Draft Regulations on Assessments and Statements*, London: DFE/WO.

DEPARTMENT OF EDUCATION AND SCIENCE (1967) *Children and their Primary Schools* (the Plowden Report), London: HMSO.

DEPARTMENT OF EDUCATION AND SCIENCE (1968) *Psychologists in Education Services* (the Summerfield Report), London: HMSO.

DEPARTMENT OF EDUCATION AND SCIENCE (1977) *A New Partnership for Our Schools* (the Taylor Report), London: HMSO.

DEPARTMENT OF EDUCATION AND SCIENCE (1978) *Special Educational Needs* (the Warnock Report), London: HMSO.

DEPARTMENT OF EDUCATION AND SCIENCE (1981) *Education Act 1981*, London: HMSO.

DEPARTMENT OF EDUCATION AND SCIENCE (1985) *Education for All* (the Swann Report), London: HMSO.

DEPARTMENT OF EDUCATION AND SCIENCE (1988) *Education Reform Act 1988*, London: HMSO.

DEPARTMENT OF EDUCATION AND SCIENCE (1989) *Special Schools for Pupils with Emotional and Behavioural Difficulties (Circular No. 23/89)*, London: HMSO.

DEPARTMENT OF EDUCATION AND SCIENCE/DEPARTMENT OF HEALTH (1989) *Assessments and Statements of Special Educational Needs: Procedures within the Education, Health and Social Services (Circular 22/89)*, London: HMSO.

DEPARTMENT OF EDUCATION AND SCIENCE/DEPARTMENT OF HEALTH AND SOCIAL SECURITY/WELSH OFFICE (1974) *Child Guidance (Circular 3/74)*, London: HMSO.

DEPARTMENT OF EDUCATION AND SCIENCE/WELSH OFFICE (1989) *Discipline in Schools: Report of the Committee of Inquiry (the Elton Report)*, London: HMSO.

DEPARTMENT OF HEALTH (1990) *An Introduction to the Children Act 1989*, London: HMSO.

DEPARTMENT OF HEALTH AND SOCIAL SECURITY (DHSS) (1976) *Fit for the Future (the Court Report)*, London: HMSO.

DOCKING, J.W. (1987) 'The effects and effectiveness of punishment in schools' in COHEN, L. and COHEN, A. (Eds) *Disruptive Behaviour: A Source Book for Teachers*, London: Harper.

DOCKING, J.W. (1989) 'Elton's four questions: Some general considerations' in JONES, N. (Ed.) *School Management and Pupil Behaviour*, London: Falmer Press.

DOCKING, J.W. (1990a) *Managing Behaviour in the Primary School*, London: David Fulton.

DOCKING, J.W. (1990b) *Primary Schools and Parents*, London: Hodder and Stoughton.

DODGE, K.A. (1986) 'A social information processing model of social competence in children' in PERLMUTTER, M. (Ed.) *Minnesota Symposia on Child Psychology* (Vol. 18), Hillsdale, NJ: Erlbaum.

DODGE, K.A., PETTIT, G.S., McCLASKEY, C.L. and BROWN, M.M. (1986) *Social Competence in Children, Monographs of the Society for Research in Child Development*, 51, 2.

DOWLING, E. and OSBORNE, E. (1985) *The Family and the School*, London: Routledge and Kegan Paul.

DOYLE, P. (1988) 'On the road back', *Special Children*, 21, pp. 10–11.

DREW, D. (1990) 'From tutorial unit to schools' support service', *Support for Learning*, 5, 1, pp. 13–21.

DUNHAM, J. (1986) 'Helping with stress' in MARLAND, M. (Ed.) *School Management Skills*, Oxford: Heinemann Educational.

DUNN, J. (1980) 'Individual differences in temperament' in RUTTER, M. (Ed.) *Scientific Foundations of Developmental Psychiatry*, London: Heinemann Medical.

DUNN, J. and McGUIRE, S. (1992) 'Sibling and peer relationships in childhood', *Journal of Child Psychology and Psychiatry*, 33, 1, pp. 67–105.

DWECK, C.S. and REPUCCI, N.D. (1973) 'Learned helplessness and reinforcement responsibility in children', *Journal of Personality and Social Psychology*, 25, 1, pp. 109–16.

DYGDON, J.A. and CONGER, J.A. (1990) 'A direct nomination method for the identification of neglected members in children's peer groups', *Journal of Abnormal Child Psychology*, 18, 1, pp. 55–74.

EDWARDS, V. and REDFERN, A. (1988) *At Home in School*, London: Routledge.

EISER, C. (1990) 'Psychological effects of chronic disease', *Journal of Child Psychology and Psychiatry*, 31, 1, pp. 85–98.

ELLIOTT, K. and CARTER, M. (1992) 'The development of the East Devon behaviour support team', *Support for Learning*, 7, 1, pp. 19–24.

ELLIOTT, M. (1986) *Kidscape Training Pack: For Use with Primary Children*, London: Kidscape.

ELLIOTT, M. (1991) *Bullying: A Practical Guide to Coping for Schools*, London: Longman.

ERAUT, M. (1989) 'Review of research on in-service education: A U.K. perspective' in WILSON, J. (Ed.) *The Effectiveness of In-Service Education and Training of Teachers and School Leaders*, Amsterdam: Swets and Zeitlinger for The Northern Ireland Council for Educational Research.

ERIKSON, E. (1950) *Childhood and Society*, New York: Norton.

EVANS, R.I. (1969) *Dialogue with Erik Erikson*, New York: E.P. Dutton.

FARRELL, M. and STRANG, J. (1991) 'Substance use and misuse in childhood and adolescence', *Journal of Child Psychology and Psychiatry*, 32, 1, pp. 109–28.

FARRINGTON, D.P. (1980) 'Truancy, delinquency, the home and the school' in HERSOV, L. and BERG, I. (Eds) *Out of School*, Chichester: John Wiley.

FARRINGTON, D.P. (1993) 'Understanding and preventing bullying' in TONRY, M. and MORRIS, N. (Eds) *Crime and Justice, No. 17*, Chicago, IL: University of Chicago Press.

FARRINGTON, D.P., GALLEGHER, B., MORLEY, L., ST. LEDGER, R.J. and WEST, D.J. (1988) 'Are there any successful men from criminogenic backgrounds?', *Psychiatry*, 51, 2, pp. 116–30.

FEINGOLD, B.F. (1975a) 'Adverse reactions to food additives with special reference to hyperkinesis and learning difficulty (H-LD)' in STEELE, F. and BOURNE, A. (Eds) *The Man-Food Equation*, London: Academic Press.

FEINGOLD, B.F. (1975b) 'Hyperkinesis and learning disabilities linked to artificial food flavors and colors', *American Journal of Nursing*, 75, pp. 797–803.

FELDMAN, L. and MITCHELS, B. (1990) *The Children Act 1989 — A Practical Guide*, London: Longman.

FERGUSSON, D.M., HORWOOD, L.J. and LAWTON, J.M. (1990) 'Vulnerability to childhood problems and family social background', *Journal of Child Psychology and Psychiatry*, 31, 7, pp. 1145–60.

FERGUSSON, D.M., HORWOOD, L.J. and LYNSKEY, M.T. (1993) 'The effects of conduct disorder and attention deficit in middle childhood on offending and scholastic ability at age 13', *Journal of Child Psychology and Psychiatry*, 34, 6, pp. 899–916.

FISH, J. (1984) 'The future of the special school' in BOWERS, T. (Ed.) *Management and the Special School*, London: Croom Helm.

FISHBEIN, H.D. (1984) *The Psychology of Infancy and Childhood: Evolutionary and Cross-cultural Perspectives*, Hillsdale, NJ: Lawrence Erlbaum.

FITTON, J.B. (1972) 'Use of the Rutter behaviour scales', *Journal of Association of Educational Psychologists*, 3, pp. 45–7.

FOGELMAN, K. (1978) 'School attendance, attainment and behaviour', *British Journal of Educational Psychology*, 48, 2, pp. 148–58.

FOGELMAN, K. (1992) 'The long term effects of truancy', *Association for Child Psychology and Psychiatry Newsletter*, 14, 2, pp. 57–61.

FONTANA, D. (1985) *Classroom Control*, London: British Psychological Society and Methuen.

FONTANA, D. (1990) *Social Skills at Work*, London: British Psychological Society and Routledge.

FONTANA, D. (1994) *Managing Classroom Behaviour*, Leicester: British Psychological Society.

FOSTER, P., ARORA, T. and THOMPSON, D. (1990) 'A whole-school approach to bullying', *Pastoral Care in Education*, 8, 3, pp. 13–17.

FOULKES, S.H. and ANTHONY, E.J. (1965) *Group Psychotherapy* (2nd edition), Harmondsworth: Penguin Books.

FRANCIS, D. and TURKINGTON, D. (1992) 'Balancing the Act', *Special Children*, 53, pp. 23–8.

FREDERICKSON, N. and SIMMS, J. (1990) 'Teaching social skills to children: Towards an integrated approach', *Educational and Child Psychology*, 7, 1, pp. 5–17.

FREDERICKSON, N., WEBSTER, A. and WRIGHT, A. (1991) 'Psychological assessment: A change of emphasis', *Educational Psychology in Practice*, 7, 1, pp. 20–9.

FRITH, U. (1989) *Autism: Explaining the Enigma*, Oxford: Basil Blackwell.

FRUDE, N. (1989) 'Sexual abuse: An overview' in LINDSEY, G. and PEAKE, A. (Eds) 'Child sexual abuse', *Educational and Child Psychology*, 6, 1, pp. 34–41.

FRUDE, N. (1990) 'Perspectives on disruptive behaviour' in SCHERER, M., GERSCH, I. and FRY, L. (Eds) *Meeting Disruptive Behaviour: Assessment, Intervention and Partnership*, London: Macmillan.

FRUDE, N. and GAULT, H. (1984) 'Children's disruption at school: Cause for concern?' in FRUDE, N. and GAULT, H. (Eds) *Disruptive Behaviour in Schools*, Chichester: John Wiley.

FURLONG, V.J. (1985) *The Deviant Pupil*, Milton Keynes: Open University Press.

GALLOWAY, D. (1985a) *Schools and Persistent Absentees*, Oxford: Pergamon.

GALLOWAY, D. (1985b) *Schools, Pupils and Special Educational Needs*, London: Croom Helm.

GALLOWAY, D. (1987) 'Disruptive behaviour in school: Implications for teachers and other professionals', *Educational and Child Psychology*, 4, 1, pp. 29–34.

GALLOWAY, D., BALL, T., BLOMFIELD, D. and SEYD, R. (1982) *Schools and Disruptive Pupils*, London: Longman.

GALLOWAY, D. and GOODWIN, C. (1987) *The Education of Disturbing Children*, London: Longman.

GALTON, M. and BLYTH, A. (1989) *Handbook of Primary Education in Europe*, London: David Fulton/Council of Europe.

GALTON, M. and SIMON, B. (Eds) (1980) *Progress and Performance in the Primary Classroom*, London: Routledge and Kegan Paul.

GALTON, M. and WILLIAMSON, J. (1992) *Group Work in the Primary Classroom*, London: Routledge.

GALVIN, P., MERCER, S. and COSTA, P. (1990) *Building a Better Behaved School: A Development Manual for Primary Schools*, London: Longman.

GALVIN, P. and SINGLETON, R. (1984) *Behaviour Problems: A System of Management*, Windsor: NFER/Nelson.

GARNER, P. (1993) 'Exclusions: The challenge to schools', *Support for Learning*, 8, 3, pp. 99–103.

GERSCH, I. (1990a) 'Behavioural systems projects in junior and secondary schools' in SCHERER, M., GERSCH, I. and FRY, L. (Eds) *Meeting Disruptive Behaviour: Assessment, Intervention and Partnership*, London: Macmillan.

GERSCH, I. (1990b) 'The pupil's view' in SCHERER, M., GERSCH, I. and FRY, L. (Eds) *Meeting Disruptive Behaviour: Assessment, Intervention and Partnership*, London: Macmillan.

GILLHAM, B. (Ed.) (1981) *Problem Behaviour in the Secondary School*, London: Croom Helm.

GILLHAM, B. (1984) 'School organization and the control of disruptive incidents' in FRUDE, N. and GAULT, H. (Eds) *Disruptive Behaviour in Schools*, Chichester: John Wiley.

GIPPS, C., GROSS, H. and GOLDSTEIN, H. (1987) *Warnock's Eighteen Per Cent*, London: Falmer Press.

GOACHER, B., EVANS, J., WELTON, J. and WEDELL, K. (1988) *Policy and Provision for Special Educational Needs: Implementing the 1981 Education Act*, London: Cassell.

GODDARD, S. and CROSS, J. (1987) 'A social skills training approach to dealing with disruptive behaviour in a primary school', *Maladjustment and Therapeutic Education*, 5, 3, pp. 24–9.

GOODYER, I. (1993) 'Depression among pupils at school', *British Journal of Special Education*, 20, 2, pp. 51–4.

GOTLIB, I.H. and HAMMEN, C.L. (1992) *Psychological Aspects of Depression*, Chichester: John Wiley and Sons.

GOW, L. (1988) 'Integration in Australia', *European Journal of Special Needs*, 3, 1, pp. 1–12.

GRAHAM, P. (1987) 'Hyperactivity and diet', *Nutrition and Food Science*, April, 2–5.

GRAHAM, P. and RUTTER, M. (1973) 'Psychiatric disorder in the young adolescent: A follow-up study', *Proceedings of Royal Society of Medicine*, 66, 1, pp. 58–61.

GRAY, J. and RICHER, J. (1988) *Classroom Responses to Disruptive Behaviour*, London: Macmillan.

GREENFIELD, P.M. (1984) *Mind and Media: The Effects of Television, Computers and Video Games*, Aylesbury: Fontana.

GREGORY, P. (1992) 'Why Louise?', *Special Children*, 53, pp. 27–8.

GRIFFITHS, A. and HAMILTON, D. (1987) *Learning At Home*, London: Methuen.

GROSS, R.T. (1984) 'Patterns of maturation: Their effects on behaviour and development' in LEVINE, M.D. and SATZ, P. (Eds) *Middle Childhood: Development and Dysfunction*, Baltimore, MD: University Park Press.

GUTEK, G.L. (1988) *Education and Schooling in America*, Englewood Cliffs, NJ: Prentice-Hall.

HACKNEY, A. (1985) 'Integration from special to ordinary schools in Oxford-shire', *Education and Child Psychology*, 2, 3, pp. 88–95.

HAIGH, G. (1990) *Managing Classroom Problems in the Primary School*, London: Paul Chapman.

HALLIWELL, M. and WILLIAMS, T. (1993) 'Towards an interactive system of assessment' in WOLFENDALE, S. (Ed.) *Assessing Special Educational Needs*, London: Cassell.

HANDY, C. and AITKEN, R. (1986) *Understanding Schools as Organizations*, Harmondsworth: Penguin Books.

HANKO, G. (1990) *Special Needs in Ordinary Classrooms: Supporting Teachers*, Oxford: Basil Blackwell.

HARRIS, P.L. (1989) *Children and Emotion: The Development of Psychological Understanding*, Oxford: Basil Blackwell.

HARRIS, J., TYRE, C. and WILKINSON, C. (1993) 'Using the child behaviour checklist in ordinary pimary school', *British Journal of Educational Psychology*, 63, 2, pp. 245–60.

HARTUP, W.W. (1983) 'Peer relations' in MUSSEN, P.H. (Ed.) *Handbook of Child Psychology (Vol. IV): Socialization, Personality and Social Development*, New York: John Wiley, pp. 103–196.

HARTUP, W.W. (1992) 'Friendships and their developmental significance' in McGURK, H. (Ed.) *Childhood Social Development: Contemporary Perspectives*, Hove: Lawrence Erlbaum Association.

HAVIGHURST, R.J. (1972) *Development Tasks and Education* (3rd edn), New York: David McKay.

HEGARTY, S., POCKLINGTON, K. and LUCAS, D. (1982) *Integration in Action*, Windsor: NFER/Nelson.

HERBERT, M. (1974) *Emotional Problems of Development in Children*, London: Academic Press.

HERBERT, M. (1981) *Behavioural Treatment of Problem Children: A Practice Manual*, London: Academic Press.

HERBERT, M. (1986) 'Social skills training with children' in HOLLIN, C.R. and TROWER, P. (Eds) *Handbook of Social Skills Training Vol. 1: Applications Across the Life Span*, Oxford: Pergamon.

HER MAJESTY'S INSPECTORATE (HMI, 1989a) *A Survey of Support Services for Special Educational Needs*, London: DES.

HER MAJESTY'S INSPECTORATE (HMI, 1989b) *A Survey of Provision for Pupils with Emotional/Behavioural Difficulties in Maintained Special Schools and Units*, London: HMSO.

HER MAJESTY'S INSPECTORATE (HMI, 1990a) *Educational Psychology Services in England*, London: DES.

HER MAJESTY'S INSPECTORATE (HMI, 1990b) *Special Needs Issues*, London: HMSO.

HERSOV, L. (1960) 'Persistent non-attendance at school/refusal to go to school', *Journal of Child Psychology and Psychiatry*, 1, pp. 130–6.

HERSOV, L. (1977) 'School Refusal' in RUTTER, M. and HERSOV, L. (Eds) *Child Psychiatry: Modern Approaches*, Oxford: Blackwell.

HERSOV, L. and BERG, I. (Eds) (1980) *Out of School: Modern Perspectives in Truancy and School Refusal*, Chichester: Wiley.

HETHERINGTON, E.M. (1991) 'Coping with family transitions: Winners, losers and survivors' in WOODHEAD, M., LIGHT, P. and CARR, R. (Eds) *Growing up in a Changing Society*, London: Routledge and the Open University Press.

HEWETT, F.M. and TAYLOR, F.D. (1980) *The Emotionally Disturbed Child in the Classroom: The Orchestration of Success* (2nd edn) Boston, MA: Allyn and Bacon.

HIBBETT, A. and FOGELMAN, K. (1990) 'Future lives of truants: Family formation and health-related behaviour', *British Journal of Educational Psychology*, 60, 2, pp. 171–9.

HIBBETT, A., FOGELMAN, K. and MANOR, O. (1990) 'Occupational outcomes of truancy', *British Journal of Educational Psychology*, 60, 1, pp. 23–36.

HIMMELWEIT, H., OPPENHEIM, A.N. and VINCE, P. (1958) *On Television and the Child*, London: Oxford University Press.

HODGE, R. and TRIPP, D. (1986) *Children and Television: A Semiotic Approach*, Cambridge: Polity Press, with Basil Blackwell (Oxford).

HOLLIN, C.R. and TROWER, P. (1986) *Handbook of Social Skills Training, Vol. 1: Applications Across the Life Span*, Oxford: Pergamon Press.

HORBURY, A. (1990) 'Procedural rules in the management of pupils in the primary school' in WEBB, R. (Ed.) *Practitioner Research in the Primary School*, London: Falmer Press.

HOULTON, D. (1986) *Cultural Diversity in the Primary School*, London: Batsford.

HOWARD, P. (1992) 'Challenging behaviour support' in BOOTH, T., SWANN, W., MASTERTON, M. and POTTS, P. (Eds) *Policies for Diversity in Education*, London: Routledge in association with the Open University Press.

HOWE, M. (1977) *Television and Children*, London: New University Education.

HOWITT, D. (1982) *Man, Media and Social Problems*, Oxford: Pergamon.

HUMPHREYS, K. and STURT, E. (1993) 'Challenging times for teachers', *British Journal of Special Education*, 20, 3, pp. 97–9.

IMICH, A. and ROBERTS, A. (1990) 'Promoting positive behaviour: An evaluation of a behaviour support project', *Educational Psychology in Practice*, 5, 4, pp. 201–9.

JOHNSON, D. (1991) 'Parents, students and teachers: A three-way relationship', *International Journal of Educational Research*, 15, 2, pp. 171–81.

JOHNSON, G., HILL, B. and TUNSTALL, P. (1992) *Primary Records of Achievement*, London: Hodder and Stoughton.

JONES, M.C. (1983) *Behaviour Problems in Handicapped Children*, London: Souvenir Press.

JONES, N. (Ed.) (1989) *School Management and Pupil Behaviour*, Lewes: Falmer Press.

JOWETT, S. (1989) 'Links between special and ordinary schools — A study of their prevalence and purpose', *European Journal of Special Needs Education*, 4, 1, pp. 23–4.

JOWETT, S. and BAGINSKY, M. with MACNEIL, M.M. (1991) *Building Bridges: Parental Involvement in Schools*, Windsor: NFER-Nelson.

KAHN, J.H., NURSTEN, J.P. and CARROLL, H.C.M. (1981) *Unwillingly to School: School Phobia or School Refusal — A Psycho-social Problem*, Oxford: Pergamon.

KAUFFMAN, J.M., LLOYD, J.W. and McGEE, K.A. (1989) 'Adaptive and maladaptive behaviour: Teachers' attitudes and their technical assistance needs', *Journal of Learning Disabilities*, 21, 1, pp. 19–22.

KENNEDY, E., SPENCE, S.H. and HENSLEY, R. (1989) 'An examination of the relationship between childhood depression and social competence amongst primary school children', *Journal of Child Psychology and Psychiatry*, 30, pp. 561–73.

KITZINGER, S. and KITZINGER, C. (1989) *Talking with Children about Things that Matter*, London: Pandora.

KNOX, P. (1990) *Troubled Children: A fresh look at School Phobia* (2nd edn), Upton-upon-Severn, Worcs: Self-Publishing Association/Patricia Knox.

KOLKO, D.J. and KAZDIN, A.E. (1991) 'Motives of childhood firesetters: Firesetting characteristics and psychological correlates', *Journal of Child Psychology and Psychiatry*, 32, 3, pp. 535–50.

KOLVIN, I., GARSIDE, R.F., NICOL, A.R., MACMILLAN, A., WOLSTENHOLME, F. and LEITCH, I.M. (1981) *Help Starts Here*, London: Tavistock Publications.

KONSTANTAREAS, M.M. and HOMATIDIS, S. (1984) 'Aggressive and prosocial behaviours before and after treatment in conduct-disordered children and in matched controls', *Journal of Child Psychology and Psychiatry*, 25, 4, pp. 607–20.

LADD, G.W. (1983) 'Social networks of popular, average and rejected children in school settings', *Merrill-Palmer Quarterly*, 29, 3, pp. 283–307.

LA FONTAINE, J.S. (1991) *Bullying: The Child's View*, London: Calouste Gulbenkian Foundation.

LAING, A.F. and CHAZAN, M. (1986) 'The management of aggressive behaviour in young children' in TATTUM, D.P. (Ed.) *Management of Disruptive Pupil Behaviour in Schools*, Chichester: John Wiley.

LAING, A.F. and CHAZAN, M. (1987) *Teachers' Strategies in Coping with Behaviour Difficulties in First Year Junior School Children*, Maidstone: Association of Workers for Maladjusted Children.

LAKE, M. (1989) 'Mind games in Milton Keynes', *Special Children*, 27, pp. 20–3.

LANE, D.A. (1989) 'Violent histories: Bullying and criminality' in TATTUM, D.P. and LANE, D.A. (Eds) *Bullying in Schools*, Stoke-on-Trent: Trentham Books.

LANE, D.A. (1990) *The Impossible Child*, Stoke-on-Trent: Trentham Books.

LANGFELDT, H-P. (1992) 'Teachers' perceptions of problem behaviour: A cross-culture study between Germany and South Korea', *British Journal of Educational Psychology*, 62, 2, pp. 217–4.

LASLETT, R. (1977) *Educating Maladjusted Children*, London: Crosby Lockwood Staples.

LASLETT, R. (1982) 'A children's court for bullies', *Special Education/Forward Trends*, 9, 1, pp. 9–11.

LASLETT, R. and SMITH, C. (1984) *Effective Classroom Management*, London: Croom Helm.

LAWRENCE, B. and BENNETT, S. (1992) 'Shyness and education: The relationship between shyness, social class and personality variables in adolescents', *British Journal of Educational Psychology*, 62, 2, pp. 257–63.

LAWRENCE, D. (1988) *Enhancing Self Esteem in the Classroom*, London: Paul Chapman.

LAWRENCE, J. and STEED, D. (1986) 'Primary school perception of disruptive behaviour', *Educational Studies*, 12, 2, pp. 147–57.

LAWRENCE, J., STEED, D.M. and YOUNG, P. (1985a) 'European opinions on disruptive behaviour in schools: Provision and facilities, causes and cures', *Cambridge Journal of Education*, 15, 1, pp. 49–58.

LAWRENCE, J., STEED, D.M. and YOUNG, P. (1985b) *Disruptive Children — Disruptive Schools*, London: Croom Helm.

LAWSON, H. (1992) *Practical Record Keeping for Special Schools*, London: David Fulton.

LEACH, D.J. and RAYBOULD, E.C. (1977) *Learning and Behaviour Difficulties in School*, London: Open Books.

LEECH, N. and WOOSTER, A.D. (1986) *Personal and Social Skills*, Oxford: Pergamon Press.

LENNHOFF, F.G. (1960) *Exceptional Children*, London: Allen and Unwin.

LENNOX, D. (1991) *See Me After School*, London: David Fulton.

LEVINE, M.D. and SATZ, P. (Eds) (1984) *Middle Childhood: Development and Dysfunction*, Baltimore, MD: University Park Press.

LEVINE, R.A. and WHITE, M.I. (1991) 'Revolution in parenthood' in WOODHEAD, M., LIGHT, P. and CARR, R. (Eds) *Growing Up in a Changing Society*, London: Routledge and the Open University.

LEWIS, A. (1991) *Primary Special Needs and the National Curriculum*, London: Routledge.

LIPMAN, M., SHARP, A.M. and OSCANYAN, F.S. (1980) *Philosophy in the Classroom* (2nd edn), New Jersey: Temple University Press.

LLOYD-SMITH, M. (1984) *Disrupted Schooling: The Growth of the Special Unit*, London: John Murray.

LOEBER, R. (1982) 'The stability of antisocial and delinquent child behaviors: A review', *Child Development*, 53, 6, pp. 1431–46.

LUK, S.L., LEUNG, P.W.L. and LEE, P.L.M. (1988) ' "Conners" teacher rating scale in Chinese children in Hong Kong', *Journal of Child Psychology and Psychiatry*, 29, 2, pp. 165–74.

LUK, S.L. and LEUNG, P.W.L. (1989) ' "Conners" teacher's rating scale — a validity study in Hong Kong', *Journal of Child Psychology and Psychiatry*, 30, 5, pp. 785–94.

LUTON, K., BOOTH, G., LEADBETTER, J., TEE, G. and WALLACE, F. (1991) *Positive Strategies for Behaviour Management: A Whole-school Approach to Discipline*, Windsor: NFER/Nelson.

MACCOBY, E.E. (1980) *Social Development: Psychological Growth and the Parent-Child Relationship*, New York: Harcourt Brace Jovanovich.

McCALL, L. and FARRELL, P. (1993) 'Methods used by educational psychologists to assess children with emotional and behavioural difficulties', *Educational Psychology in Practice*, 9, 3, pp. 164–9.

McCORD, J. (1990) 'Long-term perspectives on parental absence' in ROBINS, L.N. and RUTTER, M. (Eds) *Straight and Devious Pathways from Childhood to Adulthood*, Cambridge: Cambridge University Press.

MacFARLANE, J.W., ALLEN, L. and HONZIK, M. (1954) *A Developmental Study of the Behaviour Problems of Normal Children between 21 months and 14 years*, California: University of California Press.

McGEE, R., SILVA, P.A. and WILLIAMS, S. (1984) 'Behaviour problems in a population of seven year old children: Prevalence, stability and types of disorder — a research report', *Journal of Child Psychology and Psychiatry*, 25, 2, pp. 251–60.

McGUINESS, J. (1993) *Teachers, Pupils and Behaviour: A Managerial Approach*, London: Cassell.

McMANUS, M. (1989) *Troublesome Behaviour in the Classroom*, London: Routledge.

McMICHAEL, P. (1979) 'The hen or the egg? Which comes first — Antisocial emotional disorders or reading disability?', *British Journal of Educational Psychology*, 49, 3, pp. 226–38.

McNIFF, J. (1986) *Personal and Social Education*, Cambridge: Hobsons.

MAIER, H.W. (1969) *Three Theories of Child Development*, New York: Harper and Row.

MAINES, B. (1991) *Coping with Challenging Behaviour in the Primary School*, Bristol: Redland Centre for Primary Education.

MAINES, B. and ROBINSON, G. (1991a) 'Don't beat the bullies', *Educational Psychology in Practice*, 7, 3, pp. 168–73.

MAINES, B. and ROBINSON, G. (1991b) *Stamp Out Bullying (Video and Handbook)*, Bristol: Lame Duck Publications.

MALEK, M. and KERSLAKE, A. (1989) *Making an Educational Statement*, School of Social Sciences, University of Bath and the Children's Society.

MALIK, N.M. and FURMAN, W. (1993) 'Problems in children's peer relations: What can the clinician do?', *Journal of Child Psychology and Psychiatry*, 34, 8, pp. 1303–26.

MANNING, M., HERON, J. and MARSHALL, T. (1978) 'Styles of hostility and social interactions at nursery, at school and at home: An extended study of children' in HERSOV, L.A. and BERGER, M. (Eds) *Aggression and Anti-Social Behaviour in Childhood and Adolescence*, Oxford: Pergamon Press.

MANNING, M. and SLUKIN, A.M. (1984) 'The function of aggression in the pre-school and primary-school years' in FRUDE, N. and GAULT, N. (Eds) *Disruptive Behaviour in Schools*, Chichester: John Wiley.

MARSTON, N. and STOTT, D.H. (1970) 'Inconsequence as a primary type of behaviour disturbance in children', *British Journal of Educational Psychology*, 40, 1, pp. 15–20.

MELNICK, C.R. (1991) 'Parents and teachers as educative partners', *International Journal of Educational Research*, 15, 2, pp. 125–29.

MERRETT, F. and WHELDALL, K. (1984) 'Classroom behaviour problems which junior school teachers find most troublesome', *Educational Studies*, 10, 2 pp. 67–81.

MERRETT, F. and WHELDALL, K. (1990) *Positive Teaching in the Primary School*, London: Paul Chapman.

MINISTRY OF EDUCATION (1955) *Report of the Committee on Maladjusted Children (the Underwood Report)*, London: HMSO.

MITCHELL, C. and KOSHY, V. (1993) *Effective Teacher Assessment: Looking at Children's Learning in the Primary Classroom*, London: Hodder and Stoughton.

MITCHELL, S. and ROSA, T. (1981) 'Boyhood behaviour problems as precursors of criminality: A fifteen-year follow-up study', *Journal of Child Psychology and Psychiatry*, 22, 1, pp. 19–34.

MITTLER, P. (1992) 'Educational entitlement in the nineties', *Support for Learning*, 7, 4, pp. 145–51.

MONGON, D. and HART, S. with ACE, C. and RAWLINGS, A. (1989) *Improving Classroom Behaviour: New Directions for Teachers and Pupils*, London: Cassell.

MONTGOMERY, D. (1989) *Managing Behaviour Problems*, London: Hodder and Stoughton.

MORAN, S., SMITH, P.K., THOMPSON, D. and WHITNEY, I. (1993) 'Ethnic differences in experiences of bullying: Asian and white children', *British Journal of Educational Psychology*, 63, 3, pp. 431–40.

MORENO, J.L. (1955) *Who Shall Survive?* (3rd edn), New York: Beacon House.

MORRIS, R., REID, E. and FOWLER, J. (1993) *Education Act 93: A Critical Guide*, London: Association of Metropolitan Authorities.

MORTIMORE, P., DAVIES, J., VARLAAM, A. and WEST, A. (1983) *Behaviour Problems in Schools: An Evaluation of Support Centres*, London: Croom Helm.

MORTIMORE, P., SAMMONS, P., STOLL, L., LEWIS, D. and ECOB, R. (1988) *School Matters: The Junior Years*, Wells: Open Books.

MOSES, D. (1982) 'Special educational needs: The relationship between teacher assessment, test scores and classroom behaviour', *British Educational Research Journal*, 8, 2, pp. 111–22.

MOSLEY, J. (1991) 'A circular response to the Elton Report', *Maladjustment and Therapeutic Education*, 9, 3, pp. 136–42.

MOSLEY, J. (1993) *Turn Your School Around*, Wisbech: LDA.

MOURISDEN, S.E. and TOLSTRUP, K. (1988) 'Children who kill: A case study of matricide', *Journal of Child Psychology and Psychiatry*, 29, 4, pp. 511–16.

MUSSEN, P.H., CONGER, J.J., KAGAN, J. and HUSTON, A.C. (1992) *Child Development and Personality*, (7th edn) New York: Harper/Collins.

NABUZOKA, D. and SMITH, P.K. (1993) 'Sociometric status and social behaviour of children with and without learning difficulties', *Journal of Child Psychology and Psychiatry*, 34, 8, pp. 1435–48.

NASH, R. (1973) *Classrooms Observed*, London: Routledge and Kegan Paul.

NASH, R. (1976) *Teacher Expectations and Pupil Learning*, London: Routledge and Kegan Paul.

NEEPER, R. and LAHEY, B.B. (1988) *Comprehensive Behaviour Rating Scale for Children (CBRSC)*, Sidcup, Kent: The Psychological Corporation.

NEWTON, M. (1992) 'A changing learning support service' in BOOTH, T., SWANN, W., MASTERTON, M. and POTTS, P. (Eds) *Policies for Diversity in Education*, London: Routledge in association with the Open University.

NIAS, J. (1984) 'The definition and maintenance of self in primary teaching', *British Journal of Sociology of Education*, 5, 3, pp. 267–80.

NISBET, J. and SHUCKSMITH, J. (1986) *Learning Strategies*, London: Routledge and Kegan Paul.

NOTTINGHAM EDUCATION COMMITTEE (1991) 'Developing a coordinated approach to bullying/victim problems' in SMITH, P.K. and THOMPSON, D. (Eds) *Practical Approaches to Bullying*, London: David Fulton.

OLLENDICK, T.H., KING, N.J. and FRARY, R.B. (1989) 'Fears in children and adolescents: Reliability and generalizability across gender, age and nationality', *Behaviour Research and Therapy*, 27, pp. 19–26.

OLLENDICK, T.H., YULE, W. and OLLIER, K. (1991) 'Fears in British children and their relationship to manifest anxiety and depression', *Journal of Child Psychology and Psychiatry*, 32, 2, pp. 321–31.

OLWEUS, D. (1978) *Aggression in the Schools: Bullies and Whipping Boys*, Washington, DC: Hemisphere.

OLWEUS, D. (1984) 'Aggression, and their victims: Bullying at school' in FRUDE, N. and GAULT, H. (Eds) *Disruptive Behaviour in Schools*, Chichester: John Wiley.

OLWEUS, D. (1987) 'Bully/victim problems among schoolchildren in Scandinavia' in MYKLEBUST, J.P. and OMMUNDSEN, R. (Eds) *Psykologprofesjonen mot ar 2000*, Oslo: Universitets forlaget.

OLWEUS, D. (1989) 'Bully/victim problems among schoolchildren: Basic facts and effects of a school-based intervention program' in RUBIN, K. and REPLER, D. (Eds) *The Development and Treatment of Childhood Aggression*, Hillsdale, NJ: Erlbaum.

OLWEUS, D. (1992a) 'Bullying among schoolchildren: Intervention and prevention' in PETERS, R., MCMAHON, R. and QUINSEY, V. (Eds) *Aggression and Violence Throughout the Life Span*, Newbury Park, CA: Sage Publications.

OLWEUS, D. (1992b) *Bullying at School — What we Know and What we Can Do*, Stockholm: Liber.

O'MOORE, A.M. and HILLERY, B. (1989) 'Bullying in Dublin schools', *Irish Journal of Psychology*, 10, 3, pp. 426–41.

OSBORN, S.G. and WEST, D.J. (1978) 'The effectiveness of various predictors of criminal careers', *Journal of Adolescence*, 1, 2, pp. 101–17.

O'SHEA, L.J. and O'SHEA, D.J. (1989) 'The Regular Education Initiative in the United States: What is its relevance to the integration movement in Australia', *International Journal of Disability, Development and Education*, 36, 1, pp. 5–14.

PARKER, J.G. and ASHER, S.R. (1987) 'Peer relations and later personal adjustment. Are low-accepted children at risk?', *Psychological Bulletin*, 102, 1, pp. 357–89.

PARTINGTON, J.A. and HINCHCLIFFE, G. (1979) 'Some aspects of classroom management', *British Journal of Teacher Education*, 5, 3, pp. 231–41.

PARTINGTON, J.A. and WRAGG, T. (1989) *Schools and Parents*, London: Cassell.

PATTERSON, G.R. (1982) *A Social Learning Approach (Vol. 3): Coercive Family Process*, Eugene, OR: Castalia.

PEAGAM, E. (1993) 'Who cares about control?', *British Journal of Special Education*, 20, 3, pp. 100–2.

PEARSON, L. and LINDSAY, G. (1986) *Special Needs in the Primary School: Identification and Intervention*, Windsor: NFER/Nelson.

PERRY, D.G., KUSEL, S.J. and PERRY, L.C. (1988) 'Victims of peer aggression', *Developmental Psychology*, 24, 6, pp. 807–14.

PETERSON, D.R. (1961) 'Behaviour problems of middle childhood', *Journal of Consulting Psychology*, 25, 3, pp. 205–9.

PIDGEON, D.A. (1970) *Expectation and Pupil Performance*, Slough: NFER.

PIKAS, A. (1989) 'A pure conception of mobbing gives the best result for treatment', *School Psychology International*, 10, 2, pp. 95–104.

PISANO, S. (1991) 'Children with emotional and behavioural difficulties in the primary school', *Maladjustment and Therapeutic Education*, 9, 3, pp. 170–2.

PLESS, B. and NOLAN, T. (1991) 'Revision, replication and neglect — research on maladjustment in chronic illness', *Journal of Child Psychology and Psychiatry*, 32, 2, pp. 347–65.

POLLARD, A. and TANN, S. (1987) *Reflective Teaching in the Primary School*, London: Cassell.

PUGH, G. and DE'ATH, E. (1984) *The Needs of Parents: Practice and Policy in Parent Education*, Basingstoke: Macmillan.

PUTALLAZ, M. and WASSERMAN, A. (1990) 'Children's entry behaviour' in ASHER, S.R. and COIE, J.D. (Eds) *Peer Rejection in Childhood*, Cambridge: Cambridge University Press.

PYKE, N. (1993) 'Banished to the exclusion zone', *Times Educational Supplement*, 2 April, p. 6.

PYKE, N. (1994) 'Patten restates behaviour code', *Times Educational Supplement*, 7 January, p. 3.

REID, K. (1982) 'Disruptive behaviour and persistent school absenteeism' in FRUDE, N. and GAULT, H. (Eds) *Disruptive Behaviour in Schools*, Chichester: John Wiley.

REID, K. (1985) *Truancy and School Absenteeism*, London: Hodder and Stoughton.

REID, K. (1986) *Disaffection from School*, London: Methuen.

RENNIE, E. (1993) 'Behavioural support teaching: Points to ponder', *Support for Learning*, 8, 1, pp. 7–10.

RICHMAN, N. (1988) 'The family' in RICHMAN, N. and LANSDOWN, R. (Eds) *Problems of Preschool Children*, Chichester: John Wiley and Sons.

RICHMAN, N., STEVENSON, J. and GRAHAM, P.J. (1982) *Pre-school to School: A Behavioural Study*, London: Academic Press.

RIGBY, K. and SLEE, P. (1993) 'Children's attitudes towards victims' in TATTUM, D. (Ed.) *Understanding and Managing Bullying*, London: Heinemann.

RITCHIE, R. (Ed.) (1991) *Profiling in Primary Schools: A Handbook for Teachers*, London: Cassell.

RITTER, D.R. (1989) 'Teachers' perceptions of problem behaviour in general and special education', *Exceptional Children*, 55, 6, pp. 559–64.

ROBB, J. (1989) 'Teaching for potential', *Special Children*, 28, pp. 16–17.

ROBERTSON, J. (1989) *Effective Classroom Control*, London: Hodder and Stoughton.

ROBINS, L. (1966) *Deviant Children Grown Up*, Baltimore, MD: Williams and Wilkins.

ROBINS, L.N. (1972) 'Follow-up studies of behaviour disorders in children', in QUAY, H.C. and WERRY, J.S. (Eds) *Psychopathological Disorders of Childhood*, New York: John Wiley.

ROBINS, L.N. (1978) 'Study of childhood predictors of adult anti-social behaviour: replication from longitudinal studies', *Psychological Medicine*, 8, pp. 611–22.

ROBINS, L.N. (1981) 'Epidemiological approaches to natural history research: Anti-social disorders in children', *Journal of American Academy of Child Psychiatry*, 20, pp. 566–80.

ROBINS, L.N. (1991) 'Conduct disorder', *Journal of Child Psychology and Psychiatry*, 32, 1, pp. 193–212.

RODBARD, G. (1990) 'Going Dutch! a perspective on the Dutch system of special education', *European Journal of Special Needs Education*, 5, 3, pp. 221–30.

ROGERS, C.R. (1952) *Client-centred Therapy*, Boston, MA: Houghton Mifflin.

ROLAND, E. (1989) 'Bullying: The Scandinavian research tradition' in TATTUM, D.P. and LANE, D.A. *Bullying in Schools*, Stoke-on-Trent: Trentham Books.

ROLAND, E. and MUNTHE, E. (1989) *Bullying: An International Perspective*, London: David Fulton/Professional Development Foundation.

ROPER, R. and HINDE, R.A. (1979) 'A teacher's questionnaire for individual differences in social behaviour', *Journal of Child Psychology and Psychiatry*, 20, 4, pp. 287–98.

ROSSMAN, B.R.R. and ROSENBERG, M.S. (1992) 'Family stress and functioning in children: The moderating effects of children's beliefs about their control over parental conflict', *Journal of Child Psychology and Psychiatry*, 33, 4, pp. 699–715.

RUBIN, K.H. and PEPLER, D.J. (1980) 'The relationship of child's play to social-cognitive growth and development' in FOOT, H.C., CHAPMAN, A.J. and SMITH, J.R. (Eds) *Friendship and Social Relations in Children*, Chichester: John Wiley and Sons.

RUMBOLD, E. (1992) 'Time off for good behaviour', *Special Children*, 54, pp. 21–2.

RUSSELL, P. (1990) 'Introducing the Children Act', *British Journal of Special Education*, 17, 1, pp. 35–7.

RUSSELL, P. (1991) 'The Children Act: A challenge for all', *British Journal of Special Education*, 18, 3, pp. 115–8.

RUSSELL, P. (1992) *The Children Act 1989 and Disability*, Highlight No. 109, London: National Children's Bureau.

RUTTER, M. (1967) 'A children's behaviour questionnaire for completion by teachers', *Journal of Child Psychology and Psychiatry*, 8, 1, pp. 1–11.

RUTTER, M. (1972) *Maternal Deprivation Reassessed*, Harmondsworth: Penguin Books.

RUTTER, M. (1975) *Helping Troubled Children*, Harmondsworth: Penguin Books.

RUTTER, M. (1977) 'Brain damage syndromes in childhood: Concepts and findings', *Journal of Child Psychology and Psychiatry*, 18, 1, pp. 1–22.

RUTTER, M. (1981) 'Stress, coping and development: Some issues and some questions', *Journal of Child Psychology and Psychiatry*, 22, 4, pp. 323–56.

RUTTER, M. (1983) 'School effects on pupil progress: Research findings and policy implications', *Child Development*, 54, 1, pp. 1–29.

RUTTER, M. (1985) 'Family and school influences on behavioural development', *Journal of Child Psychology and Psychiatry*, 26, 3, pp. 349–68.

RUTTER, M. (1989a) 'Pathways from childhood to adult life', *Journal of Child Psychology and Psychiatry*, 30, 1, pp. 23–51.

RUTTER, M. (1989b) 'Isle of Wight revisited: Twenty-five years of child psychiatric epidemiology', *Journal of American Academy of Child Psychiatry*, 28, 5, pp. 633–53.

RUTTER, M., COX, A., TUPLING, C., BERGER, M. and YULE, W. (1975) 'Attainment and adjustment in two geographical areas, I: The prevalence of psychiatric disorder', *British Journal of Psychiatry*, 126, pp. 493–509.

RUTTER, M. and Quinton, D. (1977) 'Psychiatric disorder — Ecological factors and concepts of causation' in MCGURK, M. (Ed.) *Ecological Factors in Human Development*, Amsterdam: Noord-Holland, pp. 173–87.

RUTTER, M., TIZARD, J. and WHITMORE, K. (Eds) (1970) *Education, Health and Behaviour*, London: Longman.

RUTTER, M., YULE, W., BERGER, M., YULE, B., MORTON, J. and BAGLEY, C. (1974) 'Children of West Indian Immigrants, I: Rates of behavioural deviance and of psychiatric disorder', *Journal of Child Psychology and Psychiatry*, 15, 4, pp. 241–62.

RYDER, J. and CAMPBELL, L. (1988) *Balancing Acts in Personal, Social and Health Education: A Practical Guide for Teachers*, London: Routledge.

SAFRAN, S.P. and SAFRAN, J.S. (1985) 'Classroom context and teachers' perceptions of problem behaviours', *Journal of Educational Psychology*, 77, 1, pp. 20–8.

SAMPSON, O. (1980) *Child Guidance: Its History, Provenance and Future*, Leicester: British Psychological Society (Division of Educational and Child Psychology).

SARASON, I.G. and SARASON, B.R. (1986) 'Anxiety and interfering thoughts' in JONES, W.H., CHEEK, J.M. and BRIGGS, S.R. (Eds) *Shyness: Perspectives on Research and Treatment*, New York: Plenum Press.

SCARLETT, P. (1989) 'Discipline: Pupil and teacher perceptions', *Maladjustment and Therapeutic Education*, 7, 3, pp. 169–77.

SCHACHAR, R. (1991) 'Childhood hyperactivity', *Journal of Child Psychology and Psychiatry*, 32, 1, pp. 155–92.

SCHERER, M. (1988) *Schools Skills Checklist* (see chapter 5 in SCHERER, M., GERSCH, I. and FRY, L., (1990) *Meeting Disruptive Behaviour: Assessment intervention and partnership*), London: Macmillan.

SCHERER, M. (1990a) 'Assessment by baselines' in SCHERER, M., GERSCH, I. and FRY, L. (Eds) *Meeting Disruptive Behaviour: Assessment, Intervention and Partnership*, London: Macmillan.

SCHERER, M. (1990b) 'Using consequences in class' in SCHERER, M., Gersch, I. and FRY, L. (Eds) *Meeting Disruptive Behaviour: Assessment, Intervention and Partnership*, London: Macmillan.

SCHERER, M., GERSCH, I. and FRY, L. (Eds) (1990) *Meeting Disruptive Behaviour: Assessment, Intervention and Partnership*, London: Macmillan.

SCHMIDT, M.H., ESSER, G., ALLEHOFF, W., GEISEL, B., LAUGHT, M. and WOERNER, W. (1987) 'Evaluating the significance of minimal brain dysfunction — Results of an epidemiological study', *Journal of Child Psychology and Psychiatry*, 28, 6, pp. 803–21.

SCHOOl CURRICULUM AND ASSESSMENT AUTHORITY (1994) *Dearing: The Final Report*, London: SCAA.

SELIGMAN, M.E.P. (1975) *Helplessness*, San Francisco, CA: Freeman.

SEMMEL, M.I., ABERNATHY, T.V., BUTERA, G. and LESAR, S. (1992) 'Teacher perceptions of the Regular Education Initiative', *Exceptional Children*, 58, 1, pp. 9–24.

SHAFFER, D.R. (1989) *Developmental Psychology: Childhood and adolescence*, Pacific Grove, CA: Brooks/Cole Pub. Co.

SHARP, P. and DUNFORD, S. (1990) *The Education System in England and Wales*, London: Longman.

SHARP, S. and SMITH, P.K. (1991) 'Bullying in UK schools: The DES Sheffield Bullying Project', *Early Child Development and Care*, 77, pp. 47–55.

SHARRON, H. (1987) *Changing Children's Minds: Feuerstein's Revolution in the Teaching of Intelligence*, London: Souvenir Press.

SHAW, O. (1965) *Maladjusted Boys*, London: Allen and Unwin.

SILVA, P.A., HUGHES, P., WILLIAMS, S. and FAED, J.M. (1988) 'Blood lead, intelligence, reading attainment and behaviour in eleven-year-old children in Dunedin, New Zealand', *Journal of Child Psychology and Psychiatry*, 29, 1, pp. 43–52.

SKINNER, A. (1992) *Bulling: An Annotated Bibliography of Literature Resources*, Youth Work Press (National Youth Bureau).

SLAVSON, S.R. (Ed.) (1947) *The Practice of Group Therapy*, London: Pushkin Press.

SLOPER, P. and TURNER, S. (1993) 'Risk and resistance factors in the adaptation of parents of children with severe physical disability', *Journal of Child Psychology and Psychiatry*, 34, 2, pp. 167–88.

SMITH, C.J. (Ed.) (1985) *New Directions in Remedial Education*, London: Falmer Press.

SMITH, P.K. and COWIE, H. (1991) *Understanding Children's Development* (2nd edn), Oxford: Basil Blackwell.

SMITH, P.K. and THOMPSON, D. (1991) *Practical Approaches to Bullying*, London: David Fulton.

SMITH, R. (1990) *The Effective School, Vol. 2: Classroom techniques and management*, Lancaster: Framework Press.

SMITH, R. (1993) *Managing Pupil Behaviour in School and Classroom*, Lancaster: Framework Press.

SOUSSIGNAN, R., TREMBLEY, R.E., SCHAAL, B., LAURENT, D., LARIVEE, S., CAGNON, C., LEBLANC, M. and CHARLEBOIS, P. (1992) 'Behavioural and cognitive characteristics of conduct disordered-hyperactive boys from age 6 to 11: A multiple informant perspective', *Journal of Child Psychology and Psychiatry*, 33, 8, pp. 1333–46.

SPENCE, S. (1980) *Social Skills Training with Children and Adolescents*, Windsor: NFER.

SPENCE, S. and McCATHIE, H. (1993) 'The stability of fears in children: A two-year prospective study: A research note', *Journal of Child Psychology and Psychiatry*, 34, 4, pp. 579–85.

SPIVACK, G., PLATT, J. and SHURE, M.B. (1976) *The Problem Solving Approach to Adjustment*, San Francisco, CA: Jossey Bass.

SPIVACK, G. and SHURE, M.B. (1974) *Social Adjustment of Young Children*, San Francisco, CA: Jossey Bass.

STAFFORD-CLARK, D. and SMITH, A.C. (1983) *Psychiatry for Students (6th edn)*, London: Allen and Unwin.

STAINES, J.W. (1971) 'The self picture as a factor in the classroom' in CASHDAN, A. and WHITEHEAD, J. (Eds) *Personality Growth and Learning*, London: Longman for the Open University Press.

STEED, D. and LAWRENCE, J. with SCHERER, M. (1990) 'Monitoring and analysing disruptive incidents' in SCHERER, M., GERSCH, I. and FRY, L. (Eds) *Meeting Disruptive Behaviour: Assessment, Intervention and Partnership*, London: Macmillan.

STEINHAUSEN, H-C. and ERDIN, A. (1992) 'Abnormal psychological situations and ICD-10 diagnoses in children and adolescents attending a psychiatric service', *Journal of Child Psychology and Psychiatry*, 33, 4, pp. 731–40.

STEPHENSON, P. and SMITH, D. (1989) 'Bullying in the junior school' in TATTUM, D.P. and LANE, D.A. (Eds) *Bullying in Schools*, Stoke-on-Trent: Trentham Books.

STEVENSON, J., RICHMAN, N. and GRAHAM, P. (1985) 'Behaviour problems and language abilities at three years and behavioural deviance at eight years', *Journal of Child Psychology and Psychiatry*, 26, 2, pp. 215–30.

STIRLING, M. (1991) 'Absent with leave', *Special Children*, 52, pp. 10–13.

STIRLING, M. (1992) 'How many pupils are being excluded?', *British Journal of Special Education*, 19, 4, pp. 128–30.

ST. JAMES-ROBERTS, I. and WOLKE, D. (1984) 'Comparison of mothers' with trained observers' reports of neonatal behavioural style', *Infant Behaviour and Development*, 7, 3, pp. 299–310.

STONE, M. (1981) *The Education of the Black Child in Britain: The Myth of Multiracial Education*, London: Fontana Press.

STOTT, D.H. (1963) *The Social Adjustment of Children (Manual of the British Social Adjustment Guides)*, London: University of London Press.

STOTT, D.H. (1966) *Studies of Troublesome Children*, London: Tavistock Publications.

STOTT, D.H. (1975) *British Social Adjustment Guides: Manual, 5th edn*, London: University of London Press.

STOTT, D.H. (1981) 'Behaviour disturbance and failure to learn: A study of cause and effect', *Educational Research*, 23, 3, pp. 163–72.

STOTT, D.H. and MARSTON, N.C. (1971) *Bristol Social Adjustment Guides: The Child in School* (2nd edn), London: Hodder and Stoughton.

STROMMEN, E.A., MCKINNEY, J.P. and FITZGERALD, H.E. (1977) *Developmental Psychology in the School-aged Child*, Homewood, IL: Dorsey Press.

STURGE, C. (1982) 'Reading retardation and antisocial behaviour', *Journal of Child Psychology and Psychiatry*, 23, 1, pp. 21–31.

SUTTON, A. (1993) 'A framework for the future', *Special Children*, 68, September, 16–19.

TANN, S. (1981) 'Grouping and group work' in SIMON, B. and WILLCOCKS, J. (Eds) *Research and Practice in the Primary Classroom*, London: Routledge and Kegan Paul.

TANN, S. (1988) 'Grouping and the integrated classroom' in THOMAS, G. and FEILER, A. (Eds) *Planning for Special Needs*, Oxford: Basil Blackwell.

TATTUM, D. (1982) *Disruptive Pupils in Schools and Units*, Chichester: John Wiley.

TATTUM, D. (Ed.) (1993) *Understanding and Managing Bullying*, London: Heinemann.

TATTUM, D. and HERBERT, G. (1990) *Bullying: A Positive Response*, Cardiff: South Glamorgan Institute of Higher Education.

TATTUM, D. and HERBERT, G. (1993) *Countering Bullying: Initiatives in Schools and Local Authorities*, Stoke-on-Trent: Trentham Books.

TAYLOR, E. (1979) 'Food additives, allergy and hyperkinesis', *Journal of Child Psychology and Psychiatry*, 20, 4, pp. 357–63.

TAYLOR, E. (1991) 'Developmental neuropsychiatry', *Journal of Child Psychology and Psychiatry*, 32, 1, pp. 3–47.

TAYLOR, M. and GARSON, Y. (1982) *Schooling in the Middle Years*, Stoke-on-Trent: Trentham Books.

THOMAS, A. and CHESS, S. (1977) *Temperament and Development*, New York: Brunner/Mazel.

THOMAS, D. (1978) *The Social Psychology of Childhood Disability*, London: Methuen.

THOMAS, D. (1985) 'The dynamics of teacher opposition to integration', *Remedial Education*, 20, pp. 75–88.

THOMAS, G. (1985) 'Room management in mainstream education', *Educational Research*, 27, 3, pp. 186–93.

THOMSON, G.O.B., RAAB, G.M., HEPBURN, W.S., HUNTER, R., FULTON, M. and LAXEN, D.P.H. (1989) 'Blood-lead levels and children's behaviour — Results from the Edinburgh lead study', *Journal of Child Psychology and Psychiatry*, 30, 4, pp. 515–28.

TIZARD, B., BLATCHFORD, P., BURKE, J., FARQUHAR, C. and PLEWIS, I. (1988) *Young Children at School in the Inner City*, Hove: Lawrence Erlbaum Ass.

TIZARD, J. (1973) Maladjusted children and the child guidance service', *London Educational Review*, 2, 2, pp. 22–7.

TODMAN, J., JUSTICE, S. and SWANSON, I. (1991) 'Disruptiveness and referral to the educational psychology service', *Educational Psychology in Practice*, 6, 4, pp. 199–202.

TOPPING, K. (1988) *The Peer Tutoring Handbook*, London: Croom Helm.

TOPPING, K. (1990) 'Disruptive pupils: Changes in perception and provision' in SCHERER, M., GERSCH, I. and FRY, L. (Eds) *Meeting Disruptive Behaviour: Assessment, Intervention and Partnership*, London: Macmillan.

TOPPING, K. and WOLFENDALE, S. (Eds) (1985) *Parental Involvement in Children's Reading*, London: Croom Helm.

TOULIATOS, J. and LINDHOLM, B.W. (1981) 'Congruence of parents' and teachers' ratings of children's behaviour problems', *Journal of Abnormal Child Psychology*, 9, 3, pp. 347–54.

TRAVERS, C. (1992) 'Teacher stress in the U.K. — A nationwide survey', *British Psychological Society Education Section Review*, 16, 2, pp. 78–82.

TREMBLAY, R.E., DESMARAIS-GERVAIS, L., GAGNON, C. and CHARLEBOIS, P. (1987) 'The preschool behaviour questionnaire: Stability of its factor structure between cultures, sexes, ages and socioeconomic classes', *International Journal of Behavioural Development*, 10, 4, pp. 467–84.

TRIANDIS, H.C. (1971) *Attitude and Attitude Change*, New York: John Wiley and Sons.

TROWER, P., BRYANT, B. and ARGYLE, M. (1978) *Social Skills and Mental Health*, London: Methuen.

TROWER, P., CASEY, A. and DRYDEN, W. (1988) *Cognitive–Behavioural Counselling*, London: Sage Publications.

TROYNA, B. and HATCHER, R. (1992) *Racism in Children's Lives*, London: Routledge and the National Children's Bureau.

TYLER, S. (1984) 'Carrying out assessment with young children' in FONTANA, D. (Ed.) *The Education of the Young Child* (2nd edn), Oxford: Basil Blackwell.

UPTON, G. (1981) 'The early years controversy and its implications for teaching maladjusted children', *New Growth*, 1, 2, pp. 11–20.

UPTON, G. (1992) 'No time for complacency', *Special Children*, 58, pp. 23–7.

VAN DER MOLIN, H. (1990) 'A definition of shyness and its implications' in CROZIER, W.R. (Ed.) *Shyness and Embarrassment*, Cambridge: University Press.

VENABLES, P.H., FLETCHER, R.P., DALAIS, J.C., MITCHELL, D.A., SCHULSINGER, F. and MEDNICK, S.A. (1983) 'Factor structure of the Rutter "Children's Behaviour Questionnaire" in a primary school population in a developing country', *Journal of Child Psychology and Psychiatry*, 24, 2, pp. 213–22.

VERHULST, F.C., ACHENBACH, T.M., ALTHAUS, M. and AKKERHUIS, G.W. (1988) 'A comparison of syndromes derived from the child behaviour checklist for American and Dutch girls, aged 6–11 and 12–16,' *Journal of Child Psychology and Psychiatry*, 29, 6, pp. 879–95.

VERHULST, F.C. and AKKERHUIS, G.W. (1989) 'Agreement between parents' and teachers' ratings of behavioural/emotional problems of children aged 4 to 11', *Journal of Child Psychology and Psychiatry*, 30, 1, pp. 123–36.

VEVERS, P. (1992) 'Getting in on the Act', *British Journal of Special Education*, 19, 3, pp. 88–91.

VIKAN, A. (1985) 'Psychiatric epidemiology in a sample of 1510 10-yr-old children — 1. Prevalence', *Journal of Child Psychology and Psychiatry*, 26, 1, pp. 55–75.

VISSER, J. (1993) *Special Educational Needs and Legislation: A Guide to the Education Act 1993 and OFSTED inspections*, Stafford: National Association for Special Educational Needs.

WALFORD, G. (1989) 'Group therapy for sexually abused children', *Newsletter of Association for Child Psychology and Psychiatry*, 11, 6, pp. 7–13.

WEBSTER-STRATTON, C. (1991) 'Strategies for helping families with conduct-disordered children', *Journal of Child Psychology and Psychiatry*, 32, 7, pp. 1047–62.

WEINER, B. (1974) *Achievement Motivation and Attribution Theory*, Morristown, NJ: General Learning Press.

WEINER, G. (Ed.) (1990) *The Pimary School and Equal Opportunities*, London: Cassell.

WEISZ, J.R., SUWANLERT, S., CHAIYASIT, W., WEISS, B., ACHENBACH, T.M. and TREVATHAN, D. (1989) 'Epidemiology of behavioural and emotional problems among Thai and American children: Teacher reports for ages 6–11, *Journal of Child Psychology and Psychiatry*, 30, 3, pp. 471–84.

WELLER, K. and CRAFT, A. (1983) *Making Up Our Minds: An Exploratory Study of Instrumental Enrichment*, London: Schools Council.

WERRY, J.S. (1972) 'Organic factors in childhood psychopathology' in QUAY, H.C. and WERRY, J.S. (Eds) *Psychopathology Disorders of Childhood*, New York: John Wiley.

WEST, D.J. (1982) *Delinquency its Roots, Careers and Prospects*, London: Heinemann.

WEST, D.J. and FARRINGTON, D.P. (1977) *The Delinquent Way of Life*, London: Heinemann.

WEST, R. (1989) 'The work of the Swindon Behavioural Support Team', *Links*, 14, 2, pp. 15–17.

WHELDALL, K. (1989) 'The forgotten "A" in behaviour analysis: The importance of ecological variables in classroom management' in THOMAS, G. and FEILER, A. (Eds) *Planning for Special Needs: A Whole School Approach*, Oxford: Basil Blackwell.

WHELDALL, K. and GLYNN, T. (1989) *Effective Classroom Learning*, Oxford: Basil Blackwell.

WHELDALL, K. and MERRETT, F. (1984) *Positive Teaching: The Behavioural Approach*, London: Allen and Unwin.

WHELDALL, K. and MERRETT, F. (1988a) 'Packages for training teachers in classroom behaviour management: BATPACK, BATSAC and the Positive Training Packages', *Support for Learning*, 3, pp. 86–92.

WHELDALL, K. and MERRETT, F. (1988b) 'Which classroom behaviours do primary school teachers say they find most troublesome?', *Educational Review*, 40, 1, pp. 13–25.

WHITE, A. (1990) 'Alternative work strategies at an off-site adjustment unit for pupils with behaviour problems', *Links*, 13, 3, pp. 8–9.

WHITNEY, I. and SMITH, P.K. (1993) 'A survey of the nature and extent of bullying in junior/middle and secondary schools', *Educational Research*, 35, 1, pp. 3–26.

WIGGINS, J.S. and WINDER, C.L. (1961) 'The Peer Nomination Inventory: An empirically sociometric measure of adjustment in preadolescent boys', *Psychological Reports*, 9, pp. 643–77.

WILKINSON, M. and PRIEST, S. (1991) 'The N.E. Derbyshire Bullying Project: A multi-disciplinary support network' in SMITH, P.K. and THOMPSON, D. (Eds) *Practical Approaches to Bullying*, London: David Fulton.

WILLIAMS, T. and HALLIWELL, M. (1992) '1981 and all that', *Special* (Bulletin of National Association for Special Educational Needs), June, pp. 24–6.

WILLS, D. (1960) *Throw Away Thy Rod*, London: Gollancz.

WILSON, M.D. and EVANS, M. (1980) *Education of Disturbed Pupils*, London: Methuen Educational.

WILSON, M.D. (1981) *The Curriculum in Special Schools*, London: Schools Council.

WOLFE, D.A., JAFFE, P., WILSON, S.K. and ZAK, L. (1988) 'A multivariate investigation of children's adjustment of family violence' in HOTALING,

G.T., FINKELHOR, D., FITZPATRICK, J.T. and STRAUS, M.A. (Eds) *Family Abuse and its Consequences: New Directions in Research*, Beverley Hills, CA: Sage Publications, pp. 228–43.

WOLFENDALE, S. (Ed.) (1989) *Parental Involvement*, London: Casell.

WOLFENDALE, S. (1992) *Empowering Parents and Teachers*, London: Cassell.

WOLFF, S. (1973) *Children Under Stress* (rev. edn), Harmondsworth: Pelican Books.

WOOD, D., GOTT, J. and JAMES, D. (1993) 'EBD — criteria or aide-memoire? Devising a service model for the assessment of emotional and behavioural difficulties', *Educational Psychology in Practice*, 9, 3, pp. 156–63.

WOODHEAD, M. (1991) 'Psychology and the cultural construction of 'children's needs' in WOODHEAD, M., LIGHT, P. and CARR, R. (Eds) *Growing Up in a Changing Society*, London: Routledge and the Open University.

WOODS, P. (1981) 'Strategies, commitment and identity: Making and breaking the teacher' in BARTON, L. and WALKER, S. (Eds) *Schools, Teachers and Teaching*, Lewes: Falmer Press.

WOODY, R.H. (1969) *Behavioural Problem Children in the Schools: Recognition, Diagnosis and Behavioural Modification*, New York: Appleton-Century-Crofts.

WRAGG, E.C. (1993) *Classroom Management*, London: Routledge.

WRAGG, E.C. (1994) *An Introduction to Classroom Observation*, London: Routledge.

YULE, W. (1970) Personal communication.

YULE, W., BERGER, M. and WIGLEY, V. (1984) 'Behaviour-modification and classroom management' in FRUDE, N. and GAULT, H. (Eds) *Disruptive Behaviour in Schools*, Chichester: John Wiley.

YULE, W., URBANOWICZ, M.A., LANSDOWN, R. and MILLAR, I.B. (1984) 'Teachers' ratings of children's behaviour in relation to blood lead levels', *British Journal of Development Psychology*, 2, 4, pp. 295–305.

ZIMBARDO, P.G. (1977) *Shyness*, New York: Addison-Wesley.

Index of Case Studies of Children

Index